Sister Revolutions

Also by Susan Dunn

★

The Deaths of Louis XVI: Regicide and the French Political Imagination

Nerval et le roman historique

SISTER REVOLUTIONS

French Lightning,

American Light

★

SUSAN DUNN

FARRAR, STRAUS AND GIROUX

NEW YORK

Farrar, Strauss & Giroux
18 West 18th Street, New York 10011

Designed by Abby Kagan

First paperback edition, 2000

Library of Congress Cataloging-in-Publication Data
Dunn, Susan.
    Sister revolutions : French lightning, American light / Susan Dunn.
        p.   cm.
    Includes bibliographical references and index.
    ISBN 0-571-19989-5 (pbk.)
    1. United States—History—Revolution, 1789–1799—Influence.
2. France—History—Revolution, 1789–1799—Influence.   3. United
States—Politics and government—1775–1783.   4. France—Politics and
government—1789–1799.   5. Democracy—History—20th century.
6. Political culture—History—20th century.   I. Title.
E209.D85   1999
973.3—dc21   99-18178

P1

FOR JIM

Contents

Illustrations

Acknowledgments

I am deeply grateful to many friends and colleagues for their help and encouragement in this project. Gita May, Michael McGiffert, Carol Blum, Gary Jacobsohn, MacAlister Brown, Michael Mac-Donald, Robert F. Dalzell, Jr., Jeff Weintraub, Ralph Lerner, and Richard K. Matthews all generously offered constructive criticism of portions of this manuscript. Igor Timofeyev provided knowledgeable help in researching the French sources of the Russian Revolution.

I am indebted to the National Endowment for the Humanities for a senior fellowship and to Williams College for financial assistance. I would also like to thank Donna Chenail and her colleagues in the Faculty Secretarial Office as well as Phyllis Cutler, Alison O'Grady, and Walter Komorowski at the Williams College Library for their able and cheerful assistance. My friend and agent Fifi Oscard also played an indispensable role.

Some parts of this book appeared in *The William and Mary Quarterly* (3d Series, Vol. LIII, No. 4, October 1996) and in *Partisan Review* (Vol. LXV, No. 2, Spring 1998).

Finally, I would like to express my profound gratitude to James MacGregor Burns for his insightful suggestions, his careful readings of my manuscript, his wise lessons in history and politics, and much more.

Sister Revolutions

★

Sister Revolutions

F or months in 1777 it was the talk of Paris: a young nobleman, the sole heir to the prestigious title and immense fortune of one of France's most ancient families, had mysteriously vanished. He was a man who possessed, they said, all that one could dream of in life. True, he had already lost his father and his mother, but he was happily married to the pretty daughter of the Duc d'Ayen, and they were expecting their second child.

Their world was one of luxury and elegance: Paris was their home, and the glittering, pleasure-filled salons of Marie Antoinette in Versailles were open to them. They dined with the queen and her young set, danced at lavish balls, placed bets at gaming tables, attended chamber concerts and plays along with the other royal guests. They were welcome in England at the court of George III, where the young woman's uncle, the Marquis de Noailles, served as the French ambassador. The young man was a captain in the Noailles regiment and could expect many promotions.

Without bidding farewell to his wife and daughter, he had surreptitiously set out for Bordeaux, where the ship he had purchased and crew he had hired were waiting for him. The king, Louis XVI, heard that he had left his regiment without permission and signed an ominous *lettre de cachet* for his immediate capture and arrest.

But the nobleman made his way safely to Bordeaux and set sail. In the middle of the Atlantic, aboard the *Victoire,* he composed a letter to his wife, Adrienne, finally explaining why he was repudiating everything that tradition and his heritage had destined for him: "Dear Heart, It is from very far away that I am writing to you. . . . Have you forgiven me by now? . . . Soldier of freedom, the freedom I idolize, I come as a friend to offer my help to this very interesting republic, bringing with me only my sincerity and my good will. I have no desire for personal gain. By laboring for my glory, for my own eternal reputation, I labor for their happiness. . . . The happiness of America is intimately tied to the happiness of all humanity; America will become the respected and secure haven of virtue, honesty, tolerance, equality, and a peaceful freedom."

Fearful that he might be detained on the king's orders if the ship stopped in the French West Indies, the young man insisted on sailing directly to the American mainland. In June 1777, the *Victoire* landed in South Carolina, and he slowly made his way to Philadelphia. He introduced himself to the members of the Continental Congress as Marie-Joseph Paul Yves Roch Gilbert Motier, Marquis de Lafayette. To the members of his family he was simply Gilbert. Nineteen years old, he spoke little English. The reception in Philadelphia at first was cool.

A distressed George Washington had complained a few months earlier that swarms of noble French officers were arriving from old France and the Islands, eager to enlist in the American cause. Though they spoke no English, they were all demanding commissions as officers. How could he distinguish men of merit from "mere adventurers"? He knew that some, seeking adventure, had left France out of boredom, tired of the court routine. Others, royalists loyal to their king, were motivated by hatred for England. It was not clear that any of the young noblemen were passionate about a struggle for freedom. "It is by the zeal and activity of our own people that the cause must be supported," Washington confided to a friend, "and not by a few hungry adventurers." But Lafayette seemed different. He stunned Congress by asking nothing more than to serve without pay as a volunteer. Washington himself was impressed by his disinterested zeal for the revolutionary cause. Tactful and unassuming, the young man emphasized that he had come "to learn, and not to teach." His engaging manners and modesty won the Americans over. Despite Louis XVI's formal request that Lafayette not be employed in military service in America, within days the marquis received the commission of major general, becoming the youngest general in the American army.

"I do most devoutly wish that we had not a single Foreigner among us," Washington wrote to Gouverneur Morris, "except the Marquis de la Fayette who acts upon very different principles than those which govern the rest." An intimate friendship between Washington and Lafayette blossomed. For the young man whose father died when he was two, Washington had become a father, and for the childless general, the eager and chivalrous marquis had become a son; there were few others for whom Washington felt the warmth he expressed for Lafayette. Washington confided to friends that he regarded Lafayette as his child.

On the battlefield, Lafayette's ardor and courage compensated for his lack of experience. In September 1777, at the battle of Brandywine, he valiantly continued to lead his troops though seriously wounded. Two months later, he was honored with the command of a division in the Continental Army. At the battle of Monmouth, Lafayette and Washington, fighting side by side, succeeded in turning the tide and trouncing the British. The night after their victory, father and adopted son fell asleep, side by side, under a tree on the battlefield.

In the beginning of 1779, with the outcome of the war still far from certain, Lafayette returned to France to secure more aid for his American confreres. Just a few months earlier, France had recognized the United States. Lafayette found his native country deeply sympathetic to the American cause, his own letters to his wife having played a role in exciting people's interest and enthusiasm. The French had been following the dramatic events closely; they cheered at American victories, they wept over defeats. The captivating revolution provided not only an absorbing pastime but a new vocabulary as well: "freedom" was a novel and intriguing word, and in wishing it for the Americans, the French began to contemplate it for themselves.

In addition to Lafayette, one other person residing in Paris incarnated the American Revolution. Plainly dressed, bespectacled, and unpowdered, Benjamin Franklin had brought the spirit of the new nation to France in 1776. During the nine years he lived in Paris, the French responded to his warmth, humor, and simplicity by making him the toast of Paris. People came from all over France to consult with him, and soon he became the center of a new cult, the cult of freedom and revolution. Franklin himself wrote to his daughter that he had become "i-doll-ized" by the French. "Your father's face," he confessed, "is as well known as that of the moon."

Even the king was swept away by the revolutionary vogue. His advisers warned that it was a grave risk for an absolute monarch to support a colonial uprising and embrace principles of freedom and equality. Turgot, the king's finance minister, fearing that the American venture would force the king to incur more debt, tried to steer him toward domestic affairs. But the thrilling struggle of a young people against tyranny outweighed prudent counsel. Finally the king's desire to inflict upon England a humiliating defeat tipped the scale: Louis XVI decided to make a major contribution to the American cause. To finance France's donation, Necker, the new finance minister, probably borrowed even more than the 530 million livres he admitted borrowing; by 1789 the interest alone on France's debt would become staggering. But in 1779, in a country heady with the excitement of a distant revolutionary struggle, Louis XVI could not imagine that within a decade his generosity would egregiously worsen the economic crisis in France, subvert all traditional values, destabilize the monarchy, and put his own life in jeopardy. In 1789, the anguished king admitted that he never thought about the American affair "without regret."

In March 1780, Lafayette returned to America with the assurance that fleets of vessels as well as admirals, generals, sailors, and soldiers would soon follow. The arrival of the French forces in America proved indeed to be the turning point of the war. Their military and naval prowess helped make the battle of Yorktown—at which French soldiers outnumbered Americans and at which Lafayette helped prevent the escape of Cornwallis's troops—the decisive victory of the war.

Benjamin Franklin at the Court of France, 1778.
Engraving by W. O. Geller

Hardly four years after his arrival in Philadelphia, General Lafayette, now all of twenty-four years old, stood with General George Washington at Yorktown to witness the spectacle of the British surrender. Together they watched as Major General Benjamin Lincoln formally accepted the sword of the defeated General O'Hara, standing in for the redoubtable Lord Cornwallis, who was unwilling to attend the ceremony of capitulation. No one doubted that the Revolution had been won. The following day, Washington congratulated the army, careful to thank first Louis XVI and the French fleet and army. At a church service the next day, the sermon was dedicated to the Marquis de Lafayette, the "friend of mankind."

"The play is over," Lafayette wrote. The young nobleman had come to America in search of glory. Now it was his.

A hero's welcome greeted Lafayette when he returned to France. He was hailed by all as the French Washington. Louis XVI's minister of war, the Marquis de Ségur, showered him with compliments, raising him to the heights of France's legendary conquerors: "Our old warriors admire you," he told the marquis, "the young ones take you as their model." The king himself bestowed laurels on the revolutionary victor.

Would the seeds of revolution sprout in France too? The French Revolution began, one French observer wrote, when Lafayette first left French shores for America. "Monsieur de La Fayette . . . rushed forth from our ports and . . . opened to the young soldiers of France the school of American liberty," he commented, adding that "in promoting the freedom of the thirteen United States, we prepared our own." Now a generation of returning officers, proudly wearing the blue-and-white ribbons of the elite Franco-American "Order of the Cincinnati," could share with others their experiences in the young democratic land, spreading the contagion of liberty.

General Rochambeau, the commander of the French forces in America, returned to France eager to recount his stories about the hospitable Americans, whose bold thinking he admired. Their government even reminded him of ancient Greece and Rome. Another French officer, the Count de Ségur, whose parents had prevented him from going to America with Lafayette in 1777 and who only succeeded in crossing the Atlantic in 1782, returned to France impressed by American soldiers. "I had expected to see in this democratic camp unkempt soldiers and officers without training," he later wrote. "One may imagine how surprised I was when I saw a well-disciplined army presenting in every detail the very image of order, reason, training, and experience." The dignity and self-respect of the soldiers, he concluded, sprang from their love of liberty and their feelings of equality. Ségur loved reminiscing about America with his friend the Marquis de Chastellux. Chastellux, who preferred studying American customs to fighting, returned to France with a wealth of information about the young nation. Indeed, the account of his travels and observations about America, published in 1786, attracted wide attention. Chastellux praised religious freedom, the energy of Americans, and the rapid development of the country. He was especially impressed by the great opportunities afforded to hardworking, entrepreneurial Americans to purchase land and lead independent lives.

Surrender of Lord Cornwallis at Yorktown, 19 October 1781,
by John Trumbull

Stories about America intoxicated the French. They found in the Revolution in the New World the most compelling intellectual subject of the times. The Boston Club, founded by the king's cousin, the Duc d'Orléans, met regularly in the elegant Palais Royal to discuss American freedom and democracy. And the Société des Amis des Noirs, founded by the future political leaders Brissot and Mirabeau, was devoted to the abolitionist cause. People applauded the Revolution across the sea as the most important event since Columbus's discovery of the New World.

The American Revolution was not only *à la mode* in Paris; it had become virtually a new religion. Washington, Franklin, and Jefferson acted as the apostles, and Jefferson's Declaration of Independence replaced the Bible. The French needed to look no further than this lofty document, the philosopher Condorcet asserted, to find a "sublime exposition of sacred rights that have too long been forgotten." It towered, people said, as a "beacon" for humanity. Thomas Jefferson, the new American minister in Paris, could write to George Washington without exaggeration that France "has been awaked by our revolution, they feel

Washington, Lafayette, and Tilghman at Yorktown,
by Charles Willson Peale

their strength, they are enlightened." In May 1789 the Paris newspaper *Mercure de France* announced that America was "the hope and the model of the human race."

Indeed, there was much to admire during the 1780s and early 1790s, as the American Revolution was proceeding healthily from stage to stage, accomplishing its goals. The war of the 1770s had brought independence. The Philadelphia Convention of 1787 created stable democratic institutions and a venerated Constitution, to which the founders added a Bill of Rights in 1791. Throughout the 1790s, political parties were slowly evolving, preparing the political terrain for the watershed election of 1800, when the defeated incumbent party, the Federalists, would peacefully turn over the reins of government to their adversaries, the Jeffersonian Republicans, a transfer of power rare in the history of modern revolutions.

But could Americans reasonably expect the French to learn and profit from their example? Or were the lessons the Americans had to offer and the requirements of the French "hopelessly different" from each other, as some historians contend? The French seemed to face a far more complex challenge than had the Americans. Americans, after all, were content with their legal system; they had no feudal heritage to extirpate, no hereditary social orders to combat, no privileged leisure-class aristocracy to democratize and integrate into society, no tradition of religious intolerance to oppose, no wretched poverty to eliminate, and few domestic insurrections to quell.

According to Lord Acton, both Jefferson and Madison admitted that a few seats for the Americans in both houses of Parliament in England would have set at rest the whole question of revolution. As Jefferson made clear in the Declaration of Independence, Americans wanted to return to the rights and freedoms they had long enjoyed before Parliament and King George III violated them. In this sense, their revolution signified a *return*, as the literal astronomical meaning of the word "revolution" suggests—"a circuit around a central axis, ending at the point from whence the motion began."

But for some in France, revolution denoted not return but total transformation. The goal of French radicals was to reconceive and reorganize the political, legal, and social structure of the nation, to overthrow the nation's institutions, to break with a thousand years of history.

And yet, as different as the historical, military, and social circumstances were, as different as the size of their populations—24 million people in France, fewer than 4 million in the thirteen colonies—the two revolutions shared significant features. The whole Atlantic civilization, the historian R. R. Palmer commented, "was swept in the last four decades of the eighteenth century by a single revolutionary movement that shared certain common goals." In America and in France, revolutionary leaders wanted to install representative governments based on popular sovereignty and the will of the majority. They called for conventions and drafted constitutions. They composed Declarations or Bills of Rights that posited the same inalienable human rights—life, liberty, and the pursuit of happiness—and upheld the principle of citizens' equality before the law. The purpose of government, they declared, was to protect the rights and freedom of citizens.

Leaders in both countries were convinced that they were constructing a "new order for the ages." The French created a new calendar in 1792, beginning time with the year of the abolition of the monarchy and the crowning of the people as sovereign. They were convinced that they could "regenerate" humanity. Americans too conceived their revolution as a radical beginning, not just for America but for the entire world. "Happily for America, happily we trust for the whole human race," Madison trumpeted in *The Federalist* No. 14, we "pursued a new and more noble course . . . and accomplished a revolution that has no parallel in the annals of human society."

The American model was France's for the taking—after all, she had paid for it, and her officers and soldiers had fought and died for it. When the French set about drafting a constitution and establishing unfamiliar political and judicial institutions, advice and wisdom from thoughtful Americans might not have been unseasonable. Lafayette, for his part, was intent on following as closely as possible lessons from America. At one Paris dinner party in June 1789, he listened to Gouverneur Morris's suggestions. "I [took] the opportunity to tell him," Morris wrote in his

diary, "that if the [Third Estate] are now very moderate they will probably succeed, but if violent must inevitably fail."

But mostly Lafayette listened to Jefferson. In the summer of 1789,
Lafayette brought his friends to Jefferson's spacious town house on the
Champs-Elysées, where, over dinner and port, they debated the makeup
of the new government. Aware of the diplomatic necessity of appearing
"neutral and passive," Jefferson listened, saying little. But in private
Lafayette and Jefferson spent hours together discussing their ideas for a
constitution and a Charter of Rights for France. Eager to assist, Jefferson
sketched out his recommendations, advising the creation of a representative body that, with the consent of the king, levied taxes and made
laws, and an independent judiciary. In lieu of an itemized Bill of Rights,
he offered some general principles of freedom and legal process.

"I have never feared for the ultimate result," Jefferson wrote to the
young marquis the following spring, "tho' I have feared for you personally. Take care of yourself, my dear friend, for tho' I think your nation
would in any event work out her salvation, I am persuaded were she to
lose you, it would cost her oceans of blood, & years of confusion & anarchy." Jefferson was convinced that Lafayette had a major role to play and
that, more than anyone else, he was the Revolution's American anchor.
Without Lafayette, the Revolution might fail. Jefferson had always
admired the Frenchman's "zeal," "good sense," and "sound genius." If
Lafayette had a "foible," it was his "canine" appetite for popularity and
fame, but Jefferson believed that he would get over this.

Jefferson was buoyantly optimistic about the prospects for change
in France. To his friend Maria Cosway he admitted that the cutting
off of heads was so "à la mode" that he was happy, upon awakening, to
feel his own head attached to his shoulders. Nevertheless, even mobs
roaming through the streets scarcely diminished his enthusiasm for
the Revolution. Agreeing with their goals, he congratulated himself on
having slept quietly through the night, as peaceably as ever. "So far it
seemed that your revolution has got along with a steady pace," he confi-
dently wrote to Lafayette in the spring of 1790, though reminding him
that "we are not to expect to be translated from despotism to liberty in a
feather-bed."

The Chaillot Gate, by F. N. Martinet.
Looking eastward down the Champs-Elysées.
Jefferson lived in the Hôtel de Langeac (*left*)
from October 1785 until he left Paris for good in September 1789

On July 15, 1789, the day after the storming of the Bastille, Lafayette was asked by the National Assembly to command the National Guard. Though his task was to assure law, order, and security in Paris, he always stressed his own view that the overriding function of the Guard was to unify the people. The oath of loyalty that he swore promised that the Guard's members would "remain united with all Frenchmen by the indissoluble bonds of brotherhood."

Lafayette proved adept at calming angry mobs, restoring order, and saving lives. His talent for finding just the right mediating gesture defused many incendiary situations. He astutely ordered the demolition of the Bastille, the hated prison that symbolized the feudal past. Once, when the king's guards were threatened by a mob, Lafayette handed one of the guardsmen the revolutionary ribbon from his own hat, appeasing and delighting the crowd. The insignia he had chosen for the National Guard was also a diplomatic masterstroke; it combined blue and red, the colors of Paris, and the white of the Bourbons, a marriage of revolution and monarchy. Remembering the skill with which Washington had carefully created his public persona of disinterested leader, he too declined any salary.

And yet, Lafayette failed in his mission. His paramount wish had been to unite all revolutionary factions around a constitutional monarchy that embraced revolutionary values of equality and freedom. But unity proved an elusive dream. On the right, royalists condemned him for insulting the royal family and tolerating mob demonstrations. On the left, radicals attacked him for quelling popular demonstrations, defending the king, and seeking power for himself. His popularity was completely destroyed in July 1791 when he ordered the Guard to fire on demonstrators demanding the abolition of the monarchy. "I verily believe that if M. de La Fayette were to appear just now in Paris unattended by his army," Gouverneur Morris wrote to George Washington a few weeks later, "he would be torn to pieces. Thank God we have no populace in America." Resigning from the Guard, Lafayette accepted the king's appointment to head the army in the north. But when the monarchy was abolished in the fall of 1792, knowing that his situation was hopeless, Lafayette fled France. He hoped to reach the Belgian coast, from where he could sail to America, but Austrian troops refused to allow him free passage and had him arrested. Lafayette was imprisoned in Austria for five harsh years.

While Lafayette languished in one lugubrious, damp prison after another, his health steadily deteriorating, the Revolution in France was plunging into a downward spiral, devolving into Terror, devouring its children and its leaders. Devastating news of the guillotining of the pitiable monarch and Queen Marie Antoinette as well as frightening reports of summary arrests, mass drownings, and the decapitation of thousands of French men and women trickled in to him. When his wife, Adrienne, visited him in his dungeon, she recounted the hideous details of the guillotining of her cherished mother.

Americans, still grateful to Lafayette for his role in their revolution, followed his misfortunes with deep sympathy. During the decade of the 1790s, the young American government displayed considerably more appreciation toward the valiant marquis than toward the French nation that had played a decisive role in the American victory over England— and this despite the Treaty of Amity and Commerce that the Americans and French had signed in 1778. Indeed, the treaty, which had stipulated that France and the United States would defend each other against England and that neither nation would conclude a formal truce with England without the consent of the other, had become an embarrassment. Despite the enthusiasm of many Americans for the French revolutionary cause, Washington's policy of neutrality, buttressed by his own immense prestige and by Federalists' antipathy for regicide in France and commonsensical reluctance to plunge their country back into war with England, succeeded in relegating the treaty to oblivion.

In 1793, Washington, though reluctant to intervene officially in European politics, instructed Gouverneur Morris, the minister to France, to express "informally the sentiments and the wishes of this country regarding M. de La Fayette." Again in 1796 Washington made his objections about Lafayette's imprisonment known to the Austrian ambassador in London, and finally he wrote to the emperor himself, all to no avail. Only when the new moderate Directory government in France demanded Lafayette's release was the prisoner finally freed. The fragile Directory, which had been set up in 1795, a year after the "Thermidorean" counterrevolution had finally put an end to the Revolution and the Terror, feared Lafayette's return to France but felt strongly that the world-famous French citizen should no longer be arbitrarily imprisoned in Austria. Thus the Directory asked Citizen General Napoleon Bonaparte, fresh from his victory in Rivoli, to negotiate for Lafayette's freedom, on condition that he not live in France.

Forty years old, worn, drained from his suffering, most of his fortune confiscated, Monsieur Lafayette (he had given up his noble title and the aristocratic "de") and his wife waited for two more years in Prussia and Holland before it was safe for them to return to France. The great French writer Chateaubriand wrote of Lafayette, "This man has lived."

When he could finally reenter France in 1800, Lafayette found a country transformed by many of the Revolution's accomplishments. Virtually all the vestiges of feudalism had been abolished. Citizens were

Lafayette Released from Prison.
Lithograph by Smith

equal before the law; the aristocracy was no longer a privileged elite exempt from taxes; the right of all children to share equally in inheritance had replaced primogeniture; Church property had been confiscated and sold; Jews and Protestants had been granted civil rights; illegitimate children had won full legal status; married couples could divorce; a meritocracy had replaced the hegemony of the aristocracy; and the principles of the "rights of man" were universally respected.

And yet Lafayette also found an exhausted people for whom the term "republic" had become a smear word. In a plebiscite in 1799, the people of France had voted for the constitution that guaranteed the autocracy of Napoleon. The vote was 3,011,007 to 1,562. The nation wanted, first and foremost, order and the rule of law, and Napoleon and then the Restoration Bourbons would supply them in their ways. France would not know republican government until 1871.

And how had the American Revolution fared in French opinion? Preceding Lafayette's flight and the downfall of the French Revolution came the eclipse of the American "beacon." The Revolution that had been extolled by the French as the model and hope for humanity had soon lost its authority and radiance. Perhaps that model was not perfect after all, the French began to muse. Maybe they could improve upon it, maybe even surpass it. The Americans, they pointed out, had ratified in 1787 a constitution that did not contain a Bill of Rights, and they still tolerated slavery. And were they not setting the clock back by retaining a Senate that mirrored the English hereditary House of Lords? Perhaps the Americans' esteem for English tradition was the problem. The French wanted no part of a system of checks and balances that thwarted the people's will. The French representative Lanjuinais mocked "the Anglo-American Mr. Adams, the Don Quixote of nobility," asserting that American Anglophiles "have lost their influence over us; they impose upon us no longer." The philosopher Mably joined the chorus, expressing disappointment with an America preoccupied with wealth and commerce.

So would it be the French and not the Americans who were destined to dazzle the world with perfection? Duke Mathieu de Montmorency, a veteran of the American Revolutionary War, acknowledged that the Americans had created a worthy precedent, but, he grandly added, "they have given a great example to the new hemisphere. Let us give it to the universe!" For Condorcet, another French *philosophe*, the American Revolution had merely paved the way for the French Revolution, which would be based on truer, purer, and more profound principles. "Why speak of the best that exists?" the *philosophe* Dupont asked in 1788. "Why not speak of the best that is possible?"

Many people dreamt of a clean sweep of tradition, a government founded solely on Enlightenment truths. "O nation of France, you are not made to receive an example, but to set it!" declared loftily the representative Rabaut Saint Etienne. The tables had quickly turned. Jacobin leaders believed that France no longer needed to look to America for guidance. Saint-Just pitied the American "federal" nation. Why, it was not even a republic, he scoffed, but a hopelessly fragmented conglomeration. Anacharsis Cloots, the self-styled "representative of humanity" from Prussia, triumphantly divulged that the Americans were secretly envious of the French system of government and reproached themselves daily for lacking the political insight of the French!

Prey to increasingly grandiose notions, the French began to claim that America should look to France for her own salvation. Whereas Jefferson, with a certain generosity of spirit, had written to his friend George Mason that he "consider[ed] the establishment and success of the [French] government as necessary to stay up our own," Robespierre chose a different tone: "And you, brave Americans, your freedom was won with our blood and is protected by your alliance with us. What would be your fate if we no longer existed? You would crumble once again under the yoke of your enemy!" The marriage of revolutions ended in divorce. The French abandoned American theories of government. Neither the institutions of the young republic nor the thoughtful ideas behind them held any attraction for revolutionaries in France.

Lord Acton wrote that "what the French took from the Americans was their theory of revolution, not their theory of government—their cutting, not their sewing." The cutting—whether colonial war or regicide, declaration of independence or tennis court oath—is the easy part. The art is in the sewing.

In 1824, Charles X, the brother of the decapitated Louis XVI, reigned in France. A superannuated monarchy had survived the guillotine. In America, an energetic republic, though stained by the abomination of slavery, was flourishing. That year, President James Monroe and both houses of Congress invited Lafayette back to America as "the Nation's Guest." He alone embodied two revolutions, the two events that had transformed modern history. At sixty-seven, his hair was thinner and he walked with a limp, but he had managed to recapture much of his early vigor. When his ship reached New York in August 1824, a flotilla of steamships in the harbor welcomed him and his son, George Washington Lafayette. A tumultuous crowd of 30,000 people onshore cheered. As Lafayette and his son journeyed through all twenty-four states, they were showered with honors, feted with banquets, speeches, and reenactments of revolutionary battles.

People were wild with excitement. Here was the American Revolution in flesh and blood, the general who had ridden alongside his commander-in-chief in defeat and in victory, at Brandywine, Valley Forge, Monmouth, West Point, and Yorktown. "Half a century had carried nearly all of his contemporary actors of the Revolution into the great abyss of time," wrote James Fenimore Cooper, remarking that Lafayette now stood alone, "like an imposing column" commemorating sacred deeds and principles.

It was during this year that towns, villages, and counties all over the map renamed themselves Fayette, Fayetteville, Lafayette, and La Grange, after Lafayette's estate in France. Monuments to the Revolution were erected in Boston, Camden, and Savannah; triumphal arches—constructed out of plywood and papier-mâché—quickly sprang up in towns and villages. Portraits of the hero were painted by the great artists of the day: Samuel Morse, Thomas Sully, and others. His image appeared on fans, medallions, buttons, quilts, handkerchiefs, bowls as well as furniture and banknotes. Men vied with horses for the privilege of drawing his carriage. Citizens, wrote an astounded Thomas Jefferson, were simply thrown into "delirium."

After stopping in Yorktown, Lafayette spent ten days at Monticello with Jefferson. The two old friends, who had not met since the beginning of the French Revolution, embraced warmly. At sunset, James Madison joined them for dessert, and conversation about French and American politics ran late into the night. Madison later commented that Lafayette appeared in fine health and spirits but so much increased in bulk and changed in aspect that he hardly recognized him. The following day, the three compatriots celebrated the opening of the Rotunda at the University of Virginia. In Montpellier, Lafayette spent a week with James and Dolley Madison, and at Mount Vernon, he kneeled at the tomb of the man he called his "beloved General."

In Boston, he met with John Adams. At ceremonies at Bunker Hill, Lafayette laid the cornerstone of the new monument as Daniel Webster solemnly addressed him: "Heaven saw fit to ordain that the electric spark of liberty should be conducted, through you, from the New World to the Old." When Lafayette departed for France, four American Presidents, his friends, had already wished him Godspeed, and a fifth, John Quincy Adams, delivered the farewell address.

Lafayette Laying the Cornerstone of the Bunker Hill Monument,
by Langlumé

To the Americans who jubilantly feted and celebrated the hero of two revolutions it did not matter that Lafayette had not been a key leader in either. Neither a politician comfortable wielding power nor a talented orator nor a political theorist, Lafayette had been essentially a military man, not an architect of revolution. He bore little resemblance to the galaxy of American founders—Adams, Hamilton, Madison, and Jefferson—who were simultaneously experienced politicians and thoughtful political theorists, or to the fiery band of radical visionaries in France—Sieyès, Robespierre, and Saint-Just.

Still, the role Lafayette was able to play to perfection during his visit to early-nineteenth-century America was the one that had always eluded him during the French Revolution, that of national mediator and unifier, the role of a Washington. Lafayette's travels in America coincided with a chaotic and fiercely bitter presidential campaign. Competing for the presidency were five candidates: Andrew Jackson, John Quincy Adams, William Crawford, John Calhoun, and Henry Clay. While these politicians waged a rancorous free-for-all, Lafayette, high above the fray in the stratosphere of immortal heroes, could remind Americans of their common past and the founding principles of the republic. As if descending from the Mount Olympus of legendary gods, he alone was powerful enough to unite, at least temporarily, a divided country.

Americans appreciated the unique gift that the Frenchman could bestow upon them. James Fenimore Cooper observed that "at the public dinners instead of caustic toasts, intended to throw ridicule and odium on some potent adversary, none were heard but healths to the guest of the nation, around whom were amicably grouped the most violent of both parties." Another observer agreed that the only surviving general from the Revolution "turns this whole people from the . . . troubles and bitterness of our manifold political dissensions . . . [and] carries us back to that great period in our history, about which opinions have long been tranquil and settled."

Jefferson remarked to a friend that, at a crucial time in American history, Lafayette "rall[ied] us together and strengthen[ed] the habit of considering our country as one and indivisible." Toward the end of his journey, Lafayette too spoke of the feelings of fellowship his visit had engendered, expressing "satisfaction . . . that [his] presence has promoted many reconciliations between the political parties; men who have not spoken to one another for more than twenty years . . . revive together their common memories of the Revolution."

Jefferson and Lafayette knew well that for the young republic, a sense of unity was essential. But what did they mean by "unity"? Neither had in mind the kind of unity that issues from a homogeneous nation, a land where citizens share a common history along with similar ethnic and religious backgrounds. John Jay's vision, in *The Federalist* No. 2, of Americans as "one united people—a people descended from the same ancestors, . . . professing the same religion, very similar in their manners and customs," was clearly at odds with the reality of American diversity. Did "unity" evoke for Jefferson and Lafayette ideological unanimity, a community whose citizens transcend partisan conflict and find consensus? Or did they hope that citizens would experience collective, emotional feelings of fraternity and oneness?

Jefferson knew that as Americans pursued their happiness, they would disagree on all manner of social, political, and economic issues and would engage in partisan conflict. After all, he himself had been the principal leader of the earliest opposition party. And as President he had presided over a government whose checks and balances—the collision of the different branches of government—made unity all but impossible. The unity that Jefferson prized was based neither on ideological consensus nor on fraternal communion. For the third President of the United States, unity meant citizens' allegiance to the political and moral principles expressed in the nation's founding documents. Jefferson never confused this kind of shared commitment to institutions that aspired to guarantee life, liberty, and the pursuit of happiness for citizens with citizens' ideological unanimity.

Unity for Jefferson could only mean a shared commitment to core democratic values and to a republic that, though "indivisible," permitted political fragmentation and unruly—though moderate—ideological division. Lafayette's presence in America could enable all Americans to remember and celebrate the quasi-mythic founding epoch when those luminous political and moral principles were first declared.

And what did Lafayette mean by "unity"? The "reconciliation between the political parties" that he wished to promote may have signified a temporary respite from party war, or perhaps a sense of harmony and good feeling as people experienced the fellowship of their common participation in the American political experiment. Lafayette certainly did not harbor any hidden, nefarious motives in wishing to be a unifying national figure during the French Revolution or in relishing that same role in the United States of the 1820s.

And yet the term "unity" had earned the darkest of reputations during the French Revolution. "The republic, one and indivisible," was the shibboleth on every French citizen's lips for four years. Unity represented the Revolution's highest goal but also explained its calamitous descent into repression and terror.

The kind of unity cherished by the French was something quite alien to the American mentality. After centuries of the wrenching inequality of a rigid, elitist caste system, revolutionaries in France hungered first and foremost for equality. While the Americans' driving passion was for freedom, in France people longed for a nation of equal citizens. And was it not logical, revolutionaries reasoned, that equal citizens would share the same revolutionary ideals and goals? What would propel and guide the Revolution if not the people's oneness and unanimity? Their unity constituted the motor, the sine qua non, of radical political and social change. But unity could not be achieved as long as division and opposition persisted. Divisions of any kind became anathema, so many reminders of the prerevolutionary society deeply divided along class, or rather caste lines.

Tumult, division, and competing interest groups in the United States vs. concord, unity, and community in France. Here were the antithetical concepts of democracy and nationhood that shaped the core values of both revolutions, influencing, as we shall see, their notions of individual rights and freedoms, coloring their political discourse and style, and setting the stage for the success or failure of the two revolutionary projects. During the next two centuries, those divergent revolutionary traditions and visions would galvanize leaders of liberation movements around the world, inspiring some to install a system of adversarial political parties, imbuing in others the idea of "one-party democracy."

We live in a world shaped by—sometimes still reeling from—the political ideas of a generation of eighteenth-century revolutionary leaders. Throughout much of the twentieth century, the French revolutionary vision of the nation as a unitary and organic whole has colored French political culture. "Since the dawn of our history," Charles de Gaulle declared in 1947, "our misfortunes occur in proportion to our division; but good fortune has never betrayed a unified France." De Gaulle's message of unity never varied, not during World War II, not during the Fourth Republic, and not during the Fifth Republic. It was also a message with which any radical revolutionary leader in France in 1793 would have been comfortable. "There is only one duty and one law," de Gaulle proclaimed, "and that is French unity. There is only one interest that counts, that of France. There is only one duty that exists for us, and that is to unite and rally around her."

In the United States, tumult and conflict have been as American as baseball and town meetings. The American system has always worked best when stimulated by the creative tension of sharply adversarial politics. Jefferson could define and defend his vision in contrast with a Hamilton, Lincoln with a Douglas, Roosevelt with a Hoover. In 1936, FDR, railing against the businessmen, bankers, and financiers who rabidly attacked the New Deal, declared to a tumultuous Madison Square Garden crowd, "They are unanimous in their hate for me, and I welcome their hatred!" Conflict, not consensus, produced the meaningful change and progress that occurred in the 1930s.

But more recently, the French longing for unity has produced what many in France feel is a contentless consensus. And in the United States politicians have been extolling a centrist course, hoping to rise above political conflict, as if the French revolutionary dream of a harmonious, fraternal realm free from political strife were gaining new disciples on the other side of the Atlantic.

The sister revolutions of the eighteenth century hold invaluable lessons for our contemporary democracies. Not only do they illuminate our political assumptions, beliefs, and ideas, but they also help us to take the temperature of our political cultures, to diagnose our political ills, and to prescribe remedies for them.

Indeed, in the late 1850s, two decades after completing his famed *Democracy in America*, Alexis de Tocqueville, the great historian and social analyst, finally began planning another book. This time he wanted to write about his own period. "Basically, only affairs of our own times interest the public and interest me," he confessed, not unlike many writers with an eye on the marketplace. But what would be the focus of Tocqueville's new study? "When I try to find the crux of such a subject, the point where all the ideas that it generates meet and tie themselves together, I cannot find it."

Tocqueville ultimately discovered that the key to the present lay in the past. Only a book about "the long drama of the French Revolution," he realized, would provide him with a framework for his reflections on contemporary French political culture. His readers, focusing on their eighteenth-century revolution, would "reflect . . . unceasingly on themselves," grasping on the one hand "the sentiments, the ideas, the mores that alone can lead to public prosperity and liberty [and] . . . the vices and errors that, on the other hand, divert them irresistibly from this end." Tocqueville suggested that beneath the historian's text lies a subtext—a commentary on the present. In other words, we are always writing the history of our own times.

2

Revolutionary Leadership

In July 1788, nine months after the Constitutional Convention in Philadelphia, King Louis XVI convened a different kind of constitutional convention in France. At the brink of financial collapse, France was sinking into chaos. The nation's debt, along with interest on that debt, was reaching astronomical figures; the collection of taxes was breaking down. Nobles, defending their financial privileges and refusing to accept royal edicts, fomented riots in Bordeaux, Dijon, Pau, Toulouse, and Grenoble. Poor harvests sparked bread and grain riots all over France; gangs of marauding peasants were terrorizing the countryside, and starving rural workers were flocking to the towns, where they added to the numbers of the already unemployed. The king, unable to commit himself to a firm course of action, had seen an array of highly talented and competent finance ministers—the idealistic, progressive Turgot, the circumspect Necker, the courageous, reform-minded Calonne—come and go.

When Louis's fourth finance minister, Cardinal Loménie de Brienne, proposed the same reforms and taxes on the privileged nobility as had Calonne and met with the same resistance in the provincial parliaments, things were truly at a standstill. Louis felt he had no choice but to convene the Estates General, a kind of National Assembly comprising elected representatives of the three orders of France—the nobility, the clergy, and the "Third Estate," composed of all the other inhabitants of France. The king's advisers hoped that somehow the Estates General would help resolve the desperate crisis.

But whose memory was long enough to remember what a meeting of the Estates General would entail? So static and lifeless was the political culture of France that the Estates, the equivalent of the English Parliament, had not met in a hundred and sixty years. No one knew what should be the number of deputies, the relationship among the orders, the mode of election, or the procedure for deliberation. Only Louis had the authority to say what the guidelines would be, but the hapless, ineffective monarch said nothing.

That summer, Cardinal Brienne, a month before he too would be dismissed, had one of the most extraordinary ideas in the history of constitution making. He convinced Louis to invite all of France's "men of learning" to enter an intellectual competition on the subject of the Estates General, its makeup and procedures. They were asked to consider a variety of issues. For example, should the entire gathering be large or small? Should the orders meet together or separately? Should they be equal or unequal in their rights? The call was heard, and since France was the most literary country in Europe, the king was inundated with writings. One man counted twenty-five hundred political pamphlets.

The idea of an academic competition for a nation's constitution astonished Alexis de Tocqueville. He thought that the king, by treating a new constitution as an intellectual exercise, had given carte blanche to theoreticians who possessed virtually no experience in government: Louis himself bestowed authority on inventors of experimental blueprints for the total overhaul of France! Though lacking any understanding of political process in a government of representative institutions, these "men of letters" did not shrink from propounding theories for the wholesale restructuring of French society and politics.

And yet, if there is to be meaningful progress, truly significant political and social change, who will articulate visions for a better society, who will formulate those lofty goals, who will chart the course of change? Experienced political leaders and government ministers whose careers are rooted in archaic and stagnant political systems? Or people of imagination, insight, and daring? Or individuals who are simultaneously the political as well as the intellectual leaders of their day?

Tocqueville acknowledged the importance of vision and theory in forging more just and open societies. Abstract ideas, he was convinced, can play a vital, creative role in politics, nourishing a political culture, invigorating it with fresh possibilities and goals. He attributed the failure of the French Revolution not to the utopian theories of men of letters but rather to their lack of experience in politics and government and to the monarchical regime that had excluded them—along with the rest of the population—from participation in the political life of the nation.

How different was the gathering of founders in Philadelphia! At their Constitutional Convention in 1787, there was no abyss, as Richard Hofstadter remarked, between political intellect and political power. Thirty-one of the fifty-five men present had been educated at colonial colleges or at similar institutions abroad. Many were scholars and scientists, two were college presidents, and three were college professors. They were for the most part intellectual men who also possessed years of experience in self-government.

American founders such as Madison had respect for experience, practical knowledge, the lessons of the past, and especially for America's English inheritance, but they also knew that history could not always provide wisdom and direction for the future. In certain cases, such as the drafting of the Constitution, men—aided by their experience—had to embark courageously upon political experimentation based on their own ideas. These forward-looking leaders would shape their own political system and national future. Their goal was to conceive a constitution and a federal union based on rational philosophic ideas and intellectual creativity, on what Alexander Hamilton termed "reflection and choice." The founders were "children of the Enlightenment," notes one constitutional scholar. "Otherwise they would never have tried to write a Constitution whose few thousand words contained a host of untried ideas and institutions." Thomas Jefferson, hailed by Tocqueville as "the most powerful apostle that democracy has ever had," believed that progress would issue from experiment, innovation, and continual political renewal.

The 1780s were a brief and privileged moment in American history, a luminous period when a galaxy of brilliant politicians of extraordinary intellect and integrity drafted an unparalleled Constitution and shaped enduring democratic political institutions. English Prime Minister William Gladstone called their Constitution "the most remarkable work known to me . . . to have been produced by the human intellect." The achievement of the founders is breathtaking.

What was it about that period that enabled it to produce such exceptional leadership? One persuasive explanation offered by the historian Gordon Wood holds that social stratification in eighteenth-century America produced an elite class of educated gentlemen who, by virtue of their birth, were destined to be the social leaders of the day. Their intellectual and political leadership, Wood argues, was a consequence of their social leadership. They took their rank seriously, accepting its privileges as well as its responsibilities. Civic-minded, committed to lives of public service, "they thought they ought to lead the society both politically and intellectually—indeed they could not help but lead the society—by the sheer force of their position and their character." The founding period was unique because, according to Wood, "somehow . . . ideas and power, intellectualism and politics, came together—indeed were one with each other—in a way never again duplicated in American history."

Was the confluence of these men's extraordinary intellectual leadership and their years of experience in their states' legislatures, assemblies, and houses of burgesses the key to the success of their revolutionary enterprise? Was the founders' ability to synthesize political vision and political experience the fountain from which sprang the unequaled accomplishments of the American Revolution? Does Tocqueville's prescription for the happy marriage of practical knowledge and theoretical daring explain why political ideas in America led to an enduring Constitution and lasting democratic institutions and in France led to political repression and terror?

TOCQUEVILLE'S PRESCRIPTION FOR CHANGE

Alexis de Tocqueville's family bore bitter scars from the French Revolution. Tocqueville's great-grandfather, Lamoignon de Malesherbes, had served valiantly as Louis XVI's defense lawyer during his trial for treason; the ineffably painful task also fell to him of having to inform his forlorn royal client of the harrowing verdict. A few months later Malesherbes himself was guillotined. Tocqueville's mother and father were imprisoned during the Revolution and probably would have been executed had the Terror lasted any longer. Alexis himself grew up in an aristocratic milieu imbued with nostalgia for the prerevolutionary past. His father—also a historian of the Revolution—was an old-fashioned royalist. But Alexis's attitude toward the Revolution, unlike his father's, was very nuanced. Though emotionally and temperamentally drawn only to members of his own elite class, intellectually he understood very well the frustrations and aspirations of revolutionaries in France.

Tocqueville perceived that it was widespread dissatisfaction with the status quo that called change into being. Wherever people looked, ancient institutions seemed no longer to correspond to the new situation and needs of the French. French men and women, disgusted with their own times, intuitively felt that change was imminent, though no one could imagine how things could be altered or the shape that change would take. But disgust had engendered hope, and at the center of everyone's consciousness glowed the hope for change. It was as if there were some "internal force of energy with no discernible motor," mused Tocqueville, that disrupted the entire public life of France, making people question all their assumptions and habits.

Tocqueville understood that the entrenched system of abusive, ridiculous, and arbitrary privileges drove people naturally toward the idea of equality and toward a bold plan for reshaping the country. For his part, Tocqueville concurred with the new principles of equality and the sovereignty of the people; he saw no value in the vestiges of feudalism. The necessity of change was a given. Even the king of France and his advisers, Tocqueville noted, acceded to change. But embracing its novelty and energy, they failed to grasp its meaning and implications. They could not see "where they were going: they held on to each other's hands in the dark."

Ironically, the people who were least open to change—and therefore least able to understand and seize control of history—were those supposedly "wise and practical" men who had acquired decades of political experience. Tocqueville emphasized that experience is insufficient to help people comprehend a changing world. The men who possessed experience in government—administrators, ministers, and magistrates—had no true insight into the nature of politics.

They had experience, but it was the wrong kind. In a monarchical state, in the absence of any vital and inclusive political culture, no member of the government could become knowledgeable about politics, for, concluded Tocqueville in a concise formulation of his political credo, "only the interplay of *free institutions* can really teach men of state this principal part of their art." Only political experience in representative democracies like England and America could be valuable.

Ultimately, the men who were attuned to change, who had insight into the movement of society, were not men of experience or power but rather men of imagination and vision: France's men of letters. Whereas experienced politicians dismissed as a preposterous fantasy the idea of radically changing France's political and social structure, intellectuals possessed the audacity and imagination to believe that people could transform French society. Only they had the creativity and vision to think that they could build, on top of the ruins of the old order, a just society.

The impetus for real, comprehensive, and lasting change, Tocqueville concluded, comes from human creativity. The ideas and passions of men propel human affairs. "It is always within the *minds of men*," he wrote, "that we find the mark of the events that will be produced outside."

Imagination and vision constitute the motor of history. Tocqueville revealed the frequent miscalculation made by people wishing to grasp the events swirling around them: they pay attention to what men of experience are thinking. But these men who are considered "wise" and "practical" continue to judge, according to their own rules, those others whose goal is precisely to destroy and change those very rules. In times of turbulence and great historical change, "it is less important to know what men of experience are thinking," Tocqueville advised, "than to pay attention to what is preoccupying the imaginations of the dreamers."

And yet, French men of letters went too far. Tocqueville deplored their plan to replace in one swift move complex and ancient institutions with abstract systems, with "simple and elementary rules." The basic societal changes that took place may have been both inevitable and desirable, but Tocqueville thought it neither inevitable nor desirable that they should be brought about through convulsive and traumatic means. It was the brutal and violent character of the Revolution, not its underlying political principles, aims, or vision, that Tocqueville condemned and for which he faulted, not politicians, but men of letters. He did not blame intellectuals for wanting to destroy the hated abuses of the Old Regime, he explained, but he did blame the naïve, arrogant manner in which they went about this "necessary destruction."

THE POLITICS OF THE IMPOSSIBLE

The "terrifying spectacle" of intellectuals constructing an entirely new society through reason and logic alone horrified Tocqueville. But his intention was not merely to condemn men of letters and their abstract, ahistorical theories. His real aim was a sociological examination of the conditions in French society that made it possible for French intellectuals, people with no experience whatsoever in politics, to wield political authority and to prescribe a new government for France.

Intellectuals in eighteenth-century France—along with everyone else—were excluded from the political life of the period. The complete absence of political freedom, Tocqueville contended, made the world of political affairs not only "unfamiliar to them, but invisible." Even so, the absence of political freedom had not caused intellectuals to withdraw into pure philosophy or literature. On the contrary, Tocqueville noted, they wrote passionately about social and political questions. But they possessed no practical knowledge of politics to temper their ardor for theory or warn them about the obstacles of political and social reality. They created their own imaginary society, in which everything was simple and rational.

England and the United States could claim to be governed by people like Lord Bolingbroke, David Hume, Edmund Burke, and James Madison—intellectuals who played active political roles. But in France the sphere of government and the sphere of ideas were separate. Some men administered, others theorized in a vacuum about government. Tocqueville pointed out that if French men of letters, like their English counterparts, had been engaged in politics and obliged to work at modifying and reforming institutions, they would not have needed to imagine entirely new ones. Unfortunately, they believed that their only choice was between accepting all the injustices of the past and destroying the political and social fabric of the country.

Tocqueville's luminous good sense led him to pose a fundamental question concerning these *philosophes*. Why, he asked, did anyone listen to them? Why did the king and everyone else take them seriously? Why did speculative theories of government penetrate French society so deeply?

In England, few people would have wasted time on theoretical discussions of social and political issues, but in France, the people were as distant from the political process as the intellectuals. Tocqueville believed that if the French had participated in their government, as they had years earlier in the Estates General, if they had continued to be involved in the daily administration of the country through provincial assemblies, they never would have let themselves be carried away by writers' abstract ideas. People would have been knowledgeable about politics and skeptical of pure theory.

Tocqueville's insight was that the decisive political life of France took place outside of the sphere of politics, in the domain of literature and ideas. Looking for the sociological causes for the split between political power and intellectual authority, he perceived that the French nation, while alienated from its own affairs, disgusted with its institutions yet powerless to reform them, was at the same time the most literate of all nations and the most enraptured with high culture. This schizophrenic situation, Tocqueville believed, explained how intellectuals became a political power and ended up being the number one power.

Radical ideas furnished an entertaining social pastime for the aristocracy, but neither they nor anyone else discerned that all of France's institutions as well as its social fabric would face a devastating assault. When he finished compiling a list of the grievances contained in the *Cahiers de doléances* (the 60,000 pamphlets written in response to the king's request for comments on the state of the nation), Tocqueville was thunderstruck. "I realize with a kind of terror that what is being demanded," he wrote with stupefaction, "is the simultaneous and systematic abolition of all the laws and customs of the country. I see that it will be a question of one of the most dangerous revolutions that ever took place in the world."

And yet the proponents of this radical change, who would be its unwitting future victims, had no notion of the violence that would accompany such a total and sudden transformation of French society. They naïvely thought that the whole process could be carried out through "reason" alone.

At the time of his death, Tocqueville was working on a sequel to *The Old Regime and the Revolution*. In his notes he discussed the violence that can be produced by ideas, depicting intellectuals and theoreticians gone haywire. "The Convention, which did so much harm to its contemporaries by its wrath, did eternal harm by its examples," he wrote, revealing a prophetic understanding of the far-reaching and ominous repercussions of the French Revolution. "It created the politics of the impossible, the theory of madness, the cult of blind audacity." Tocqueville recognized that the leaders of the French Revolution formed a new international "turbulent and destructive race, always ready to strike down and incapable of setting up, that stipulates that there are no individual rights, indeed that there are no individuals, but only a mass which may stop at nothing to attain its ends." Their revolutionary religion was "one of the most singular, the most active, and the most contagious diseases of the human mind."

A successful revolution, according to Tocqueville's prescription, calls for the marriage of bold political vision and practical experience in representative political institutions. Unfortunately, it was a prescription that could not be applied in France. There existed neither an inclusive political culture nor representative institutions in which men of letters could have gained crucial experience. To whom could the French have turned to draft a constitution, establish new institutions, and create a vital political culture? Tocqueville's assessment is logical and pessimistic: it was virtually impossible for eighteenth-century France to produce leaders capable of installing democracy. The appropriate course, under such circumstances, would probably have been not revolution but patience and gradual reform. France would have been propelled by the tide of industrialization, urbanization, modernization, and capitalism to evolve incrementally and nonviolently toward equality and democracy.

When Tocqueville looked at America, he saw a different political panorama. The kind of revolutionary mentality that, undermining all traditional beliefs, opens up before people the sense of "an empty, virtually limitless space" for social and political experiment never existed, he believed, in America. He was convinced that Americans had not staged a democratic revolution. On the contrary, he saw them as having arrived in their new land "more or less as we see them," already imbued with democratic principles. As for radical theories, he was persuaded that the participation of Americans in representative institutions had moderated their taste for abstract political ideas.

French intellectuals, at the time of the revolutions, however, far from perceiving the significant differences between France and America, discerned in the Revolution on the other side of the Atlantic the confirmation of all their own theories of government. They congratulated Americans for acting upon the theories of French intellectuals, for giving the "substance of reality" to French dreams. But Tocqueville knew that there were profound differences between the two revolutions. Indeed, he remarked that political philosophy had led in America to liberty, while in France it merely invented new forms of servitude. The French saw in America the realization of their revolutionary principles, not recognizing that the American founding fathers were men not only of profound learning but also of decades of experience in government and nonviolent political conflict.

THE AMERICAN SYNTHESIS

Years before the American Revolution, the men who would become the new nation's founding fathers were already versed in representative government. John Adams: Massachusetts legislator and one of the Massachusetts delegates to the First Continental Congress. Samuel Adams: member of the Massachusetts assembly. John Hancock: Boston selectman, then representative to the Massachusetts legislature. Gouverneur Morris: elected to New York's provincial congress in 1775. George Washington: member of the Virginia House of Burgesses. Thomas Jefferson: member of the Virginia House of Burgesses. Clinton Rossiter estimated that as a group they had had more political experience than any gathering of the leaders of a newly independent nation at any time in history. But these were also highly educated men whose political experience was complemented by their intellect. George Washington, though not a "man of letters," hailed the revolutionary era that wedded the wisdom of political philosophers with that of working legislators. It was a period, he wrote, "when . . . the researches of the human mind, after social happiness, [and] the Treasures of knowle[d]ge, acquired by the labours of Philosophers, Sages and Legislatures . . . are laid open for our use, and their collected wisdom may be happily applied in the Establishment of our forms of Government." Not all the founders were equally enthusiastic about political theory, but they all—to a greater or lesser degree—respected the value of both experience and ideas.

No one in America more than Alexander Hamilton combined practical experience, respect for tradition and historical continuity, and political vision. An aide to George Washington during the Revolutionary War, the commander of an artillery battery at Yorktown, Hamilton also served in the New York legislature and as a delegate to the Constitutional Convention. As the first Secretary of the Treasury he worked to create a national bank as well as a dynamic capitalist economy for the young nation. He envisioned America as a great commercial empire, sharing ideological as well as economic ties with England.

Hamilton was one of the first Americans to precede Tocqueville in expressing alarm about abstract political philosophy—especially in

The Constitutional Convention, by Howard Chandler Christy

France—that was not complemented by experience in representative government. Just as events in Paris were beginning to unfold, Hamilton conveyed to the Marquis de Lafayette his apprehension about the role of philosophers in those events. "I dread the reveries of your Philosophic politicians," he wrote, warning Lafayette that these theoreticians seemed to have lost contact with reality.

Like Washington, Hamilton believed in the "collected wisdom" of philosophers and legislators. He was convinced that good government should be a matter of "reflection and choice" and innovation, but he also prized continuity in government along with strong and stable institutions. Thus he expressed wariness of visionary men who were immune to the lessons of experience. Viewing innovation and "enthusiasm" with suspicion, he wrote to George Washington that "prodigious innovations" and "excessive fermentation" did not augur well for the order and health of French society. He felt deeply that governments needed a more stable foundation than the "ebullitions" of philosophers. And, though one of the architects of the new constitution and federal system, he insisted that "experience" was "the least fallible guide of human opinions."

Nor was imagination in politics a positive value for the politician, businessman, and diplomat Gouverneur Morris. A witness to early revolutionary events in Paris even before he was named America's minister to France in 1792, Morris took a dim view of attempts to democratize France. The traditional ways of France charmed Morris. Unlike the Anglophile Hamilton, Morris was an enthusiastic visitor in Paris, finding French society "the delight of Life" and missing few dinner parties or plays. Still, he was unimpressed by the French "Leaders of Liberty" who seemed to wish to annihilate much that was precious in France. Morris dryly remarked that "the best heads" among the revolutionaries in the French Assembly "would not be injured by *Experience*, and unfortunately there are a great number who, with much *Imagination*, have little Knowledge, Judgment or Reflection." Like Hamilton, Morris valued practical experience in government, but the French, he wrote, "have taken Genius instead of Reason for their Guide, adopted *Experiment* instead of *Experience*, and wander in the Dark because they prefer Lightning to Light."

Morris informed Washington that there were three parties in the National Assembly: the aristocrats, the madmen, and another party consisting of friends to good, free government. Unfortunately, this "middle party" could not be counted on for political leadership, for its members, Morris commented, acquired their ideas of government from books alone. "The Men who live in the World are very different from those who dwell in the Heads of Philosophers," Morris noted, recommending that the *philosophes'* systems and theories be put back into the books from which they came. The abstract and fallacious ideas of these "literary People" were leading them to misconstrue human nature in general and the nature of the French in particular.

From books emerged the abstract, universal, rational political principles that the revolutionaries dreamed of applying equally to all countries, regardless of a people's particular traditions and history. Such revolutionaries, Morris complained, seemed to want to bring everything to the same "Roman standard," refusing to recognize that the different societies on the "Face of this Planet" require "Different Constitutions of Government." Ultimately, "metaphysic" theories of government, he felt, did nothing less than undermine all the moral and religious underpinnings of society.

For Hamilton and Morris, the strength of American democracy lay in its continuity with its colonial past and English institutions. Experience and practical wisdom were purely positive values. Neither man thought that experience dulled the mind with routine, stale formulas or worn ideas. They preferred well-trodden routes to pathbreaking experimental, visionary, or utopian plans. Their ability to combine an openness to political experiment with caution and a desire to preserve rather than to destroy put them irremediably at odds with a revolution in France that aspired to begin even time anew.

At the end of the century, Americans were still echoing Morris's preference for experience over experiment. Even though "experiment" represents an interesting middle ground between experience on the one hand and theory on the other, and even though the American experiment was showing every sign of success, many preferred to cling to the security of the already known. Celebrating the anniversary of American Independence in New Haven in 1798, Noah Webster declared: "Never . . . let us exchange our civil and religious institutions for the wild theories of crazy projectors; or the sober, industrious moral habits of our country, for *experiments* in atheism and lawless democracy. *Experience* is a safe pilot; but *experiment* is a dangerous ocean, full of rocks and shoals."

Voltaire was "a liar"; Rousseau, a "coxcomb," "a satyr"; the utopian philosopher Condorcet, "a quack" and a "fool"; d'Alembert, a "louse" and a "tick"; Turgot, "not a judicious practical statesman." The outspoken John Adams did not hide his contempt for utopian theorists. Indeed, he blamed the French *philosophes'* abstract systems, lack of practical experience in politics, presumption, and arrogance for the disastrous Revolution in France.

As the American minister in Paris in 1778, Adams met and dined with all the renowned thinkers of the day, the respected finance minister and *philosophe* Turgot, the progressive social thinker La Rochefoucauld, and Condorcet, the mathematician and humanitarian *philosophe*. He admitted that they were learned, honest, and well-meaning, but, he added, not only were they blindly infatuated with a "chimera," they were totally ignorant of the science of government.

The axiomatic slogans that the French loved repelled Adams. Turgot's fanciful political abstractions, especially about a government that was "one and indivisible," were as meaningless as they were "mysterious." As for Condorcet, Adams felt that if he had remained a philosopher, he would have been harmless, but unfortunately as a legislator he helped destroy all the good he had aimed at. Adams ridiculed Condorcet's dogmas about the limitless perfectibility of man and unstoppable progress. But especially he disdained Condorcet's belief that intellectuals were humanity's "eternal benefactors." This cult of genius, Adams warned, constituted a mischievous new mythology that substituted infallible men for gods. And so shocked was Adams when he read Condorcet's Francocentric judgment that the principles of the French constitution were more pure, accurate, and profound than the principles informing the American Constitution, that in the margin of his book he only scribbled: "Pure! accurate! profound! indeed!"

When Adams and Jefferson reminisced in their correspondence about hours spent in Paris with early leaders of the French Revolution, Adams never failed to comment on their appalling lack of experience and knowledge. He recalled in particular one memorable evening spent in Jefferson's *hôtel* with his son John Quincy and their friend Lafayette. While Adams and Jefferson sat silently, Lafayette "harangued" them for the entire evening, outlining his ideas for reform in France. Adams's verdict was unequivocal and harsh: "I was astonished at the Grossness of his Ignorance of Government and History."

Not only did the French *philosophes*, according to Adams, contribute nothing to the creation of lasting democratic institutions (they were "totally destitute," he noted, of "Common Sense"), but they actually set history on a backward course. The "fantastical projects" they invented, according to Adams, actually retarded any improvement in the condition of mankind for a hundred years. The vestiges of feudalism and slavery were already disappearing, knowledge was expanding, governments were making critical reforms. But none of this, Adams lamented, was enough for the *philosophes!* They demanded immediate perfection! "They rent and tore the whole garment to pieces and left not one whole thread in it."

The events of his own times inspired little but gloom in Adams. Recalling political instability on both sides of the Atlantic, ignorance in France, revolt in America, American enthusiasm for violent events in France, and the hurtful misrepresentations of his own political positions, he expressed bitter disenchantment with an entire decade of political experiment. "I was determined," he wrote, "to wash my own hands as clean as I could of all this foulness."

Though in 1776 Adams hailed his own times for providing the opportunity for unparalleled political creativity, for the forming of "the wisest and happiest" government that human wisdom could contrive, he also wrote that same year, "I dread the Spirit of Innovation." By the 1780s, his political ideas—his desire for a bicameral legislature that would house separately an aristocratic order, his affinity for hereditary institutions, and his belief that the people possessed only "an essential share" in the nation's sovereignty—placed him outside of the mainstream of American political thought. While the American experiment in government was evolving, Adams, disabused and sour, took comfort in retreating backward in time.

ARCHITECTS AND DREAMERS

If there was a philosopher who was also the principal architect of the new American government, it was the studious, vigorous James Madison—though he himself regarded the Constitution as the work of "many heads and many hands." This Virginian was truly a voice of reason—of respect for experience and of enthusiasm for visionary ideas. He was an intellectual interested not only in political theory but in every aspect of American society, from taxes to trade, industry, and the construction of new canals. He also possessed a deep understanding of the relationship between political thought and action. At the Philadelphia Convention, one admiring delegate from Georgia remarked that the Virginian blended "the profound politician with the scholar."

Although wary of "theoretic politicians" who acquire knowledge "in a man's closet," separated from human agents and events, and fully aware of the limits of human sagacity, Madison nevertheless saw an important place in politics for speculation and abstract theory. In even the most imperfect theories there could be germs of truth. When Madison read of Rousseau's hopeful proposal for a kind of league of nations, a council of sovereigns that would assure perpetual and universal peace, his first reaction was one of skepticism. Such utopian dreams, he thought, exist only in the imaginations of visionary philosophers. Yet so dreadful were the realities of war that an appeal to rationalist schemes could not be summarily rejected. "Much is to be hoped from the progress of reason," he sensibly wrote, "and if any thing is to be hoped, every thing ought to be tried." Similarly, the writings of Montesquieu might contain inaccuracies, but Madison recognized that Montesquieu "lifted the veil from the venerable errors which enslaved opinion" and applauded him for having pointed the way to "those luminous truths of which he had but a glimpse himself."

The reservations Madison harbored about political theories were not fundamentally different from his reservations about the value of practical experience. Indeed, he discerned fallibility and flaws in all facets of human understanding and endeavor. Language itself—more basic than human rationality and experience—was flawed. No language, not even English, is so copious as to supply "words and phrases for every complex idea." Thus the wisest course was to have only moderate expectations and hopes for the efforts of human intelligence.

In this imperfect world, experience and history could instruct people as to what systems of government would *not* work, and in those cases, Madison held, "experience is the oracle of truth." Seldom, however, did historical precedents offer lessons for the future. They "furnish no other light than that of beacons," he remarked, "which give warning of the course to be shunned, without pointing out that which ought to be pursued." Open to experiment and innovation, Madison knew well that men had no choice but to use their rational faculties and imagination to shape the political future.

The "glory" of the Americans, according to Madison, was that they "have not suffered a blind veneration for antiquity, for custom." In creating a Constitution and political institutions, they embarked upon a course that quite simply had "no parallel in the annals of human society." Madison even called Americans the first free people to deliberate on a form of government since "the creation of the world."

An optimistic Madison expressed confidence in people's ability to shape freely and rationally their own political future. The American Constitution, he emphasized, was an experiment, probably not "a faultless plan," inasmuch as its drafters—like its critics—were fallible men. But he was excited rather than deterred by the idea of seizing the moment and setting out on an untried path. "I can see no danger," he said at the Virginia ratifying convention, "in submitting to practice an experiment which seems to be founded on the best theoretic principles." Defending the Constitution, he stressed the value of openness to innovation. "Is it not agreed," he asked his fellow Virginians, "that a reform is necessary? If any takes place, will it not be an experiment?"

Indeed, Madison believed that men of letters were as important to politics and progress as experienced politicians. "The class of literati," he wrote, "is not less necessary than any other. They are the cultivators of the human mind—the manufacturers of useful knowledge—the agents of the commerce of ideas . . . the teachers of the arts of life and the means of happiness."

Politician and intellectual par excellence, Madison inhabited both the abstract and the empirical worlds. He hailed the rational, creative minds that "invented" America's republican government but also expressed the hope that experience would confirm and strengthen the American experiment, that America's "glory be completed by every improvement to the *theory* which *experience* may teach; and her happiness be perpetuated by a system of administration corresponding with the purity of the *theory*." His goal was government founded on reason, but, he added prudently, "the most rational government will not find it a superfluous advantage to have the prejudices of the community on its side."

★   ★   ★

Thomas Jefferson was a firebrand. He neither shared the negativity toward the French *philosophes* of Hamilton, Adams, and Morris nor admired Madisonian prudence and caution. On the contrary, he was unusual in his openness to change, innovation, and experiment in politics.

When in 1787 an alarmed Abigail Adams in London wrote to Jefferson in Paris that the "mobish insurgents" of Shays's Rebellion in western Massachusetts were destroying the fabric along with the foundation of American society, taking the country to the brink of chaos, Jefferson greeted the news cheerfully. "I like a little rebellion now and then," he replied. "It is like a storm in the Atmosphere." Jefferson bestowed his warm approval not only on resistance to government oppression but on the revolutionary enterprise in general.

When Jefferson first arrived in Paris and frequented the intellectual salons of the late 1780s, he encountered French wit and the French passion for puns and *bons mots*. He was not impressed. "This nation," he decided, "is incapable of any serious effort." Uninterested in vacuous verbal acrobatics, he wrote to Abigail Adams, not without wit of his own, that all one might do for the French was "pray that heaven send them good kings."

Two years later, however, life in Paris had changed dramatically and Jefferson remarked that the frivolities of conversation had given way to a more serious awareness of politics. Now Jefferson found himself praising the men of letters who belonged to the "Patriotic party," asserting that they constituted the intelligent part of France. Those who had leisure to think were in a position to initiate change and reform an abusive government. A believer in the power of reason to shape history, Jefferson admired the new writings, noting that they give "a full scope to reason, and strike out truths as yet unperceived and unacknoleged [sic] on the other side of the channel." Still, he admitted that the lack of political experience of men of letters prevented them from fully appreciating the value of the American model. French intellectuals, versed only in theory and new in the practice of government, were making some unfortunate proposals. Ideally, theory and experience would complement each other.

Jefferson, the prudent diplomat, calmly observing events unfold in Paris, counseled Lafayette to proceed step by step. Should the French

Shays's Rebellion, by Howard Pyle. A group of farmers, led by Daniel Shays, takes possession of the courthouse in Northampton, Massachusetts, in 1786

attempt more than their established habits were ripe for—that is, more than a constitutional monarchy—they would lose all and postpone indefinitely the realization of their goals. In a letter to George Washington, he expressed his hope that the Estates General would neither "shock the dispositions of the Court" nor "alarm the public mind." All improvements should "follow from the nature of things."

For Jefferson the cautious and practical statesman, progress would have to be gradual and incremental, but for Jefferson the revolutionary, the part-time *philosophe*, the ultimate aim was nothing less than "perfection." The two sides of his political personality—circumspection and idealism—were wedded in this extraordinary pronouncement: "We must be contented to travel on towards perfection, step by step."

In American politics too Jefferson proved himself to be an idealistic as well as a realistic and practical politician. When news about the proposed Constitution for the new federal union finally reached him in Paris, he was deeply disappointed. The absence of a bill of rights, something that "no just government should refuse," was a stinging omission. Though he was tempted to suggest to Madison that the draft Constitution be sent back to the convention for further revision, he declared instead that the will of the majority should prevail and that he would concur with that will. Even so, he remained optimistic that there would be future amendments. "We must be contented with the ground which this constitution will gain for us," Jefferson wrote to the French ambassador, adding that he hoped "that a favorable moment will come for correcting what is amiss in it."

Still, revolution exhilarated Jefferson. The Estates General, he wrote to Thomas Paine in 1789, showed "through every stage of these transactions a coolness, *wisdom,* and resolution to set fire to the four corners of the kingdom and to perish with it themselves, rather than to relinquish an iota from their plan of a total change of government." Jefferson's ardent letter reveals his audacious, passionate commitment to political experiment and transformation. The "coolness" and "wisdom" he praised are not synonymous with compromise and patience, but rather with a purposeful determination to "set fire to the four corners of the kingdom" and to perish rather than retreat from a "plan of a total change of government."

This idyll of fire, blood, self-sacrifice, and radical revolution is a precursor to Jefferson's striking "Adam and Eve" letter of 1793, in which he wrote that "rather than [that the French Revolution] should have failed, I would have seen half the earth desolated. Were there but an Adam and an Eve left in every country, and left free, it would be better than as it now is." His enthusiastic though ill-considered and naïve apologia for political violence may shock, but Jefferson's dream of a new race of free men is also powerful testimony to the boldness of his revolutionary vision. Indeed, Jefferson never renounced his faith that there were goals "worth rivers of blood, and years of desolation." Jefferson's intrepid and spirited embracing of change exemplifies what Bernard Bailyn termed a "freshness and boldness in the tone of the eighties, a continuing belief that the world was still open, that young, energetic, daring, hopeful, imaginative men had taken charge" and were creating a civilization "free from the weight of the past."

Jefferson's radical perception that "the earth belongs always to the living generation" inspired in him the hope that each generation, not just his own, would possess the freedom and creative energy to renew society. This doctrine of perpetual revolution appears to be an enthusiastic version of Machiavelli's concept of *rinnovazione*, the community's periodic recovery of its original vigor and citizens' active recommitment to the society's founding principles—though to *rinnovazione* Jefferson significantly added a healthy dose of *innovazione*. As Machiavelli proposed, periodic revolutions would assure the health, vitality, and longevity of the republic which, without *rinnovazione* or renewal, would inevitably stagnate and ultimately cease to exist. Jefferson similarly favored "tumult" and even uprisings because they would keep leaders true to the founding principles of their government.

In the next century, Abraham Lincoln followed Jefferson's advice, urging his countrymen to look "away back of the constitution, in the pure fresh, free breath of the revolution." There, in Jefferson's Declaration of Independence, they could rediscover the abstract founding truths—"applicable to all men and all times"—that would assure the renewal of American society. "I have never had a feeling politically," wrote Lincoln, "that did not spring from the sentiments embodied in the Declaration of Independence." In the Declaration, Lincoln believed he had found the unchanging principles of change.

While Jefferson was electrified by the idea of the sovereignty and political autonomy of the living generation, many continued to view society in terms of a partnership among generations. After reading Jefferson's letter to him in which he proclaimed that the earth belonged solely to the living, a disconcerted Madison attempted to calm his fellow Virginian by suggesting, first, a continuity between generations. Second, though in *The Federalist* Madison defended the people's right to alter or abolish a government that was "utterly defective," he expressed reservations about a proliferation of political experimentations. The success of the American experiment notwithstanding, Madison cautioned that "experiments are of too ticklish a nature to be unnecessarily multiplied." The sensible Madison may have swayed Jefferson, who, as he grew older, came to believe in periodic, nonviolent constitutional revision instead of periodic revolution.

Jefferson's radical advocacy of rebellion and change may appear reckless next to Madison's measured reflections on government, but his love of political experiment is also testimony to his bold and resilient optimism and faith in the future. Indeed, so passionate about innovation was Jefferson that in his later years he happily described the American Revolution in the same way that Alexis de Tocqueville viewed the French Revolution—that is, as the product of men of theory who had no practical experience in politics and who used the nation as a blank slate for their ahistorical speculations and abstractions. "Our Revolution . . . presented us an album on which we were free to write what we pleased," observed Jefferson. Portraying a revolution unencumbered and un-enlightened by the past, he added, "We had no occasion to search into musty records, to hunt up royal parchments or to investigate the laws and institutions of a semi-barbarous ancestry. We appealed to those of nature, and found them engraved on our hearts." Finally he congratulated the politicians of his generation for spontaneously inventing all they knew. "We had never been permitted to exercise self-government. When forced to assume it, we were *novices* in its science. Its principles and forms had entered little into our former education."

Jefferson, Adams, Madison, Washington, Hamilton, Morris, novices? unskilled and inexperienced in government? Had Jefferson forgotten his own political past, his service in the Virginia House of Burgesses? Had he forgotten his own efforts as archivist of Virginia's constitutional and legal record? his admiration for the Saxon constitution? Two years before his death, Jefferson astonishingly transformed in his mind the American Revolution into the twin sister of the one in France. He imagined the American Revolution as the product of an ahistorical and theoretical political experiment conducted by men inexperienced in politics, oblivious to and even contemptuous of history. Had he forgotten that most Americans in 1776 desired a return to the enjoyment of the long-established rights and liberties they had known before Parliament and King George III deprived them of those rights?

Jefferson's delusionary statement that the American Revolution "presented us an album on which we were free to write what we pleased" can be understood only as a *dream* of escape—a dream of unlimited personal freedom as well as a dream of liberation from tradition, from experience, from the prison house of history. Innovation triumphs over renovation. Jefferson envisaged America as a new land where political theory and man's rational faculties, not history, determined the future.

While Hamilton, Morris, and Adams saw the French wandering the dark because they preferred "Lightning to Light," Jefferson was attracted and emboldened by that lightning. For him, political theorists were not reckless terrorists, inventors of dangerous blueprints for society, but visionaries whose utopian ideas were as essential and nourishing to politics as experience, pragmatism, and caution. For Jefferson, to theorize was not to destroy but, instead, to dream. "My *theory* has always been, that if we are to *dream*, the flatteries of hope are as cheap, and pleasanter than the gloom of despair."

REVOLUTION VS. EVOLUTION

Although Jefferson's fanciful idea that the American Revolution shared the French Revolution's contempt for history and experience reveals his passionate commitment to political experiment, it also curiously ignores the true genius of the founding fathers—their ability to synthesize experience and ideas. Indeed, their unique double vision can be found in Jefferson's own Declaration of Independence, a document simultaneously backward- and forward-looking, upbraiding the king for interfering with Americans' traditional freedoms and boldly announcing a new society based on the individual's unalienable rights. Unlike the older Jefferson who would yearn for freedom from history, the younger Jefferson anchored his Declaration in tradition and history. He discovered a synthesis of preservation and innovation, thereby merging into one breathtaking act of revolution the two contrary meanings of revolution—return and transformation.

Similarly, whereas one Jefferson in 1789 advocated periodic rebellion if not periodic revolution, another Jefferson in 1816 perceived that the healthy synthesis of experience and experiment would make revolution superfluous. Leaders possessing experience as well as theoretical insight would understand that laws and institutions must continually renew themselves according to the progress of the human mind. He pointed out that if eighteenth-century monarchs had yielded to the "gradual change of circumstances, favoring progressive accommodation to progressive improvement," their subjects would not have had to seek, through blood and violence, "rash and ruinous innovations." Ideally leaders would be able to protect their societies from the traumatic and violent upheaval of revolution by assuring continual change and progress.

For Jefferson, all things and beings change. He maintained that, as human intelligence evolves, as new discoveries are made and new truths disclosed, and as mentalities also change, "institutions must advance also, and keep pace with the times." In America where all is new, he wrote in 1813, no innovation should be feared that offers some good.

On the other hand, in England stagnation seemed to reign. "The dread of innovation there," he observed, "has, I fear, palsied the spirit of improvement."

Twenty years later, Tocqueville also concluded that the spark of new ideas revitalizes and reenergizes a society. Predicting that egalitarian democracies like America, where men are inclined to promote social stability and political moderation in order to protect the enjoyment of their wealth and property, would eventually become prey to intellectual enervation and political and social stagnation, he counseled that only new ideas and theories could rescue and refresh such societies. "I cannot help fearing," he wrote, "that men may reach the point where they look on every new theory as a danger, every innovation as a bothersome problem, all social progress as the first step toward revolution. . . . Personally, I am afraid that the human race will stop and clip its own wings and that . . . humanity will progress no farther."

For Jefferson and Tocqueville, successful revolutions and, even more important, healthy democratic societies call for leaders who possess the crucial combination of political experience and political imagination. People—experienced in representative institutions and, at the same time, courageous, farsighted, idealistic, and hopeful—can assure the perpetual renewal and thus the survival of their societies.

But the remarkable synthesis of ideas, experience, and experiment that took place in America could simply not have been reproduced in eighteenth-century France. French intellectuals would have had to temper their theories with some practical understanding of representative political institutions, but those institutions did not exist.

Ideas gone amok doomed the Revolution in France. As we shall see, one blinding idea in particular—the idea of unity—mesmerized revolutionaries, preventing them from creating a political culture more democratic, inclusive, and open than the lifeless and closed government of the *Ancien Régime.*

3

Conflict or Consensus?

The harmony and consensus that reigned at the Constitutional Convention in Philadelphia in 1787 delighted James Madison. The delegates, he marveled, managed to deliberate without conflict or faction and "with a unanimity almost as unprecedented as it must have been unexpected." Throughout the stifling summer months of July and August, the windows of the State House closed, the curtains drawn, these leaders toiled six days a week on the new Constitution, hammering out compromise measures, from the problem of representation in Congress for smaller states to the issue of counting slaves in the representation of the South.

Such concord, Madison knew, was a rare achievement, almost a miracle. One could plausibly believe, he remarked, that God himself had intervened. He could discern in the Constitutional Convention no evidence whatsoever of "pestilential" party influence, the disease considered inherent in virtually all deliberative bodies, always threatening to contaminate and undermine them.

How had such amity and unity been possible? Perhaps the members of the Convention approved the Constitution, Madison hypothesized, because they possessed "a deep conviction of the necessity of sacrificing private opinions and partial interests to the public good." Ironically, such willingness to sacrifice one's own interests for the good of all was not to be expected of citizens of the new federal union. Unless there were some extreme crisis and overwhelming sense of shared purpose, Madison anticipated neither consensus nor unity in the new republic.

The Convention represented a privileged moment in American politics, a moment of harmony that produced a Constitution incorporating and even enshrining the principles of disharmony and conflict. After that founding moment, unity would never again be the goal of government. On the contrary, the new federal government was carefully structured so that people and interest groups would collide rather than concur. Consensus *and* conflict would coexist. The American *constitutional consensus,* in the words of one historian, presents "an invitation to conflict," an agreement to disagree.

Indeed, as soon as the Constitution was agreed to and signed in Philadelphia, conflict over it commenced. Would the state legislatures vote in favor of the new federal government? Antifederalists were galvanizing their followers and drumming up opposition. James Madison was troubled that even in Virginia distinguished men such as Patrick Henry, Arthur Lee, Benjamin Harrison, and others were opposed to the Constitution. On the one hand, he could only regret this dissent, but on the other, he knew well that just such pluralism and conflict were the fundamental underpinnings of his political vision. When Alexander Hamilton proposed that he, Madison, and John Jay help strengthen the Federalist position by publishing a series of essays in New York newspapers, Madison readily agreed. Returning to New York that November, he drew up, in less than a week, one of the masterpieces of modern political thought. Two words describe the import of The Federalist No. 10: "diversity" and "conflict."

Madison's plan for American government gave free rein to citizens to act in their self-interest, to form factions, to enter into conflict with one another, and the predictable result would be disorder and tumult. The government would make no attempt to eliminate conflict—that is, nonviolent and rational contention—only to moderate it and provide channels for it.

In France, however, the momentum of the Revolution was toward order, not tumult, toward oneness, not multiplicity. Far from accepting diversity and conflict, the French worshipped homogeneity and unanimity. Their leaders believed that the salvation of the Revolution depended above all on the absolute unity and solidarity of the people. According to their revolutionary agenda, three orders—nobility, clergy, and Third Estate—would become one, 25 million citizens would form one unitary people. All would sacrifice their self-interest for the common good of all; diverse opinions would yield to consensus.

AMERICAN TUMULT

Madison's brilliant and novel plan for the federal republic stemmed from his fundamental belief that citizens are individuals and that as individuals they are all different. He explicitly rejected the idea of regarding Americans as "one homogeneous mass." He knew well that people would never agree unanimously on anything. A vast variety of "unavoidable" factors—wealth and property, social class, religion, geography, political ideas, etc.—would always divide people into different interest groups and factions. Indeed, the principle of diversity seemed embedded in human nature—that is, in human rationality. Madison argued that rational people view issues in different ways because reason is essentially imperfect. "As long as the reason of man continues *fallible*," he maintained, "and he is at liberty to exercise it, different opinions will be formed."

Could differences and factions be removed from society? Madison asked. Could conflict be eliminated and unity achieved? Certainly, unity and unanimity could be created by summarily outlawing factions, but such an option was completely unsatisfactory and unacceptable, since its cost would be freedom itself. People would be forced to sacrifice the very liberty that was "essential to political life." Thus the remedy would be worse than the disease. "Liberty is to faction," Madison said in a superb simile, "what air is to fire. . . . But it could not be less folly to abolish liberty, which is essential to political life, because it nourishes faction, than it would be to wish the annihilation of air."

Was there any other way to achieve unity? No. The dream of unity, he noted with disdain, was a fantasy that only "theoretic politicians" could find fruitful. Only cloistered philosophers could imagine imposing the same opinions, passions, and interests on every citizen. In the "civilized communities" of real life, no such "perfect homogeneousness of interests, opinions & feelings" would ever be found. Division and conflict were inevitable because "the latent causes of faction are . . . sown in the nature of man." Not "reason" but passion and self-interest would always dominate human affairs. "In all very numerous assemblies," Madison wrote in *The Federalist* No. 55, "passion never fails to wrest the scepter from reason. Had every Athenian citizen been a Socrates, every Athenian assembly would still have been a mob."

Madison's acceptance of the reality of human nature was itself a crucial feature of the American Revolution. He was never tempted to remold or "regenerate"—as the French would have said—human beings to suit utopian political blueprints. "What is government itself," he wrote, "but the greatest of all reflections on human nature. If men were angels, no government would be necessary."

Madison was influenced by the mentality—if not by the words—of Niccolò Machiavelli, the great Florentine political thinker. Though he was celebrated as the author of *The Prince*, a training manual in realpolitik for power-driven, hard-nosed rulers, the kind of government that Machiavelli himself preferred and wished to see return to his native Florence was a republic, a government by the people. In *The Discourses*, his writings on republican government, Machiavelli offered the gleaming insight that a republic is energized by conflict: without conflict there is no politics and no freedom. Tumult, he wrote in 1513, was "the guardian of Roman liberties" and "deserved the highest praise." When tumult is absent, when everyone in a state is tranquil, he noted, "we can be sure that it is not a republic."

Machiavelli described ancient Rome as a kind of unruly "theater of turbulence"—plebs hurling accusations against the Senate, senators railing against the plebs, angry crowds milling through the streets, people locking up their houses and fleeing the city. While accounts of this tumult and unrest horrified many of his contemporaries, Machiavelli alone recognized the value of conflict. The people, he explained, demonstrate and clamor for their rights when they experience or fear oppression. Their demands, far from being harmful, eventually produce "all legislation favorable to liberty." Looking for the reasons behind the achievements of ancient Rome, Machiavelli contended that the greatness of the republic depended on and even required internal dissension. If Rome had been "more tranquil," she simply would have lost her energy and her capacity for expansion. "Continued tranquillity," he remarked, far from stabilizing or consolidating a republic, would in fact have the contrary effect of enervating and undermining it.

Machiavelli understood that conflict is the foundation of freedom and politics. The very nature of politics is *conflictual,* and only tolerance for political conflict can guarantee the survival of political freedom. Nearly three hundred years later, James Madison not only revived Machiavelli's ideas but acted upon them, making the people's right to form factions and engage in conflict the foundation of his theory of republican government.

Like Machiavelli, Madison embraced disorder. The Virginian's political genius lay not merely in his realization that diversity and division were inevitable but in his further insight that they could be useful in government, that they could be an effective bulwark against tyranny. This was the lesson he had learned when he worked with Jefferson to secure the right of religious freedom in Virginia. He discovered that the ultimate protection of religious freedom lay not in statements of principles or in deeply held convictions or even in laws, but surprisingly in a power situation. Divisions among a variety of religious groups, and even conflict among them, made it unlikely that one "overbearing" religious group would seek to oppress or infringe upon the rights of others. A multiplicity of religions and sects—Protestant, Catholic, Jewish— ensured the freedom of all.

Applying this principle to political power and factions, Madison believed that self-interested and passionate factions, given free rein, would check and balance one another, making it virtually impossible for one faction to dominate the others, thus creating "social and political equilibrium." Although political theorists had for centuries viewed factions and parties as so many sicknesses eating away at the body politic, for Madison, factions were stabilizing rather than disruptive. He counted on factions to perform a task of paramount importance: resistance to any concentration of power, especially the power of an "overbearing" majority. He was convinced that the more diverse the society, the more it was broken down into "so many parts, interests and classes," the more likely it would be that any majority would become broad and hence moderate in its goals, and the less likely it would be that the rights and interests of individuals would be threatened by "the combinations of the majority."

This same notion of division, conflict, and equilibrium also became the foundation for Madison's plan for the structure of American government. The government would be structured around institutions that checked and balanced one another; it would be divided against itself, institutionally split "between different bodies of men, who might watch and check each other." Power would always be fragmented and a certain balance and stability in government could be achieved.

THE FRENCH NATION, ONE AND INDIVISIBLE

In January 1789, in the middle of a turbulent winter, pregnant with anticipation, a small political pamphlet began circulating in Paris. People read it aloud in cafés, passed it excitedly around to their friends, discussed it in intellectual salons, and speculated about who the anonymous author could be. Soon people talked of little else. Within weeks thirty thousand copies were sold; three more editions were printed that same year. The fourth edition revealed at last the author's name: Emmanuel Sieyès.

The pamphlet that took Paris by storm, *What Is the Third Estate?*, contained the radical concepts that would mold the Revolution and chart its course. Sieyès was a forty-year-old priest and church administrator, surprisingly indifferent to religion and spirituality but passionate about philosophy and politics. Reserved, perpetually clothed in black, his face pale, his health fragile, he seemed to come alive only when he spoke out about freeing France from her history. Then his weak voice would gain strength as his abstract ideas gained audacity, his eyes ablaze as he attacked with trenchant words the predatory aristocracy that he despised. Sieyès was Madison's French counterpart, the artisan of revolutionary ideology.

That winter, a sudden economic crisis rocked France. Every day people demonstrated in the streets over taxes and food shortages. Everyone awaited the momentous meeting of the Estates General, hoping that this body could restore financial order as well as address burning questions of liberty and equality. Representatives of the three social and legal orders—the nobility, the clergy, and the Third Estate—would meet, each order deliberating separately. Spokesmen for the Third Estate were already objecting to this antiquated structure. Looking for a strategy that would guarantee them a majority, they were demanding that the three estates meet together rather than separately and that the Third Estate be accorded representation equal to the two other orders combined.

But in his pamphlet Sieyès had gone even further, making a far more radical demand. Bitterly denouncing the entire anachronistic institution of the Estates General, he declared that there should be a single National Assembly comprised solely of representatives of the Third Estate. The aristocracy and the clergy together included about 200,000 members; the Third Estate, 25 million. The nation and the Third Estate, he insisted, were one and the same.

"What is the Third Estate?" Sieyès demanded in his lapidary style. "Everything. What has it been in the political order up to now? Nothing. What is it asking for? To become something." Instantaneously Sieyès excluded the two privileged orders from membership in the nation. Their representatives, he claimed, spoke not for different orders but for different nations. Even the clothes they wore, he added, proved that they were foreign. The aristocracy, judged Sieyès, were "enemies" and "traitors." Thomas Jefferson, always buoyed by upheaval and revolution, commented that Sieyès's words "electrified France." Tocqueville later called the pamphlet a "war cry."

"How easy it would be to do without the privileged orders!" Sieyès predicted. "How difficult it will be to turn them into citizens!" The first two orders detracted from the nation. Without them, France would be more, not less. Without them, the nation would flourish. Though he briefly entertained the possibility of permitting the first two orders to join the National Assembly, since they would constitute only a powerless minority, he determined that it was pointless to incorporate a permanent obstructionist minority party that would constantly vote against the majority. He approved, however, of the idea of the other two estates renouncing their privileges and joining the rest of the nation as equals—as he himself would do, winning election to the National Assembly as a representative of the Third Estate, not the clergy. Separate, privileged orders, he noted, were like malignant fluids attacking a sick body: they had to be "neutralized."

When the Estates General convened that spring, Sieyès, by then a celebrity in Paris, audaciously proposed that the Third Estate declare itself the National Assembly. Not only did his profoundly revolutionary motion pass by a vote of 491 to 90, but two days later, the clergy agreed with the representatives of the "Third," and voted to join them. The next morning, Louis XVI locked them all out of their meeting room, insisting that the traditional three separate orders of France be respected. Refusing to disperse, the representatives went en masse to an athletic court, the Jeu de Paume, where they took an oath not to leave until a new constitution for France was written and enacted.

"I order you, Gentlemen, to disband," commanded the king. But after some nobles defected to the Third Estate, the king, realizing that he had little choice but to accept the legitimacy of the new National Assembly, invited his "faithful clergy and faithful nobility" to join the Third Estate. In August, all privileges and feudal rights were abolished. The Declaration of the Rights of Man and Citizen, composed that month, decreed that the nation was sovereign. Just eight months after the publication of his ideas, Sieyès's theoretical blueprint for France had become the new reality. His printed words and radical ideas had metamorphosed into the revolutionary acts of a nation, proving that ideas and theories can shape events and institutions.

The key to Sieyès's vision of a new France—and the concept that shaped the Revolution's politics and became its mantra—was *unity*. The refrain—repeated in every possible context over the course of the Revolution—always remained the same: "the nation, one and indivisible." People swore oaths to it, agreed to die for it, and denounced traitors to it. The salvation of France and the success of the Revolution appeared to hinge on the indivisibility of the nation. "It is through union and concord," one representative asserted, "that prosperity occurs; . . . if you are united, the nation is invincible. If you are divided, the nation becomes a slave."

Underlying this doctrine of "oneness" lay Sieyès's radical new definition of the nation as consisting solely of the Third Estate, the new sovereign. Composed of this one order, the nation would possess one single will and could therefore deliberate and legislate purposefully and effectively. "There cannot be one will as long as we permit three orders," he patiently explained. "At best, the three orders might agree. But they will never constitute *one* nation, *one* representation, and *one* common will."

Can 25 million people possess one single will? The answer for Sieyès was "yes." He conceived the Third Estate *not* as a diverse population of heterogeneous individuals each acting in his own self-interest, but rather as a homogeneous mass devoted to the common good. This philosopher-politician, more comfortable with abstract ideas than with unruly human beings, envisioned all members of the Third Estate not only as equal but also as like-minded, sharing the same opinions, ideals, and revolutionary goals. Indeed, the hallmark of a citizen was the commonality he shared with other citizens. Individuals might differ from one another in their private lives, Sieyès allowed, but those differences occur "beyond the sphere of citizenship."

Significantly, Madison had already criticized in 1787 the leap that Sieyès made in 1789—that is, the leap from the idea of citizens' equality before the law to the idea of citizens' similarity in everything else. "Theoretic politicians," Madison wrote in *The Federalist* No. 10, "have erroneously supposed that by reducing mankind to a perfect equality in their political rights, they would at the same time be perfectly equalized and assimilated in their possessions, their opinions, and their passions." For Madison, there was no single common good or "General Will" in society, only the interests and wills of diverse citizens and factions, all competing for influence and power.

But the French were mesmerized by a dream of unanimity and harmony that had come down to them from Jean-Jacques Rousseau. Sieyès, Robespierre, Saint-Just, and others proved to be diligent and devoted pupils of Rousseau; they had studied his books, especially *The Social Contract*, absorbing his central notion of the General Will, taking for granted its validity.

Democratic societies, the Genevan philosopher had claimed, possess a General Will, tantamount to the common interest of all. This "will" reflects what enlightened citizens would want if they were able to make decisions solely as social beings and citizens and not as private individuals. *Individuals* may possess private wills that express their particular interests, but *citizens* must recognize and concur with the General Will that mirrors the good of all. The General Will is not tantamount to the will of all citizens. Nor is it the sum of all individual wills or the expression of a compromise or consensus among them. Nor is it the equivalent of the will of the majority, for even the majority can be corrupt or misguided. The General Will is *general*, not because a broad number of people subscribe to it but because its object is always the common good of all.

Thus, hovering strangely yet absolutely and infallibly above and beyond the wills of all, the General Will is "always constant, unalterable, and pure," always mirroring perfectly the common good of all members of the community. The ultimate authority—and ultimate sovereignty—thus reside not really in the people, who may err in their estimation of the General Will, unable to transcend their private wills, but rather in the General Will itself—the power of Reason, the enlightened collective moral conscience.

True freedom, Rousseau maintained, consists in *choosing* to *obey* the General Will. But how can freedom be equated with obedience?

For Americans like Madison, liberty meant the right of individuals to be autonomous, to act as they wished, in a variety of diverse ways, and pursue their self-interest and happiness as they conceived them. But Rousseau proposed a radically different concept of freedom. It was not a Madisonian kind of "negative freedom," freedom *from* constraint, that inspired him, but rather "positive" freedom, freedom *for* some higher good, for the enjoyment of a moral life as a citizen devoted to the common good. This kind of freedom paradoxically implied *obedience* to the General Will. People were free to *concur* with the General Will, not to oppose it. For Rousseau, true freedom could belong only to citizens who were able to suppress their private wills, sacrifice their private, selfish interests for the good of all, and consciously choose the common good over their own desires. Freedom was the province of citizens who had mastered themselves, becoming moral and hence free beings.

This was a radically original society, geared not to individuals interested in maximizing their own private interests, but instead to citizens who possessed a strong moral sense of their responsibilities and duties toward one another and toward the community. The blossoming of their humanity is inseparable from their citizenship and their conformity to the state's prescription for the "good life." By identifying fully with the community, by choosing to live as parts of a whole, citizens have a chance at real fulfillment and peace of mind. They are free and equal, not because they own equal property or possess equal talents, but rather because they share an equal measure of civic rights and responsibilities. By renouncing their autonomy and participating in and obeying the General Will, they assure that they will all be treated fairly and with equal consideration and respect.

The General Will has come to dominate all of society and its laws. Every citizen must submit to its infallible, unlimited authority. What king ever ruled so absolutely?

Indeed, Rousseau's utopian, ethical, democratic polity includes no channels for the expression of dissent or opposition. Having defined the General Will as infallible and sovereign, Rousseau could not logically imagine any legitimate opposition to it. Political "freedom" in such a solidary, unified society requires submission and obedience to the General Will. In Rousseau's utopia, those who disagree with the General Will are simply in error, expressing selfish, "particular" interests that perversely thwart the common good of all. There can be no role for minority opinion. Neither dissenting individuals nor groups, political parties, or factions can be tolerated by the cohesive whole. To persist in questioning or opposing the General Will is to abdicate one's membership in the polity and give up one's political rights. Those who have difficulty recognizing the General Will must be made to see the light. "Whoever refuses to obey the general will," Rousseau decreed, "shall be constrained to do so by the whole body: which means nothing else than that he shall be forced to be free."

Forced to be free? These paradoxical words are shocking, for they cast their dark shadow on some of the grimmest periods of history. The concept of the General Will, we have come to realize, is arbitrary, illusory, and coercive. Yet Rousseau's goal was freedom, community, and morality, not mass repression. Rousseau would contend that if society constrains people to be free, socializes them to suppress their animal instincts and selfish desires, and educates them to choose the General Will over their private wills, it is in the name of their own human dignity.

Following Rousseau, Sieyès would similarly claim that French citizens must choose the General Will in the name of their nation and their Revolution. And, not surprisingly, the coercive and repressive policies that he and other French revolutionary leaders would derive from their understanding of Rousseau's political thought would lead them slowly but inexorably to the Terror.

Sieyès, like Rousseau, viewed citizens' rights and freedoms as springing from their status as equal and concurring members of society, from their submission to the General Will. Any individual who "exits from the common quality of citizen" cannot "participate in political rights." For Sieyès, as for Rousseau before him, there could be no legitimate role for dissenting individuals or minority factions to play in self-government. Sieyès contended that all citizens, by virtue of having accepted and entered into their society's social contract, agree to be bound by the will of the majority. A citizen has the obligation to "view the common will as his own." Should he refuse to yield to the majority, his only alternative is to leave the polity. Thus the sole solution envisaged by Sieyès to the problem of possible political conflict between an individual and the group was expatriation. Similarly, a minority faction has no right to oppose the majority, since the majority could be assumed to speak for the General Will. Sieyès impatiently insisted that if someone could not clearly see that the General Will was the will of the majority and not the

Allegory of the Revolution, by Jeurat de Bertry.
Jean-Jacques Rousseau and the symbols of the Revolution. The flags read "French Republic" and "Love of the Fatherland." The obelisk at the left reads "Equality." The pillar at the center reads "strength," "truth," "justice," and "union." The tree is labeled "Liberté." The short column at the right reads "Regeneration of Mores"

will of the minority, "there is no point in trying to reason with him." The minority must simply join the majority. So much for opposition!

Patriotic citizens would always place the public interest above their private interest. "Everyone must forget his own interest and pride," instructed Saint-Just, the most radical ideologue among the Jacobins. "Private happiness and interest are a violence against the social order. You must forget yourselves. . . . Your interest demands that you forget your interest; the only salvation is through the public good." Life, liberty, and the pursuit of happiness were thus conceived in collective terms. "The social union has as its object not just the freedom of one or several individuals," Sieyès declared to the National Assembly in July 1789, "but the freedom of all." Similarly, the goal of society was the "common happiness" of all, not individuals' pursuit of their own personal happiness.

Underlying Sieyès's coercive and antipluralist vision of united citizens, all concurring with the General Will, are certain assumptions about human rationality. While Madison's theory of the *fallibility* of human reason had led him to deduce the inevitability of diversity and factions, the French embraced an entirely different theory of human reason that predisposed them to a doctrine of unity.

The seventeenth-century philosopher Descartes's famous treatise on human reason, *Discours de la méthode,* buttressed Sieyès's vision of citizens happily sacrificing their self-interest for the good of all. The opening sentence of Descartes's book had announced simply that "good sense is the best shared thing in the world." All human beings possess "reason." It is what distinguishes us from animals; it is an essential part of our very being, the determining feature of our humanity. And because reason—like an essential chromosome—is what defines human nature, all human beings, Descartes concluded, must therefore possess reason in equal amounts.

When there is diversity of opinion, it occurs not because some individuals are more rational than others, but rather because they take different approaches to reflecting on the same problems. If all people adopted the same method for analyzing a problem, Descartes continued, they would all arrive at the same truths. Certain objective "truths" exist, and human reason, with the help of disciplined, methodical thinking, can provide the path to them. Thomas Jefferson commented that Descartes's theoretical "fancies" retarded the progress of science in France for generations.

Ironically, Descartes had specifically tried to dissuade his readers from applying his method to politics. "Reason" might only change things for the worse, he cautioned, recommending instead that imperfections in the political system be tolerated, for they were probably more bearable than would be the consequences of efforts to improve upon them. But so convincing was his demonstration of the universality of reason and its power to discern the "truth" that his own warnings went unheeded.

It was only logical, according to this vision of human reason, that citizens would agree on the same principles and ideals. "One must have a poor idea of the march of reason," Sieyès wrote, "to imagine that an entire people could remain blind to its true interests." With rational people thinking correctly, the Revolution's goals would be easily accomplished: "If everyone thought right," Sieyès hopefully remarked, "the most significant changes . . . would not be difficult to make."

Sieyès was especially confident in his own ability to "think right." Not only were there certain objective political and social truths, but he sensed that he himself had privileged access to them. "My own personal role," he commented without irony, "consists in presenting the truth. . . . That my principles are true, that my deductions are flawless, I have no doubt." Harboring no reservations about his ability to discern truth from error, he conceived his revolutionary role as that of prophet and guide. Rational, grateful citizens would accept his enlightenment and guidance.

Fortunately, the people would not require very much guidance, for they too occupied a privileged position in French revolutionary mythology. Like the nation, "the people" was conceived as one and indivisible, an organic collective being. Over and over, revolutionary orators extolled the new divinity, "the people," in whose name they claimed to speak. The people were taken to be the source of all virtue and goodness. Ultimately Jacobins were willing to sacrifice real people—rowdy, imperfect, Catholic, royalist, apolitical—to their abstract, rational concept of an ideal "people."

Curiously, all the qualities that had traditionally been attributed to the quasi-divine king—oneness, indivisibility, infallibility—were transferred to the revolutionary "people." For centuries, the king had been conceived essentially in terms of his "oneness." Louis XIV's tutor, the theologian Bossuet, had taught his royal pupil that "any realm that is divided will be devastated" and that "monarchical government is the most antithetical to division." Just as the king's body incarnated the indivisible nation, Sieyès also conceived the indivisible nation as a person, asserting that "one must conceive the nations of the earth as individuals." In addition, age-old dogma had emphasized that "the king can

Necker leads Louis XVI to the three united orders beneath medallions of Henry IV and his minister, Sully. The three orders are nobility, clergy, and Third Estate

do no wrong." Like the infallible monarch, the people's General Will could also never be in error.

Oddly, on the basis of the resemblance of people and monarch, Sieyès defended the French monarchy against radical republicans like Thomas Paine. After Louis XVI's abortive attempt to flee France in 1791, Paine and some other representatives demanded that the king be deposed. But Sieyès favored forcing the recalcitrant king back on the throne, telling Paine that the "individual unity" of the king constituted a perfect executive for the "collective body" of the people. "I think that unity of action," he informed the American, "must not be separated from the unity of an individual person." Sieyès even advised Paine that "one is freer under a monarchy than under a republic." The two unitary beings, king and people, meshed well, for Sieyès was convinced that "the monarch's obvious and palpable interest will always, but always, be inseparable from that of the majority." Only after the abolition of the monarchy, in the fall of 1792, would the people reign alone. The beheading of Louis XVI was the crowning of the people as the new indivisible, infallible sovereign.

STABILITY VS. ENERGY

A system of two legislative chambers? Why, it was "like putting one horse before a cart and the other behind it and whipping them both," exclaimed Benjamin Franklin. "If the horses are of equal strength, the wheels of the cart, like the wheels of government, will stand still; and if the horses are strong enough, the cart will be torn to pieces." A legislative body divided against itself? A patently foolish idea.

The specter of governmental deadlock—Franklin's two horses—did not haunt James Madison. In designing a plan for the new federal union, Madison knew that he had to make the fundamental choice between energetic government and stable government. Ideally government would be both stable and energetic, but Madison realized that energy posed an insurmountable problem: it requires the concentration of power either in the hands of the few or in the hands of the many. In the most energetic form of government, power is executed "by a single hand." But such an "energetic" leader, Madison noted, can all too easily become a dictator.

Why, he wondered in *The Federalist* No. 38, did the ancient Greeks, a people who cherished their freedom, place "their destiny in the hands of a single citizen," allowing individuals such as Draco, Solon, and Lycurgus to frame or reform their government and laws? He surmised that they must have feared discord and disunion more than they feared "treachery . . . in a single individual." But like Machiavelli, Madison preferred "discord and disunion" to despotism. His greatest fear was tyranny, and he came to view conflict and tumult as the guardians of liberty. Thus, faced with the choice between energy and stability, Madison easily opted for stability in government. He concluded that only stability and not energy could be counted on to coexist with liberty.

Stability came at a high price: energetic, dynamic government would have to be sacrificed. But given Madison's realistic if not pessimistic appraisal of human nature, that was a small cost to pay for freedom.

The Madisonian system of checks and balances was a perfect way to fragment authority and prevent a concentration of power. "Ambition must be made to counteract ambition"—with this terse sentence Madison ensured that conflict would endure within the government and that any popular majority would be thwarted by checks and balances. Thus a bicameral legislature would fragment power, protecting citizens from a tyrannical majority. The House and Senate, one based on population, the other on geography, would each reflect two differently constituted and potentially opposing majorities. In addition, the President—originally elected "indirectly" by a deliberative body called the "Electoral College"—represented still another form of majority.

This creation of different majorities illustrated Madison's conviction that the voice of the majority was not necessarily the voice of the common good, since different organs—all representing different majorities—could speak for the people at the same time. Moreover, it proves that Madison sought institutional ways to foil the majority and strengthen the rights of minority groups. And still another form of division and fragmentation of power was the split between state and federal governments, though the federal government had the ultimate power to veto state laws.

The Madisonian system, in the words of Gordon Wood, represented a "kinetic theory of politics"—such an atomization and partition of political and social interests and of power itself "that no combination of parts could hold, no group of evil interests could long cohere." Not only were homogeneity and unanimity not expected, the new government was designed specifically to prevent unity or oneness.

Madison turned traditional political thought upside down. Political theorists had always warned that factions would inevitably degenerate into conspiracies intent on overthrowing the republic itself. According to these theorists, the republic itself stood for and defended the common good against the claims of interested factions. But Madison rejected the idea that there could be a "neutral" agency in government that voiced the public good. He was convinced that every participant in government represented some interest or faction. "What are the different classes of legislators," he asked, "but advocates and parties to the causes which they determine?" He confessed that it would be highly desirable to have some kind of "dispassionate umpire in disputes between different passions & interests in the State," but he knew that hopes for such a neutral referee were vain. Factions did not exist in opposition to government: they *constitute* government. Conflict among different factions was not merely tolerated *by* government: conflict *was* government.

ENERGY AND IMPACT IN FRANCE

The French, Thomas Jefferson remarked to John Jay, had less patience than any other nation in the world, and, in the late summer and fall of 1789, the little patience they did possess was "worn threadbare." Unemployment was increasing, gangs of marauding beggars were terrorizing the countryside, local governments were overthrown, fears of famine as well as of aristocratic conspiracies raised tension to a fever pitch. People were clamoring for change, for reform, for bread.

While Americans had opted for governmental stability, the French hungered for energetic, decisive, effective government. It was stagnation that they feared, not the concentration of power. The American solution—factions and conflict, the separation of powers, checks and balances—seemed wildly inappropriate to most French revolutionaries, certain that it would only thwart the radical steps they wanted revolutionary government to take. Although in retrospect one can imagine that revolutionaries in France, scarred if not traumatized by centuries of monarchical absolutism, might also have sought to divide and fragment power, in fact the opposite was the case. They had learned from Sieyès that the nation could act purposefully and effectively only if it possessed one roaring voice and one indomitable will.

What kind of government would the National Assembly set up in 1789? That the king would constitute the "executive branch" was accepted by virtually all, but Louis would not have an absolute veto on the legislature. "The will of one cannot outweigh the General Will of all," declared Sieyès.

But what about the legislature? Would it have two chambers along the lines of the English and American models or one, as in Benjamin Franklin's state of Pennsylvania? Would France turn to England and the United States for proven political wisdom or would she strike out on her own and create original institutions for an entirely new kind of egalitarian society? The debates were passionate, divisive, and complex.

The choice seemed momentous. But was it really a pivotal decision?

One group, the "Anglomen," forcefully advocated the English system of a House of Commons and a House of Peers. They reasoned that France was a heterogeneous society consisting of different social classes, factions, and interests, and they felt that a bicameral configuration could reflect those different orders and interests. The Anglomen were also well acquainted with Montesquieu's theory of checks and balances. Montesquieu's political dream was inertia. He envisaged two houses happily producing "rest" and "inaction."

For their opponents, the "Américanistes," a simple one-house legislature appeared the only logical choice. Since revolutionary France was composed of only one social order, the Third Estate, it was superfluous to have more than one legislative chamber. There was no need, wrote Turgot, for a balance of powers in a classless republic founded on the equality of all citizens.

"Américanistes" was an odd misnomer, because the French Américanistes were far more radical than their American counterparts. In America, almost every state had adopted a bicameral legislature, though a single house had existed briefly under the Articles of Confederation. The Américanistes could more accurately have called themselves "Franklinians." Still, the name Américanistes indicated their opposition to English institutions that evoked a class system and a feudal past.

French radicals were probably right to suspect that any bicameral system would have made it more difficult to transform and reorganize French society. What they wanted from revolutionary government was the opposite of inertia and deadlock. They demanded innovation, action, impact. They yearned for immediate, deep, and lasting change. Neither governmental stability nor complicated procedures nor lengthy debates held any appeal for them. The proposal for a single legislative chamber won overwhelmingly, by a vote of 849 to 89. The new motto was "One God, one King, one National Assembly."

Years later, John Adams placed much of the blame for revolutionary catastrophes in France on the "fatal" choice of a unicameral legislature. The "blind love" of revolutionary leaders for "the Constitution of Mr. Franklin," Adams contended, had led to disaster. Adams and others were convinced that the concentration of all power in one body was a prescription for dictatorship. But a unicameral legislature was not, in itself, enough to doom the French Revolution. After all, both the American and English systems of government would probably be able to function in approximately the same ways with only one legislative body.

In 1848, when Tocqueville was a member of the Constituent Assembly that would create a short-lived republic, he argued desperately in favor of two houses, exhorting his colleagues to find that "this question of two chambers is the question of *freedom*, it is the future of a free government. A single Chamber is dictatorship."

Ironically, however, Tocqueville's insistence on a bicameral legislature contradicts the crucial distinction that he himself made between institutions and what he called the "habits of the heart." Political societies, Tocqueville stressed, are ultimately not what their laws make them, but are shaped by the people's own emotional and intellectual commitment to democratic values, their tolerance for diversity of opinion, their desire to participate in self-government. "Would to God I believed more in the omnipotence of institutions!" he wrote in 1853 to a friend. "Then I would have more hope for our future, because by chance we might, someday, stumble onto the precious piece of paper that would contain the recipe for all wrongs, or on the man who knew the recipe. But, alas, there is no such thing."

The French National Assembly became a monster that destroyed the Revolution, not because it consisted of only one chamber, but because it swallowed up all the other branches of government, permitting no independent judiciary and creating no legitimate place for dissent and opposition. But so enchanting was the idea of unity that, even as he fled the Terror and went into hiding, the philosopher Condorcet was still criticizing the American system of checks and balances, spouting that such pluralism "disfigures simplicity." A few weeks later, he committed suicide.

The outcome of democracy in revolutionary France was decided, not as Adams suggested, by the "fatal" choice of a unicameral legislature, but rather by the values—unity, consensus, indivisibility—underlying that institution of choice.

THE JEFFERSONIAN MODEL OF PARTY POLITICS

In 1800, on the day it became clear that he won a majority in the presidential election in New York City, a victory decisive for the outcome in the state as well as in the union, Thomas Jefferson called on President John Adams. "Well," Adams said, "I understand that you are to beat me in this contest, and I will only say that I will be as faithful a subject as any you will have." "Mr. Adams," replied Jefferson, "this is no personal contest between you and me. Two systems of principles on the subject of government divide our fellow citizens into two parties. With one of these you concur, and I with the other. . . . Were we both to die to-day, to-morrow two other names would be in the place of ours, without any change in the motion of the machinery. Its motion is from its principles, not from you or myself."

As Jefferson explained, the basis of party politics is ideological conflict between two competing political parties—not conflict among branches of government and not personal conflict between individuals. This new kind of conflict, driven by political visions and principles, would provide the momentum for change. Energy, through conflict, Jefferson remarked to John Dickinson, had returned to government.

Now there was a second strategy for governing the nation. Whereas the Madisonian model of fragmentation and checks and balances used conflict to impede the will of the majority, the Jeffersonian model of party politics used conflict to empower the majority. Madison and Jefferson—fellow Virginians, lifelong friends and confidants—shared many ideas about government, but one man feared a popular majority while the other sought to shape and invigorate its voice. One proved to be a master theoretician of the system of checks and balances, the other a consummate party politician.

Can a democratic election be considered a revolution? The watershed election of 1800 changed the principles of American government so dramatically that it constituted a second American Revolution. Jefferson himself called this election "as real a revolution in the principles of our government as that of 1776 was in its form."

How was this election different from earlier ones? It not only introduced politics based on two rival parties competing for power and alternately governing but also created the virtually unheard-of precedent of one defeated incumbent party peacefully turning over political power to the opposition. The recognition of the legitimacy of the opposition and the acceptance of a system of organized, adversarial political parties marked the final stage in the American Revolution.

The transition, however, from the Washingtonian desire for consensus to the acceptance of ideological party conflict would take decades. It was a process of change all the more daunting because almost no one, as political scientist James MacGregor Burns points out, had a theory of party. The evolution of parties in the United States was shaped far more by events than by design.

The English, on the other hand, were already engaged in developing a theory of political parties. Edmund Burke, a leader of the opposition Whig party, found it inconceivable that representative government could exist without political parties. Why would like-minded politicians, who want to see their ideas and principles translated into practice, not associate and cooperate with one another? He was convinced that "no men could act with effect, who did not act in concert; that no men could act in concert, who did not act with confidence; that no men could act with confidence, who were not bound together by common opinions, common affections and common interests."

The thought that men would choose *not* to act in concert with others struck Burke as "utterly incomprehensible." "Of what sort of materials must that man be made," he wondered in disbelief, "who can sit whole years in Parliament, with five hundred and fifty of his fellow-citizens, . . . in the agitation of such mighty questions . . . without seeing any one sort of men, whose character, conduct, or disposition, would lead him to associate himself with them?"

But despite Burke's insight into the importance of associations and parties, Americans were skeptical if not plainly averse to the idea of organized parties. In his conclusion to *The Federalist*, Hamilton had warned against "an obstinate adherence to party," stressing the value of consensus in a young society that was not yet unified. Adams too had judged that "a division of the republic into two great parties . . . is to be dreaded as the greatest political evil under our Constitution." Even Jefferson had once railed against parties. "If I could not go to heaven but with a party," he exclaimed, "I would not go there at all."

George Washington also hoped for a leadership that would hold itself above party. As President, Washington desired nothing more than to preside over and even symbolize a government of national unity. "I was no party man myself," he wrote to Jefferson in 1796, "and the first wish of my heart was, if parties did exist, to reconcile them." The danger of parties, Washington explained, is that they "render alien to each other those who ought to be bound together by fraternal affection." The first President's strategy for governing was consensus, not conflict. More comfortable with conciliation than with strife, Washington even pardoned the leaders of the Whiskey Rebellion.

When a policy of his was challenged, Washington charged that such opposition was the work of a "party," not realizing or not acknowledging that its supporters, as Richard Hofstadter remarked, also constituted a party. Even when Washington and other political leaders of the 1790s were engaged in conflict and factions, they rejected the idea of political parties, seemingly unaware that they were actually shaping embryonic political parties. At the end of his first term, still believing in a united government and in his own role above the political fray, Washington warned that "internal dissensions" were "harrowing our vitals." His Farewell Address alerted citizens to "the baneful effects of the Spirit of Party." His antagonism toward parties mirrored the mentality of his generation.

Even so, the deep and bitter discord within Washington's own cabinet ultimately evolved into two opposing parties, the Federalists and the Republicans. Alexander Hamilton, the Secretary of the Treasury, and Thomas Jefferson, the Secretary of State, differed violently over almost everything—banks, tariffs, fiscal policy, foreign policy, presidential power. Attempting to mobilize congressional support for the Administration's economic policies, Hamilton began to form a political party around his fellow Federalists. Ironically, through his party-building efforts, he unwittingly galvanized the Republican opposition, which soon surpassed the Federalists in their organizational and propagandizing skills.

Between 1791 and 1792, Madison published a dozen newspaper articles outlining the principles of his and Jefferson's opposition to Federalist policies. Republicans, led by Madison, skillfully created party structures at all levels—local, state, and national. In comparison, the Federalists neglected the building of a widespread, grassroots party establishment. Not only did they prefer, as Burns notes, the "high road" of political principles to the nitty-gritty of majoritarian electoral politics, but their feeling that they possessed a certain "entitlement" to govern and that they acted in the name of the Constitution rather than a party ideology inhibited them from committing themselves to new, imaginative electoral and party strategies.

The antipathy between the two burgeoning parties exploded in the early 1790s, in reaction especially to their opposing stands on the political turbulence and violence in revolutionary France. While Federalists looked on with horror and revulsion at the shocking guillotining of Louis XVI and the lawless executions of the so-called enemies of the people, enthusiastic Republicans cheered their French brethren, hailing the radical revolutionary cause. The president of Yale, Ezra Stiles, welcomed the news of the execution of the king, proclaiming it a sign that European monarchs would soon be "tamed."

Federalists branded their Republican adversaries "Jacobins," and Republicans returned the compliment by labeling the Federalists "monocrats." Each group portrayed its opponent as conspiratorial and treasonous, an ally either of reactionary England or of sanguinary France. The opposition, both groups charged, was scheming to subvert America's autonomy and republican ideals. Party newspapers issued partisan pronouncements on events in France—the Federalist *Gazette of the United States,* edited by John Fenno, and the Republican *National Gazette,* edited by Philip Freneau.

By polarizing Americans and forcing them to recognize the profound ideological differences that stood between them, the French Revolution can be credited with stimulating a large number of people to participate in foreign policy debates and thus with contributing to the development of political parties in America. Ironically, the antidemocratic nature of the Revolution in France had the effect of consolidating democracy in the United States.

The decade of the 1790s had become so contentious, passions so inflamed, and denunciations so personal and vituperative that President John Adams sought in 1798 to restore order through the repressive Alien and Sedition Acts. The stated purpose of the Sedition Act was to prohibit people from publishing or saying anything of a "false, scandalous, and malicious" nature against Congress or the President with an intent to defame them. But how many politicians have felt that criticism of them was not defamatory? The Sedition Act was clearly designed to crush the

Republicans and protect Federalists from opposition, and not, as Federalists claimed, to bar opposition to the American constitutional system.

By making political opposition illegitimate, the Federalists' Sedition Act came spectacularly close to the kind of repression practiced by the Jacobins they loathed—and perhaps, as R. R. Palmer proposed, with even less justification. Several dozen men were jailed and fined under the Sedition Act, most of their trials "travesties of justice dominated by judges who saw treason behind every expression of Republican sentiments." A stain on the precious Bill of Rights passed only seven years earlier, the Sedition Act seriously jeopardized freedom of the press and freedom of speech. President Adams and the Federalists had set the stage for the smashing of Republican printing presses and the jailing of opposition newspaper editors.

In this climate of hostility and paranoia, Federalists and Republicans battled for the presidency. Jefferson showed himself extremely adept at partisan politics. The key to his success as a party builder was his passionate commitment to democratic ideals. His ability to inspire others with his vision of popular democracy and a classless society—a vision that disputed Federalist elitism—gained him fervent followers and a broad and solid political base. The people, Jefferson believed, could be rallied to the truth, their Republican spirit resurrected if they could be educated and persuaded to resist the "dupery" practiced on them by Federalists.

So it was crucial to articulate and disseminate his party's positions. To this end, in 1799 Jefferson asked his friend Edmund Pendleton to write and distribute, on his behalf, ten or twenty thousand copies of Republican principles and positions, diligently providing him with a voluminous packet of documents and information. Jefferson also knew that it was of paramount importance to work not only for his own electoral victory but for the elections of state legislators favorable to his own candidacy. His goal was to capture not one but two branches of government. Though he himself never campaigned actively for the presidency, from behind the scenes he knew just how to pull the strings of party politics, ultimately creating strong political support in Congress and among the people.

Underlying Jefferson's belief in party politics lay his unshakable faith in majority rule, which he called a "fundamental law of nature." An organized, unified, and ideologically galvanized majority, by means of an election, could take over one, two, or even three branches of national government and proceed to fulfill—or to attempt to fulfill—its ideological agenda. The party and its leaders could conceivably govern the nation vigorously and freely. The majority could recapture its power and its voice from the antimajoritarian system of checks and balances, making energetic government a possibility.

Still, as a deft and calculating party politician, Jefferson understood that a system of two adversarial political parties could work only if each party was unified and well organized. If there was any threat to a healthy democracy, it came not from a strong opposition party but rather from party disunity. "As there will always be an opposition," he wrote, "I believe it had better be from avowed monarchists than republicans." A strong and viable opposition party was critical, for otherwise a lone and unopposed predominant party would merely splinter into new parties.

Despite Jefferson's recognition of the importance of an opposition party, his record in tolerating opposition is not unblemished. As President, he let the Sedition Act expire, but, like Adams, he was also so incensed by his critics that he proposed legal action against them. It should not be a "general prosecution for that would look like a persecution," he cautioned Thomas McKean, but rather a few selected prosecutions of only the most defamatory journalists. His fierce partisanship taking the upper hand, he wished that the opposition party would simply disappear from the face of the earth, leaving only the Republicans to absorb all citizens. His administration's policies of economy and peace would, he predicted, "sink federalism into an abyss from which there shall be no resurrection for it." Despite an occasional conciliatory remark, necessary to win over Federalist rank and file, Jefferson always retained his hostility to Federalist leaders and principles. "I wish nothing but their eternal hatred," he bristled.

And how did the defeated Federalists feel about turning the reins of government over to men they loathed and feared? Was there no way to save the republic, Alexander Hamilton wondered, "from the fangs

Thomas Jefferson,
by Cornelius Tiebout

of *Jefferson*?" Would not the transfer of power "to hands hostile to the system heretofore pursued with so much success" jeopardize the new federal union? So angry and disturbed was Hamilton at the prospect of Jefferson's ascension to the presidency that he considered calling together the exiting legislature to block the election by declaring it invalid.

"In times like these in which we live," Hamilton wrote ominously to John Jay, "it will not do to be over-scrupulous. It is easy to sacrifice the

substantial interests of society by a strict adherence to ordinary rules."
He believed that he had a "solemn obligation" to "prevent an atheist in
Religion, and a fanatic in politics, from getting possession of the helm of
state." Resorting to Jacobin-style discourse, he even declared that blocking Jefferson's election "is justified by unequivocal reason of PUBLIC
SAFETY." A few months later, however, his ambivalence toward John
Adams and his obsessive antipathy for Aaron Burr led him to support
Jefferson over Burr and to reject explicitly any attempt to thwart the
election. "Mr. Jefferson's character," Hamilton conceded with a conciliatory, almost generous tone, "warrants the expectation of a temporiz-
ing, rather than a violent system."

After an initial cooling-down period, Federalists reacted to their
defeat, not with talk of resistance, but rather as politicians who were
accustomed to power and who were intent upon recapturing it. The
game of majoritarian party politics would have to be played if Federalists were to regain control of the government. Hamilton admitted in
April 1802 that "we must consider . . . employing the weapons which
have been employed against us."

"Nil desperandum," wrote Gouverneur Morris when he learned of
Jefferson's victory. "Let the chair of office be filled by whomsoever it
may, Opposition will act as an outward conscience, and prevent the
abuse of power." Out of power, the Federalists seemed to appreciate the
essential contribution to democratic government that the "loyal opposition" can make.

The opposition party, noted the Federalist Fisher Ames, must be "a
champion who never flinches, a watchman who never sleeps." He
advised Federalists to exploit to the fullest their new role of critic. "We
must make it manifest that we act on principle," he wrote, "and that we
are deeply alarmed for the public good. . . . We should . . . enjoy [our
antagonists'] late advantages of finding fault, which popular prejudice is
ever prone to listen to. We should soon stand on high ground, and be
ready to resume the reins of government with advantage." But despite
their sophisticated remarks about new strategies for opposition, by 1812
the Federalists would collapse as a national party, unable to develop a
rank-and-file organization and grassroots support.

Party conflict had replaced the aspiration for consensus. Although Washington, Hamilton, and other founders had feared that political parties would weaken the nation, the opposite proved to be true. This early creation of organized opposition *strengthened* the young republic by according legitimacy to dissent. The nation was sufficiently unified in citizens' commitment to the Constitution to permit organized opposition to the party in power. The world of government and the world of party politics had become one.

American government would henceforth operate as a "strange hybrid," in the words of James MacGregor Burns, of the Madisonian political model, which aimed at stability in government, political equilibrium, and snail-like change, and the Jeffersonian model, which sought vigorous government and swift progress. One model envisioned change occurring through consensus and compromise, the other through ideological conflict. Although the two models continue to coexist and shape American political life, the Madisonian model—cast in a Constitution as enduring as stone—has always dominated the equation.

The cohabitation of the two political models has never been smooth or especially logical, as President Jefferson came immediately to realize. Jefferson won the election of 1800 with a solid majority and governed energetically, but he still had to accept the limitations imposed on government by Madisonian checks and balances. His famous confrontation with Chief Justice John Marshall in the case of *Marbury* v. *Madison* taught him that the Supreme Court could and would invalidate congressional action and that majoritarian party politics could not overcome checks and balances. As for Madison, he would find his own presidency weakened not only by checks and balances but also by his own personal ambivalence toward strong government and by his lack of skill as party leader.

Despite Madison's and Jefferson's fundamentally different attitudes toward political power and majority rule, what they shared—and what most distinguishes their political ideas from political thought in revolutionary France—is a core acceptance of political conflict. For Madison, conflict is organizational, taking place within the formal structure of government. For Jefferson, conflict is ideological, taking place in the realm of political ideas. Both political models tolerate and exploit division, faction, and opposition. Both models also seek to moderate conflict: one requires a wide consensus to overcome checks and balances, the other works best when parties and their ideas are broadly based.

UNITY AND REPRESSION IN FRANCE

On July 11, 1793, the celebrated French artist Jacques-Louis David dashed over to the Convention, voluminous notes and sketches in hand. He had come to lay out in detail for the members of the Convention his lavish plans for the Fête de la Réunion, the revolutionary festival of unity. It was to be an overwhelming, inspiring occasion, choreographed down to the smallest details. Every costume, every color, every song and gesture would contain some symbolic meaning. The sunrise itself would play a role in the revolutionary spectacle: people taking part in the festival would rise before dawn so that the emotional scene of their coming together in fraternity would be illuminated by the first rays of the sun.

The centerpiece of the day, the artist proudly announced, was to be a stupendous parade: first the members of political clubs would march; they would be followed by the representatives of the Convention; and finally and most important, the people themselves, the sovereign of France, would appear. This group, far larger than the others, would be drawn from all over France and from all walks of life—peasants, workers, artisans. David excitedly explained that spectators viewing the "people" on parade would not be aware of distinct individuals at all but would experience instead the merging of all identities into one, the one true collective revolutionary spirit. The majestic hero of the celebration was the oneness of the people.

When David finished outlining the scenario for the celebration, he hurriedly left the Convention to supervise final preparations. Representatives then resumed the work of the day. Billaud-Varenne spoke first. Angrily calling people's attention to a revolt taking place in Toulouse, he demanded the punishment of the citizens of Toulouse. No leniency, he sternly declared, must be shown to conspirators. Someone else denounced General Dillon. When Camille Desmoulins attempted to defend Dillon, his friends physically silenced him, insisting that they were only preventing Camille from dishonoring himself. Next the representative Mallarmé demanded the arrest of three deputies from Rhône-et-Loire, and finally on that day the representative Legendre demanded more mass arrests in Lyon.

Revolutionary business as usual—the two Janus faces of the Revolution, unity and exclusion, fraternity and terror. A combination well known to myriad revolutionary regimes, legatees of the French Revolution, that practice repression in the idealistic name of the people's unity. Why is it that unity and repression so often go hand in hand?

Tocqueville lucidly uncovered the dark, coercive underside of the fraternal desire for consensus and concord. In the people's collective elation, in the joy of their common dedication to the revolutionary cause, in the immense grandeur of the fraternal struggle, he pointed out, there was no place for opposition or conflict. The primacy of unity imposed assent. People spoke about what brought them together but were silent on the questions that divided them. "Trapped by the spirit of harmony," Tocqueville remarked, "they neglected to express and resolve their differences." Pluralism and democracy, he perceived, were the victims.

The Revolution's doctrine of unity and indivisibility polarized the nation. If there was conflict, it had to occur, as R. R. Palmer commented, between the people and something that was not the people, between the nation and something alien to the nation. People were divided into two camps; in one camp were revolutionary friends and patriots, in the other, enemies and traitors. Virtuous people were on the inside; counterrevolutionaries were on the outside. Thus the corollary of a nation's unity is the exclusion of any individuals or groups that disrupt that unity. "The psychology of purging the heretic," Palmer noted, "drew strength from this very yearning for cohesion."

Under the Old Regime in France, lèse-majesté—any kind of opposition to the king—had been a capital crime. Under the Revolution, any opposition to the unity of the revolutionary nation—lèse-nation—was similarly a capital offense. Any opinion, any proposal that could be considered divisive was anathema. Individuals who did not concur with the nation's interests and goals, who voiced their own private interests, who threatened the nation's unanimity were *enemies* to be banished or punished. Ultimately, the Convention would mandate the death penalty for any attempt to threaten *"la République une et indivisible."*

As early as June 1789, just days after the creation of the new National Assembly, a time heady with idealism and hope, the representative Barère was already urging the Assembly to stop at nothing "to uncover, thwart, and punish the disastrous schemes of the enemies of the people, the enemies of humanity, . . . the avaricious and cruel men who live off the misery of the people." The first time that Robespierre addressed the Assembly, in July 1789, he assailed "the most fatal conspiracy ever contrived." Employing the same language that he would resort to several years later at the height of the Terror, he insisted that "any conciliation with conspirators is treason against the people. . . . Do not forget that you are sworn to punish the guilty!" Four days later he demanded that men suspected of harming the nation be subjected to "exemplary judgments." "Let the people be certain," he declared, "that its enemies will not escape the vengeance of the law!"

In the midst of this impatient, reckless rush to discover and denounce omnipresent enemies, the great leader Mirabeau tried to be a calming voice of reason. Cautioning against exaggerating the number of the people's enemies, he urged his fellow representatives to refrain from condemning those who disagreed with them. Instead, they should try to "pity some of those who differ, give others the time to join us, and enlighten them all." Diversity itself, he counseled, is useful to society. But Mirabeau's plea for pluralism and tolerance fell on deaf ears.

"It is necessary for us to know," Sieyès declared in June 1791, "where are our true friends and our enemies." According to Saint-Just, "everything that is opposed to [the will of the French people] is outside the sovereign; everything that is outside the sovereign is the enemy." In 1794, in one of the last speeches he made before he was guillotined, Robespierre continued to maintain that there existed "only two parties, the party of good citizens and the party of evil ones."

FACTIONS ARE POISON

Tocqueville was of course right that from 1789 to 1794 the myth of unity was a veil behind which seethed disunity and discord. Politicians, journalists, philosophers, economists disagreed on all the major issues of the day, as ordinary, rational people in any country would. Numerous factions—monarchiens, Brissotins, Feuillantistes, Montagnards, Girondins, Jacobins, sans-culottes, chouans, enragés, Dantonistes, Hébertistes, Robespierristes, Thermidoreans—dotted the political landscape, making the simple schism in America between Federalists and Republicans seem, in comparison, positively unimaginative. But so spellbound were the French by the myth and rhetoric of unity and so cynical were political leaders who used the myth of unity to isolate their adversaries and consolidate their own power, that even when citizens and politicians disagreed passionately with one another, they continued to condemn factions and parties as well as the very idea of organized opposition. Even when it should have been apparent that nothing existed *but* dissension and conflict, revolutionary leaders in France were blind to the idea of an inclusive polity in which a variety of political visions were tolerated as well as to the idea of parties that might cut across rather than exacerbate class divisions.

In the United States, conflict among branches of government and between political parties constituted the principal feature of American political culture. But in France, factions and parties were anathema. What justification could there be for bodies that represent "partial" and private interests in a nation of equal and self-sacrificing citizens, all committed to the "common good"? Such "particularisms," moreover, constituted unwelcome reminders of the privileged, elite bodies of the Old Regime.

In April 1790, in an attempt to quash the influence of factions and political clubs that were inundating the Assembly with petitions, the Assembly decreed that the "right of petition" belonged only to individuals and "may not be exercised collectively . . . by clubs." This rule went largely ignored, the historian Isser Woloch reports, and the question of clubs was addressed again the following year. Another bill to limit them was passed in June 1791, stipulating that "no club may assume a political existence under any form whatsoever." But by 1792, when the law against political organizations was reconsidered once more, the clubs had begun to appear more helpful than dangerous. And in the fall of 1793, as Jacobin radicals gained ascendancy, clubs were finally empowered to denounce all counterrevolutionary citizens, to propose patriotic citizens for government posts, and to assure orthodoxy in the provinces. Clubs had become an "unpaid revolutionary bureaucracy," abetting political conformism to Jacobin rule.

Throughout these years when clubs were tolerated, prohibited, and empowered, revolutionary politicians never ceased denouncing factions and organized political groups. Those who would be crushed no less than those who would vanquish unanimously opposed all political associations. They all bought or swallowed the doctrine of unity. Factions, Sieyès declared, "create the most fearsome public enemies." "No one knows better than I," proclaimed Mirabeau, "that the salvation of everything and of every one resides in social harmony and in the *annihilation of all factions*." "I abhor any kind of government," Robespierre stated succinctly, "that includes factious men." "We will not permit a single heterogeneous body in the Republic," pronounced the delegate Garnier.

Revolutionary leaders compared factions to disease and poison that weakened and undermined society. "Factions are a *malady* of society and especially of republics," the representative Morisson declared. Saint-Just also weighed in, announcing that "factions are the most terrible *poison* in society." Danton echoed the party line: "You must absorb this truth: factions cannot exist in a republic." The fantasy that the solution to complex political problems lay simply in harmony and unity motivated Danton to declare that "fraternity alone . . . can give the Convention the sublime impetus that will define its path." The Jacobins, for their part, in their quest to purge all dissent and factions, never saw themselves as a party or faction but only as the self-anointed voice of the General Will.

The most universally execrated political faction proved to be neither royalists nor constitutional monarchists but "federalists," for "federalism" was seen as a crime against the "nation, one and indivisible," an attack on her political unity as well as a breach of her territorial integrity. People like Mirabeau who advocated federalism were in fact seeking to rescue the country from the crushing preponderance of Paris and the Parisian populace. The throne could be saved by detaching the provinces from the frenzy of the capital. Thus associated with monarchy on the one hand and with the American Constitution on the other, federalism evoked a purposeful, organized strategy to divide and decentralize France. The American federal state, for Saint-Just, represented the antithesis of a unified and indivisible republic. He ridiculed the American republic for containing the principle of its own dissolution. "Some day," he wrote, as if prophesying the events of the 1860s, "one state will take up arms against another."

Any individual or group that could be branded "federalist" stood automatically beyond the pale. Indeed, the epithet "federalist," like the all-purpose word "aristocrat," furnished a convenient way to dispose of political adversaries in the name of the "oneness" of France. When the moderate Girondins were put on trial in the fall of 1793, they were pronounced guilty of having tried to "federalize" the Republic, and thus some of the most able leaders of the Revolution found themselves under the blade of the guillotine.

Ironically, the Girondins were acolytes in the same cult of unity. Attacked for undermining the indivisibility of the Republic, they defended themselves not by invoking freedom of speech or freedom of conscience or parliamentary inviolability, but rather by proclaiming their fidelity to the god of unity. Jacobins and Girondins fought to the death, both groups equally unwilling to press for the recognition of the legitimacy of opposition.

TERROR

The morning after they were found guilty, the executioner came to the cell of the twenty-one moderate Girondins to tie their hands and prepare their heads for the guillotine. As five tumbrels carried them through Paris, they sang the "Marseillaise." At the scaffold, they continued their song, their ranks thinning, until only one voice, that of Vergniaud, was left.

At their weeklong trial, seventy-three Girondins—those present at the trial along with others who had fled—had been found guilty of conspiring against the unity and indivisibility of the Republic and sentenced to death. The historian Michelet remarked that no hypocrisy colored the trial, for absolutely no attempt was made to follow legal procedure. The sole purpose of the trials, he lamented, was to murder the opposition. Upon hearing the verdict, some of the Girondins reacted with fury, others with calm. One stabbed and killed himself; another, Brissot, appeared lost in thought; the most famous among them, Vergniaud, showed no emotion. One representative managed a pointed joke, remarking that there was only one way left to save their skins, to proclaim the *unity* of their lives and the *indivisibility* of their heads.

The trial was a turning point in the Revolution, probably the single most catastrophic blow to political pluralism. Such a trial could take place only because of the Convention's decision six months earlier to suspend the inviolability of its deputies. Henceforth—in flagrant violation of the act of June 23, 1789, protecting deputies' freedom of speech—duly elected representatives could be—and were—removed, prosecuted, and killed for nothing more than their minority views. The improbable argument was made that the inviolability that had cloaked the hereditary monarch must not be accorded to temporary, elected officials.

Girondins as well as Jacobins imagined that they could profit from the exclusion of their adversaries. Neither group had the political intelligence or the commitment to democracy and individual rights to create guarantees for the expression of dissent and opposition. "Let us examine the behavior of members of the Convention," Marat had declared. "Let us strike down the traitors wherever they may be." The Girondin representative Biroteau self-destructively concurred, asserting that "at a time when freedom is threatened from all sides, any kind of inviolability ceases; the people cannot place their trust in a deputy against whom numerous accusations have been made."

A few lone, defensive voices argued that there could be no freedom without the right to dissent. "If you blow a deputy's brains out," the representative Cambon declared, "just for having uttered an opinion, we will no longer dare to speak!" Cambon's courage inspired Barère to remind his fellow delegates that "you will never lay the foundation for freedom without representatives who can freely express their opinions." But virulent attacks on traitors proved more effective than well-meaning pleas for freedom of speech. Making no attempt to disguise the Jacobins' refusal to tolerate an opposition, Saint-Just proclaimed in February 1794 that "what constitutes a republic is the total destruction of everything that stands in opposition to it."

The Girondins on Their Way to Execution, by Delaroche

The journalist and representative Camille Desmoulins had taken particular pleasure in denouncing the Girondins as conspirators and traitors, urging the Convention to "vomit out" the federalist Girondins and guarantee a permanent majority to his friends. But when, months later, he heard about the death sentence pronounced against the Girondins, he woefully regretted his incendiary words. He could not have known then that he, Danton, and their friends would soon also perish on the guillotine, victims of a similar political purge.

Politics is the art of persuasion, not annihilation. What French politicians did not grasp, as they were wiping out their political adversaries, is that political majorities and minorities are forever fluctuating, new coalitions always replacing old ones. They did not seem to realize that, in the world of politics, political adversaries are potential friends, political allies are potential defectors, and politics is largely the art of the deal. None of them viewed conflict as something that might add to rather than subtract from the nation. And as they spat out their vitriolic denunciations, their rage against the "monsters" that opposed them, they insisted that political change could somehow take place in a non-conflictual, harmonious arena.

THE PURGE OF ALL FOR THE SALVATION OF ALL

The Girondins were not the sole victims of revolutionary violence in France. According to most estimates, 17,000 people were executed during the Terror, though some historians count as many as 50,000 killed. Vague and arbitrary categories had transformed every citizen into a potential customer for the guillotine.

A revolutionary Tribunal was established in March 1793 to ferret out domestic enemies—all the traitors and conspirators who threatened the nation's unity. A few months after its establishment, an emboldened Robespierre demanded that the Tribunal be unhampered by legal procedure. The original Law on Suspects had at least established specific criteria for identifying France's internal enemies—there had to be some evidence of conduct, writings, or talk to convict people of being partisans of tyranny and federalism. But within weeks, the law was expanded to include those who were merely suspected of counterrevolutionary activities or thoughts.

The list of grounds for suspicion of counterrevolutionary activities is hair-raising, for "enemies" of the Republic could be charged with acts they committed as well as with acts they failed to commit. The death penalty was mandated not only for those who spoke out against the Revolution but also for those who displayed indifference to it along with those who did not extol it with sufficient zeal. "There can be no prosperity as long as the last enemy of freedom still breathes," Saint-Just announced in a typical speech. "You must punish not only traitors, but even people who are indifferent; you must punish whoever remains passive in the Republic and does nothing for her. . . . Between the people and their enemy there is nothing in common except the guillotine." Citizens were obliged to denounce their neighbors. Laws were passed that made it a citizen's duty to "unmask the charlatans of patriotism and denounce traitors, to uphold the dignity of the French people and to spread the political principle of the unity of the Republic to all hearts and minds."

Ultimately, no sacrifice was too great—not even the sacrifice of all for the salvation of all—to make to the god of unity. "I would rather let 25 million French men and women perish a hundred thousand times," the Jacobin Hydens declared, "than let perish one single time the united and indivisible Republic." Robespierre even indicated that a purge of the majority of citizens was not unthinkable, for he had come to believe that *most of the people* in France were the dupes of the Revolution's enemies. After first reassuring his startled audience that he was "far from claiming that the majority of people in the country are guilty," he disclosed that "in truth, the majority is paralyzed and betrayed; foreign intrigue has triumphed!"

So elusive were the unity and unanimity that Robespierre pursued that he ultimately declared, in one of his most bizarre, paranoid fantasies, that France's enemies—Austria, England, Russia, Prussia, and Italy—had established within France a rival government that had achieved the unity that the French themselves were incapable of mastering.

The last speech that Robespierre made to the Convention before he was overthrown and guillotined was a 15,000-word rambling harangue about corruption and conspiracies, ending with a final exhortation to his colleagues to wake up to the vast plot against public freedom. "This conspiracy owes its strength to a criminal coalition that weaves its webs inside the Convention itself. . . . What is the remedy for this disease? Punish the traitors, . . . *purge* the Comité de Sûreté Générale, *purge* the Comité de Salut Public itself, . . . and use the full weight of national authority to decimate all factions!" Conspiracies, factions, traitors, purges, death—the monotonous, paranoid litany never varied, neither for Robespierre nor for his fellow Jacobins nor even for their more moderate adversaries.

The cult of unity that rejected political parties and nonviolent political conflict led ironically, though naturally, to the most extreme form of

Revolutionary calendar. Year II of the Republic.
"Unity, Indivisibility of the Republic.
Liberty, Equality, Fraternity, or Death"

conflict, violence and murder. But the precepts that made the Terror possible—the dogma of the oneness of the nation, the passion for equality at the expense of individual rights and freedom, the exclusion of factions and parties, the refusal to accord legitimacy to opposition—were already present in Sieyès's original definition of the unitary revolutionary nation. To Sieyès's exclusionary formula for unity and concord, the Jacobins added their paranoia, their arrogance and intellectual shallowness, their hunger for power, their taste for repression and punishment, and finally a lethal dose of violence. The fictitious idea of political unity, which mesmerized some revolutionaries while serving others as a cynical mask for political intimidation, became a terrifying and bloody reality under the blade of the guillotine.

Still, defenders of the Jacobins contend that the Terror was a necessary reaction to a crisis situation. France, they claim, was threatened with foreign invasion and rocked by counterrevolutionary domestic insurrections. But political repression is typically linked to an irrational fear of foreign infiltration. One need only think of the Alien and Sedition Acts or the "Red scare" and blacklists of the 1950s to discern the hysteria associated with the fear of foreign infiltration. In the late 1790s, the possibility of a fifth column of aliens in the United States alarmed Federalists. The Alien Act was a response to their erroneous anticipation of war with France and to their mistrust of the high numbers of immigrants who were joining the Republican opposition. The Sedition Act merely extended repression to encompass not just immigrants but all American citizens who criticized their government. This panicky overreaction, like that of the 1950s, resulted in frightening miscarriages of justice.

In France too, repression was linked more to paranoia than to real danger. The historian François Furet points out that the Republic's most critical period was the spring and summer of 1793: the Prussians and Austrians had invaded parts of France, the royalist peasant revolt in the Vendée was gaining ground, and counterrevolutionary insurgents took control of Lyon, Marseille, and Toulon. And yet these dire months did not coincide with the height of the Terror. On the contrary, the number of death sentences increased sharply that fall when the situation had significantly improved. And, in the spring of 1794, when domestic insurrections had successfully been quelled and the armies of France had taken the offensive at the borders, the Terror reached its apogee. Ultimately, the function of the Terror was not the protection of France from foreign threats but rather protection of the "oneness" of the people from the freedom of the people.

In revolutionary America, terror never took over the legal system. During the War of Independence, the wealth of loyalists was occasionally confiscated, some acts of violence and vengeance were committed, and some people were killed, but neither then nor during the late 1790s were there any political trials that ended in a death sentence.

CONFLICT AND COMMUNITY

Are political parties and conflict necessary in a democracy? In the late twentieth century, there is agreement among political scientists that the determining features of democracy are a legitimate opposition and political parties. The definition of a free government, for historian R. R. Palmer, is a regime that "can tolerate opponents and presumptive successors in office, without fears for its own existence." And political scientist Robert Dahl concurs, proposing that the "right of organized opposition to those who govern" is one of the essential characteristics of any democratic polity. The distinction between democracy and dictatorship, according to political scientist E. E. Schattschneider, can be made "in terms of party politics."

Is there a role for unity and unanimity in a democracy? Yes. Richard Hofstadter explains that in a democracy there must be a "constitutional consensus" that binds both government and opposition—that is, a shared understanding that opposition is directed against a certain complex of policies, not against the legitimacy of the constitutional regime itself. "There is only one thing about which there should be unanimous agreement," writes the political scientist Pierre Rosanvallon, "the recognition of the fact that a majority and an opposition that respect each other must confront each other and alternately hold power. This is the only consensus that is necessary, the democratic consensus."

The American constitutional consensus represents just such an agreement to disagree. The American founders bequeathed to us enduring and workable institutions that tolerate factions, protect minorities, and provide channels and rules for political conflict.

But are there other necessary ingredients in a democracy? What about a sense of community?

Indeed, some contemporary social scientists argue that the Madisonian vision underlying our constitutional consensus is not as beneficial as we might like to think. They contend that the emphasis on factions, conflict, and individual rights that dominate American politics tends to undermine a cohesive national community of citizens committed to the common good.

An "agglomeration of hostile individuals coming together for their mutual benefit" describes historian Gordon Wood's view of Madisonian society. "Madison cannot envision even as few as three individuals living together peacefully without the presence of 'rules & forms of justice,'" another political scientist remarks. For these critics, Madison's plan for government reduces the common good to nothing more inspiring and unifying than the reconciliation of conflicting interests. They fault him for relinquishing faith in fraternity and solidarity and for countenancing citizens' withdrawal from the responsibilities of citizenship to pursue their own private interests: "In such an environment, there can be reason and stability, but no community."

But are conflict and community irreconcilable? This question is a crucial one. For if the American model of government does indeed preclude the possibility of community, then it would be understandable that the French dismissed the American experience and sought their own blueprint for democracy that emphasized fraternity and community.

In the 1950s, the political theorist Louis Hartz anticipated and responded to this criticism of Madisonian democracy. There existed, according to Hartz, "a *peculiar sense of community*" in Madison's America, something more than atomized and self-interested individuals. What held men together, Hartz argued, was not the sense that they were different parts of a corporate whole, but rather "the knowledge that they were similar participants in a uniform way of life." At the core of American society, according to Hartz, stood a glacier that rested on "miles of submerged conviction." This shared conviction was the American creed of individualism and freedom. It was so powerful and appeared so self-evident that people not only conformed to it but did not even realize that they were conforming to an ideology at all. And this powerful "common standard," Hartz believed, produced a very real kind of social cohesion among citizens committed to the same common good: life, liberty, and the pursuit of happiness.

Other social scientists have also defended Madison by pointing out that, thanks to Madison's encouragement of pluralism and factions, there exists in America an unusually rich, diversified, and inclusive political community. Ever since the vote was extended to those who were not property holders, to African-Americans, and to women, the social and political arena has been able to encompass new interest groups and accommodate a vast number of voluntary associations, assuring most citizens and most emerging groups membership and representation in the national community. Indeed, one could argue that more important than an emphasis on "feelings" of "community"—a risky valorization of collective emotion that more than once in history has resulted in the eclipse of individual rights—is the freedom that guarantees and nourishes a vital and inclusive political culture.

An energetic, dynamic political community startled Tocqueville when he visited the United States in 1831. Coming from lethargic Restoration France, he was astonished by the frenetic political activity taking place at all levels of society. "As soon as you step onto American soil," he marveled, "you find yourself in the middle of a kind of tumult." Everyone was attending meetings! One group was debating whether to build a new church; another deciding whom to elect as representative; still another considering what kinds of improvements to make to their township. Farmers had left their fields to discuss the construction of a new road or a new school. Some citizens showed up at a meeting merely to declare their opposition to the government. And at another meeting citizens were passionately denouncing drunkenness, the source of all social evil. Even women went to meetings—perhaps to forget their household cares.

Meetings took the place of theater! Being part of the nation's public life became people's entertainment and pleasure. But more than that too—their involvement in public affairs affected their sense of self-worth. Active citizens, Tocqueville noticed, displayed a certain self-confidence, for people listened to them and sought their advice. They were full of ideas for improving public property—as well as their own. These observations about American society led Tocqueville to the dramatic, penetrating realization that what all these people in reality were doing was pursuing happiness.

Happiness, Tocqueville suggested, is not a state of being, but a level of engagement. When citizens join with others to promote their private interests, they discover that their own interests are inseparable from those of others. Their tireless efforts to improve their society, their energetic participation in their political community constitute their pursuit of happiness. They could hardly be working more feverishly, Tocqueville observed, at being happy.

The political community that Tocqueville admired in the United States comprised a rich array of associations and factions—clashing, cooperating, creating tumult. The unusual, dynamic activity that so astonished and impressed Tocqueville proved to him that he was visiting a land of freedom, for when freedom is absent, he remarked, "everything appears calm and immobile." "Freedom of association," he explained, "is not as threatening to public order as people suppose, and it is even probable that, after a certain period of instability, it actually strengthens the polity." Like Machiavelli, Madison, and Jefferson before him, Tocqueville came to the same sagacious conclusion that the guardian of freedom is tumult.

Men were made for life in community, Jefferson always stressed. Only through their joint activities would people fully blossom and reach their complete potential. "Without this mutual disposition [to act together]," he told his friend John Dickinson, "we are disjointed individuals, but not a society."

Despite Jefferson's belief in party conflict, even he hoped that ideological conflict would not become so intense that it would corrupt or rupture American society. "The happiness of society depends so much on preventing party spirit from infecting the common intercourse of life," he explained. Especially in "society circles," the two parties should be harmonized and "amalgamated." "The greatest good we can do our country," he wrote to Dickinson, "is to heal it's party divisions & make them one people. It is very important that the pure federalist and republican should see in the opinion of each other but a shade of his own."

Jefferson's notion of the "ward republic" presented a formula for community and self-government, if ever there was one. Jefferson had advocated dividing the nation into small "ward republics" in which "every man is a sharer . . . and feels that he is a participator in the government of affairs, not merely at an election one day in the year, but every day." In such a participatory democracy, a citizen is attached "by his strongest feelings to the independence of his country, and its republican constitution." Jefferson modeled his ideal ward republic on the New England self-governing township, which he judged "the wisest invention ever devised by the wit of man for the perfect exercise of self-government, and for its preservation."

Conflict and community prove to be eminently reconcilable. A vital, inclusive community, the Americans intuited, is founded on conflict, competing interests, engagement, and self-government. The longing of French revolutionaries for unity, fraternity, and harmony, paradoxically, only stifles a dynamic community by banishing freedom of expression, self-interest, and dissent.

But could Madison have persuaded revolutionaries in France that where there is freedom, there will be conflict? Could Jefferson have convinced political leaders in Paris that the key to community is not *unité* or *égalité* but *liberté*—the freedom to engage in self-government and in organized adversarial political parties? Unlikely. The American synthesis of conflict, community, and individual freedom set the American Revolution irremediably at odds with a French Revolution spellbound by a dream of unity.

But lest we exaggerate the wisdom of the American founders, we may ask whether Americans, had they been faced with the problems of an entrenched aristocracy, hyperinflation, food shortages, a proliferation of provincial insurrrections, radical mass street demonstrations, and extremist parties on the left and on the right, could have sustained their tolerance for conflict. The Alien and Sedition Acts as well as Jefferson's forays into suppression of criticism demonstrate that respect for opposition was a lesson that took decades to be absorbed and integrated into the political culture.

Moreover, the harmony in Philadelphia that led to the adoption of the Constitution was possible only by avoiding conflict on—and agreeing not to resolve—the wrenching issue of slavery. As is so often the case, the need for order—security through union—took far greater precedence over the crucial but longer-run questions of liberty and equality. That original consensus exploded in the 1850s, and in the ensuing Civil War, many more people died than in the Terror in France. In both those crises, convulsive violence replaced regulated, nonviolent political conflict. The sister revolutions together teach the lesson that the cost of fleeing peaceful political conflict may be higher than that of meeting it head-on.

4

Revolutionary Talk, Revolutionary Stage

Never to contradict anybody"—diplomatic advice from Benjamin Franklin that Thomas Jefferson adopted and passed down to his grandson.

The young man, Jefferson counseled, should always refrain from announcing his own opinions. Instead, he should ask questions of others. "When I hear another express an opinion which is not mine," Jefferson remarked, "I say to myself, he has a right to his opinion, as I to mine; why should I question it?" Politicians, however, strained the talents of the most tactful diplomat, for it was often impossible to reason with them. How then should the young man behave in their company? "Consider yourself, when with them, as among the patients of Bedlam needing medical more than moral counsel. . . . Be a listener only, keep within yourself, and endeavor to establish with yourself the habit of *silence,* especially on politics."

Caution and reserve were also traits that George Washington recommended to his nephew, Bushrod Washington. "Be courteous to all, but intimate with few," he warned, "and let those few be well tried before you give them your confidence." Washington's most distinctive characteristic, according to Thomas Jefferson, was prudence. He never acted,

Jefferson remarked, until he had carefully weighed every circumstance and every consideration. Jefferson was personally acquainted with Washington's high-strung and volatile temper; he had witnessed many times in private the first President's wrath. But, added Jefferson, in public Washington was a master of self-restraint. Through determined "reflection and resolution," Washington had obtained a "firm and habitual ascendancy" over his own excitable disposition.

John Adams also offered prudent, diplomatic advice: "Never to speak ill of any body." Though the irascible, outspoken Bostonian was himself temperamentally unable to wear the social mask of *politesse*, he learned to admire it in others. In old age, meditating on the glory of Washington, Franklin, and Jefferson and on his own less than mythic stature, Adams concluded that "*Silence* and *reserve* in public are more Efficacious than Argument or Oratory." He finally realized that "great caution" and "great Reserve" were necessary ingredients for "Fame and Preferment." After decades in public life, he understood that a public speaker who cannot bear to be outdone in reasoning, wit, or sarcasm will succeed only in making lifelong enemies who will in turn "humble and mortify him." To his son John Quincy, he preached the merit of "eternal taciturnity."

The language—and silence—of a gentleman was an art the founders wished to pass on to their close family members. But diplomatic speech was also a necessary skill for politicians, and they hoped that courteous, gentlemanly discourse would pervade and mold the political culture of the young nation. They knew that, as politicians discussed and debated the great issues of the day, there would be contention and conflict, but conflict did not preclude a language of self-restraint, a code of respect for others. On the contrary, civility was all the more necessary if political conflict was to remain nonviolent, normalized, and ritualized. Thus Jefferson, cultivating the art of understatement, expressed his strong disapproval of one of Hamilton's proposals by wryly admitting, "If I do not subscribe to the soundness of his reasoning, I do most fully to it's ingenuity." Especially in the 1780s, before the tumultuous passions unleashed by the French Revolution inflamed American politics, decorum and honor accompanied the expression of political convictions. Politicians could disagree with one another—but as gentlemen.

In France, however, revolutionary leaders had nothing but contempt for gentlemen and their polished language. The word *"gentilhomme"* had never lost its class connotations in France; it was a title that belonged solely to the nobility. While in England and America the term "gentleman" had acquired a broad usage and could be applied to any man who demonstrated courteous manners, genteel language, and honorable character, in France the manners and culture of a gentleman were considered a matter of birth that could not be secured in any other way. Could a bourgeois try to act like a *gentilhomme*? Why, nothing could be a more ludicrous spectacle, as the seventeenth-century playwright Molière had demonstrated in his searing social comedy *Le Bourgeois gentilhomme*.

Revolutionaries, unlike Molière's farcical Monsieur Jourdain, who yearned to be a "man of quality" and distinguish himself in the eyes of others, had no such longing to ape the language and manners of the nobility. On the contrary, committed to the idea of equality, they disdained the aristocratic language that had been used very effectively for centuries to bolster the class system. Sieyès and others deplored the courtly affectations and pronunciations that had enervated and defiled the French language, creating the impression that a mannerly nation existed within a barbarous one.

While the leaders of the American Revolution, engaged more in a political than in a social revolution, were proud to strike a gentlemanly pose of moderation and tolerance, impatient revolutionaries in France wanted nothing more than to tear the mannerly ancient aristocracy out by its roots, ending desolate centuries of institutionalized injustice and inequality. Their far-reaching social revolution required wresting the nation as well as the nation's speech from the gentlemen of the nobility.

Leaders proposed a linguistic agenda for popularizing and revolutionizing the language and restoring to it "the vigorous accent of freedom and equality." Words that had reinforced social distinctions were banished; citizens were obliged to address one another with *tu* instead of *vous,* dropping the polite form of address that had incorporated respect and ceremony. Old words acquired novel meanings. The word "people" lost its pejorative prerevolutionary connotations of poverty, illiteracy, and labor, and became synonymous with purity, self-sacrifice, and patriotism. The word "aristocrat" came to designate, not someone of an elite social class, but any ideological adversary. Synonyms for "aristocrat" included "monster," "traitor," "imbecile," "pervert," "pygmy," and more. Above all, the new people's language would be one of blunt truth and frankness.

But revolutionary, egalitarian speech came at a high price. Devolving into an incendiary language, it would propel political conflict toward violent confrontation. In America, on the other hand, the founders' language of civility and self-control contributed significantly to the establishment of a political arena in which nonviolent conflict could safely take place.

The Constitutional Convention that took place in Philadelphia during the summer of 1787 and the Virginia ratifying convention that took place in June of the following year both exemplified the mannerly politics of gentlemen. During these crucial, decisive discussions, a magnificent decorum reigned, an accomplishment all the more impressive inasmuch as the debates were shielded from public view and concerned issues as sensitive as aristocracy, popular power, and slavery. When Colonel Mason differed with Mr. Sherman at the Virginia ratifying convention, he took pains to find words of praise for his opponent, professing that there was "great weight in the remarks of Mr. Sherman." When Madison opposed a motion made by Mr. Clay, he limited himself to restrained though pointed remarks such as "Mr. Chairman, I cannot think that the explanation of the gentleman last up is founded in reason." The strongest language was heard when debate focused on slavery. Disagreeing with the proposal to give 3/5 representation for slaves, Mr. Martin said that "it was inconsistent with the principles of the revolution and dishonorable to the American character to have such a feature in the Constitution."

At the Philadelphia Convention, some delegates gave others discreet lessons in political manners. On a certain procedural issue, Mr.

Pinckney of South Carolina stubbornly refused to agree to open the question again for debate, considering it an "utter waste of time." But Gouverneur Morris decided to educate Mr. Pinckney in political courtesy and the importance of fair and open procedure. When Morris opposed one of Mr. Pinckney's own proposals, he made no attempt to bury it, as Mr. Pinckney had done. Morris declared that he himself "did not see the utility or practicability of the proposition, but he wished it to be referred to the consideration of a Committee."

Delegates often reminded one another that their mission was to ensure dispassionate and open debate. Gouverneur Morris lectured his fellow delegates in Philadelphia on the importance of being governed by reason and not by feelings. Interestingly, however, he drew a distinction between reason and civility, offering the view that "the language of Reason" often dictates "that we should not be polite at the expense of prudence." Though Morris was undoubtedly right to place reason and rational principles on a higher plane than style and manners, most delegates to the Constitutional Convention recognized that decorum, reason, and prudence were intimately linked.

These gentlemen always assumed that their audience was, as Jefferson remarked, "an assembly of reasonable men." In Philadelphia as well as at the various ratifying conventions, men would make their arguments and, through rational, civil debate, try to convince others to change their opinions. The aim was not to conquer—*vincere*, in Latin, but rather to persuade—*convincere*, to bring others along, thus "conquering" together. When Alexander Hamilton rose to discuss a certain issue, he expressed the hope that "gentlemen of *different opinions* would bear with him in this, and he begged them to recollect the change of opinion on this subject which had taken place and was still going on." And when delegates debated the issue of what kind of majority—2/3 or 3/4—should be required to override the President's veto, Mr. Williamson remarked that he himself had originally proposed 3/4 instead of 2/3, but that he had since been "*convinced* that the latter proportion was the best."

The politics of persuasion requires respect for the rationality of others and a recognition of the fallibility of one's own reason. Uncertainty about his own reason and judgment was Benjamin Franklin's extraordinary and exemplary explanation for his support of the final version of the Constitution. "I confess," Franklin said, "that there are several parts of this Constitution which I do not at present approve, but I am not sure I shall never approve them: For having lived long, I have experienced many instances of being obliged by better information or fuller consideration to change opinions even on important subjects, which I once thought right, but found to be otherwise. It is therefore that the older I grow, the more apt I am to doubt my own judgment, and to pay more respect to the judgment of others. Thus I consent, Sir, to this Constitution because I expect no better and because I am not sure that it is not the best."

Franklin, like Washington and Jefferson, believed strongly in "expressing [him]self in Terms of modest Diffidence." In his *Autobiography*, he told of his conscious decision to forswear words like "certainly" and "undoubtedly" that "give the Air of Positiveness to an Opinion." Having learned from Pope that "Want of Modesty is Want of Sense," Franklin's object was to please as well as to persuade and to avoid at all costs provocation and opposition. In his short speech to the Philadelphia Convention, the language of self-restraint and modest diffidence suited well the polite political arena, merging helpfully with values of tolerance and respect for others.

When disagreement and opposition persisted and delegates could not easily reach a consensus, often those in the minority yielded to the principle of majority rule. Gouverneur Morris admitted that he too harbored certain reservations about the Constitution. But he felt that the final plan was probably the best that could be attained, and he would take it with all its faults. In any case, the majority had determined in its favor, he concluded, and by that determination he "would abide." Another delegate in Philadelphia, Mr. Mercer, also wished it understood that he did not like the proposed Constitution, that it was weak, but that he had decided to "go with the stream."

Even the volatile Patrick Henry, passionately opposed to the Constitution at the Virginia ratifying convention, acknowledged the principle of majority rule. "If, then, gentlemen, standing on this ground, are come to that point, that they are willing to bind themselves and their posterity to be oppressed, I am amazed and inexpressibly astonished. If this be the opinion of the majority, I must submit; but to me, sir, it appears perilous and destructive." Henry's aggressive words—"inexpressibly astonished," "perilous," "destructive"—did not prevent him from binding himself to the community and to the will of the majority—"I must submit."

In the socially stratified world of the 1770s and 1780s, the gentlemen-politicians of the young republic never believed that they had to appeal to the masses and color their rhetoric to arouse popular emotion. On the contrary, as Gordon Wood remarked, they felt that it sufficed to reach and influence "only the rational and enlightened part" of the population, who in turn would bring the rest of the populace with them through the force of deferential respect. Thus emotional language was rare. Colonel Mason, who opposed the Constitution, swore that he would "sooner chop off his right hand than put it to the Constitution as it now stands." Fortunately for everyone, Mason proposed chopping off only his own hand and not someone else's! When Mr. Bedford used intemperate language, he was roundly scorned. Mr. King commented that it was not only that Mr. Bedford had uttered dictatorial language but that this intemperance had stained the honorable gentleman himself. "Mr. King was grieved that such a thought had entered *into Mr. Bedford's heart,*" the record states, "but he was more grieved that such an expression had dropped *from his lips.* Mr. King could only excuse such language on the score of passion."

Passion and emotion were never permitted to eclipse reason, tolerance, and dignity. At one point during the Virginia ratifying convention, Patrick Henry, sounding like a proto-Jacobin, extolled the value of suspicion, deeming it a democratic virtue. Not imagining what the institutionalization of suspicion would soon entail in France, he declared that "suspicion is a virtue as long as its object is the preservation of the public good, and as long as it stays within proper bounds. . . . Guard with jealous attention the public liberty. *Suspect every one* who approaches that jewel." But Edmund Randolph answered Henry's emotional call for suspicion with a few well-chosen words of restraint. "I confess that a certain degree of [suspiciousness] is highly necessary to the preservation of liberty," he judiciously remarked. "But it ought not to be extended to a degree which is *degrading* and *humiliating* to human nature and which is sufficient to *disturb a community.*" Acutely sensitive to the fine line separating suspicion from repression, Randolph impressively insisted on respect for the fundamental dignity of others and for the dignity of the community itself. His civility of speech matched well his respect for a social order based on the protection of individual freedom, demonstrating the bond between political language and political principles.

As President of the new federal union, George Washington always insisted on controlled, tactful speech and behavior in his cabinet. He recognized that the members of his government would on occasion express themselves "imprudently," their self-control shattered by the "effervescences" of the moment. But, he wrote to Gouverneur Morris, explaining his political creed, "you can run no hazard in asserting that the executive branch of this government never has suffered, nor will suffer, while I preside, any improper conduct of its officers to escape with impunity, nor give its sanctions to any disorderly proceedings of its citizens."

In the 1790s, however, language caught on fire. The change during these years of revolutionary turmoil in France and fierce ideological contention in the United States was dramatic. Vituperative attacks on him in the press astonished George Washington. "I did not believe until lately that it was within the bounds of probability [that] I would be accused of being the enemy of one nation, and subject to the influence of another," he fumed in a letter to Thomas Jefferson. Not only were the acts of his government subject to the "grossest and most insidious misrepresentations," but he himself was attacked in "indecent terms as could scarcely be applied to a Nero, a notorious defaulter, or even to a common pick-pocket."

During this most tumultuous period in American politics, political discourse in the press sank to vitriolic depths. Politicians hurled baseless charges and countercharges of conspiracy at one another. Federalists, convinced that Republicans belonged to an international Jacobin conspiracy, branded them "atheists" and "tyrants" and accused them of hatching treasonous plots. As for Republicans, they hysterically assailed Federalists for conspiring to monarchize the United States. The Republican propagandist James Callender, after having attacked Washington in the press for seeking to become the people's "infallible, immaculate, omniscient" master, turned his vitriolic pen to John Adams. "What a patriot is not Mr. Adams! . . . What a friend . . . to the *peace* of the United States is not JOHN ADAMS!" Pronounced guilty of sedition, Callender was sentenced to jail in 1800.

Studying the periodic appearances of a "paranoid style" in American politics from the 1790s through McCarthyism to the John Birch Society, Richard Hofstadter insightfully argued that the disposition to imagine that nonexistent conspiracies are a major historical force "is mobilized into action chiefly by social conflicts that involve ultimate schemes of values and that bring fundamental fears and hatreds, rather than negotiable interests, into political action." As Hofstadter suggested, the Federalists' and Republicans' paranoid belief that the adversary party was conspiring against the republic demonstrates the profound ideological differences between them.

Even so, fear and contention were not so overwhelming that Federalists were prepared to block Jefferson's ascension to the presidency, and this despite eight years of denunciations of him as a Jacobin fanatic and generally treacherous, duplicitous, and incompetent leader. Indeed, the peaceful transfer of power from Federalists to Republicans in 1800 appears all the more remarkable when placed in the context of the frenzy of talk of plots and counterplots. The fears of one another that Federalists and Republicans harbored yielded to their common understanding that, after all was said and done, they were gentlemen of the social elite who had known one another for decades and who were all committed, in their own ways, to the survival of the republic.

Jefferson's "radical" beliefs were finally less objectionable to Alexander Hamilton, his ideological adversary, than John Adams's ungentlemanly, unpredictable temperament. "It is a fact," wrote Hamilton in a pamphlet attacking Adams, "that he is often liable to paroxysms of anger, which deprive him of self command." But Hamilton's ungentlemanly vilification of a fellow Federalist, notes historian Joseph Ellis, proved to be an "act of political suicide," casting fatal doubts on his own character and turning other Federalists against him. His overwrought words demonstrated again that, at least for the founding generation, skillful, successful leadership required self-restraint and civility as well as courage and commitment to political principles.

LANGUAGE ON FIRE

The American founders were playing an old game to perfection. They had successfully absorbed invaluable lessons on moderation, ethical behavior, good humor, and wit from the virtuosic British masters of the day, especially from—according to James Madison—the essayist Joseph Addison. They had become proficient players in the game of speaking and acting as gentlemen. But French revolutionary leaders, on the other hand, scorned this game and disdainfully brushed aside its rules. Boldly they sought to reinvent the language of politics.

While the mark of a leader of the founding generation in America was self-control accompanied by a certain verbal elegance and subtlety, the contrary traits of *ardor* and *vigor* were the mark of a patriot in France. "Who can love the fatherland coldly?" Robespierre demanded. Revolutionaries impatiently dismissed reserve, understatement, and subtlety as signs of indifference to the Revolution. Their world-historical enterprise called for hyperbole and passion. If emotions were not histrionic, inflamed, excessive, volcanic, they were deemed insufficiently revolutionary. People were not permitted to have calm emotions about anything, observed Tocqueville. Words had to surpass the feelings one wanted to express.

Passion and fervor ignited language. One moment revolutionaries were extolling their own wondrous deeds, the next moment spewing rage at their enemies. They reveled in their astonishing feats. "The French people are two thousand years ahead of the rest of humanity," boasted Robespierre. "It is tempting to conclude that the French constitute a different species." "The French are the first people in the world to establish a true democracy," he improbably exulted in February 1794, in the midst of the Terror. Hyperbole applied to the paranoid hunt for traitors as well. Marat, the historian Jules Michelet commented, did not limit himself to demanding a severe verdict for the scoundrels he accused of treason. Death itself was too mild a sentence. His imagination required burning at the stake, conflagrations, atrocious mutilations. "Brand them with an iron, cut their thumbs off, rip out their tongues, etc. etc."

Curiously, such hyperbole and uncivil frankness were not the innovation of the Revolution. Despite revolutionaries' boasts that they were replacing courtly affectations with democratic candor, the standard language spoken in the Old Regime's assemblies of notables had traditionally been one of undiplomatic insolence and bluntness. So unruly were these assemblies of notables, comprised of members of the nobility, the clergy, and the *haute bourgeoisie,* that a member had once proposed a rule that there never be more than four members speaking at once. "It was an old tradition under the monarchy," Tocqueville commented, "that the Parliament, in voicing its objections, could express itself with a male frankness bordering on rudeness." Tocqueville explained this incivility by placing it in the context of the political relationship between the weak Parliament and the absolute monarch. The king was willing to grant this "linguistic license" to the Parliament because it possessed so little real power. The Parliament was accustomed to producing a great deal of noise in order to obtain little. The king, buttressed by solid and unquestioned institutions, was not harmed by brash language, especially because the language was not followed by any actions. The notables' exaggerated, overstated speech became acceptable to all parties.

But what happens, Tocqueville asked, when that same hyperbole and blunt, violent language are transported from a feudal society to a democratic one? The people, unlike weak, disempowered nobles, will produce not "ineffective whimpers," but a revolution.

Indeed, inflammatory revolutionary language in France shook society and eventually even reason itself to their roots. Revolutionaries demanded ever more zeal, energy, and soaring vigor to propel the Revolution toward new heights; reserve and self-control would only impede its flight. "We do not need to protect ourselves from an excess of energy," declared Robespierre, "but rather from an excess of weakness." Revolutionary leaders demanded *virtue* of the people as well as of themselves. Not virtue in the usual sense of "goodness," though that was part of the equation. But rather virtue in the Latin sense, *virtus,* derived from the word for man, *vir. Virtus* signified manliness, virile energy, and courage. Virile energy was the sine qua non of a successful revolution. A virtuous, patriotic citizen would stop at nothing to advance the Revolution and avenge the oppressed people. Robespierre singled out "virtue" and forceful character as the most effective guarantees of freedom and independence. Imploring citizens to crush their enemies, he urged them to "show a *firm,* patriotic as well as truly *energetic* character."

But could there be an overload of zeal? Robespierre posed the hypothetical choice between an excess of patriotic fervor on the one hand and the abyss of complete indifference to patriotism and the stagnation of moderation on the other. "Do not for a second hesitate," he advised. "A vigorous body, stimulated by an overabundance of lifeblood, has more potency than a cadaver." "The most perilous shoal we must avoid is not the fervor of zeal," he divulged, "but lassitude with doing good and fear of our own courage."

If the Revolution suffered reverses, the culprit was a lack of virtue—that is, a lack of revolutionary potency. "The cause of our ills," Robespierre diagnosed, "is in . . . our deplorable frivolity, our profound laziness, our idiotic confidence." "We must be prepared to inject energy into government," Danton asserted in 1793. "The people want terror to be the order of the day, and rightly so. . . . The time for clemency has not yet arrived. . . . I want stronger sentences, more terrifying punishments." "Crime has a softer voice than the truth," disclosed Saint-Just, recommending an end to moderation.

As early as June 1789 Mirabeau had already been pleading for moderation, urging his fellow delegates to remember that "justice and truth" are always in the wise middle, and that extreme options are the "recourse of despair." But Mirabeau was virtually alone in counseling restraint. When, during the height of the Terror, a chastened Danton tried to defend two of his close friends who had been arrested, he argued that the ardent energy that the Revolution had once required

Oath of the Tennis Court,
by Dominique Vivant Denon

was no longer necessary. But his words of moderation and restraint came too late.

In revolutionary America, references to virile energy were rare, though occasionally such Spartan language crept into political discourse. Federalists attacked Jefferson for "a want of *firmness*" and, sounding like the Jacobins they despised, they proclaimed that "the *energy* of the true federalist will stamp the character of America with *strong* and *manly* features." And, according to Samuel Adams, Americans would show the world how to conciliate republicanism and virtue by founding their own "*Christian* Sparta."

For the most part, however, the American Revolution was propelled, not by a cult of potency, but rather by strict, even tedious adherence to parliamentary procedure. While Americans produced an innovative Constitution and Bill of Rights only after long months of methodical, disciplined, and peaceable nationwide debate, in France impulsive revolutionaries ridiculed such a slow, orderly process. What were legal forms but cumbersome, archaic constraints on the virile energy of the people? "We invoke forms," deplored Robespierre, "because we lack principles; we pride ourselves on our delicacy because we lack *energy.*"

A formal, punctilious trial for the accused Louis XVI? People who insisted on fair legal procedure for the treacherous monarch, Saint-Just disclosed, "fear that later they will suffer for their *courage:* they lack all *energy.*" A slow, cumbersome trial? It entraps "that *soaring vigor* of which we have such need," he warned.

A merciful, politic verdict for the king? Why not supernatural vengeance instead? "A people does not judge as does a court of law," Robespierre explained. "It does not hand down sentences, it *hurls* down

Execution of Louis XVI, 21 January 1793

thunderbolts; it does not condemn kings, it *plunges* them into the abyss; such *justice* is as compelling as the justice of courts." A public execution? Why not a spectacular—and expeditious—assassination? "Some day men will be astonished that in the eighteenth century humanity was less advanced than in the time of Caesar," mused Saint-Just. "Then, a tyrant was slain in the midst of the Senate, with *no formality* but thirty dagger blows, with no law but the liberty of Rome." Saint-Just bestowed on all virtuous French citizens the right of assassination. "There is no citizen who does not have the right that Brutus had over Caesar," he decided.

A thoughtful Thomas Paine dared to make the humane and politically astute suggestion that the king be pardoned and exiled to America. Marat, who admired the international revolutionary from America, shouted out that this could not possibly be Paine's view, that the translation of Paine's words had to be botched. For his part, Marat was convinced that pardon would demonstrate not only weakness but "treason, wickedness, and perfidy." Those who ask for a pardon, Saint-Just scornfully observed, seek "less to persuade you than to constrain and corrupt your *energy*." Robespierre too screamed for death for the monster-king: "What scruple yet fetters your *zeal*?"

Revolutionary language spurned the oblique, courtly path. Brutal frankness was more suited to patriots laboring for the radical transformation of French society. Revolutionaries had absorbed Rousseau's preference for honesty over the exquisite courtesy, "the false veil of politeness," of eighteenth-century France. They agreed with the hero of Rousseau's famous novel, *La Nouvelle Héloïse*, that "the plain and emotive effusions of an honest soul" communicate far more authentically and effectively than the "insincere demonstrations of politeness." The other side of Rousseau—his political prescription for self-mastery and self-repression—was conveniently ignored.

"Let us be bold, ever more bold, bold forever!" roared Danton. The Revolution's role model, the polar opposite of the prudent George Washington, was Brutus. An admiring Danton praised Brutus's outspokenness, applauding him for uttering truths in the Roman Senate that the French, with their "fainthearted standards," would timorously call "personal abuse." The abbé Grégoire similarly contended that "the language of Republicans must stand out by frankness."

Revolutionary frankness smashed the artificial, decorous forms of civility. Blunt criticism of adversaries, revolutionary leaders believed, would demonstrate candor and courage. Now bold representatives could freely indulge in ad hominem attacks on their colleagues. Citing the merit of frankness, Danton publicly impugned a variety of his fellow politicians: Marat, Roland, Brissot, and many others. When Danton himself was denounced by the representative Lasource for conspiring with the treasonous General Dumouriez, Lasource also claimed that *frankness* obliged him to reveal his true feelings about Danton.

In English parliamentary democracy, the kind of personalized attacks that took place in France were rare, in part because speakers were required to address the chair, not their colleagues. But in France representatives raged unhampered at one another, incited by the presence of rowdy spectators. The rotation every two weeks of the Assembly's president and secretaries also promoted instability and the absence of procedure.

Was parliamentary procedure unknown in France? In 1789 Mirabeau had helpfully presented to the National Assembly the translation of a book drawn up by his English friend Sir Samuel Romilly on the rules of Parliament. Unable to find a book of rules for Mirabeau, Romilly had decided to compile them himself. Later he recalled the reception his work received in France. "[My book] never was of the smallest use," he wrote in his memoirs. "No regard whatever was paid to it by the National Assembly." Romilly understood that French politicians were little disposed to borrow anything from England. They were not inclined to adopt English rules, nor were they interested in adopting rules of their own. Proceedings conducted with "order and regularity," Romilly concluded, might have allayed many of the rash and violent measures that prevailed in the Assembly. For his part, Robespierre readily admitted his dislike of elaborate parliamentary procedures, specifically equating political debate with "intrigue." "I don't like this new science that is called the strategy of large assemblies," he declared. "It bears too much resemblance to intrigue. *Truth* and *reason* alone must reign in legislative assemblies."

"Truth" and "reason" called for a new repertoire of revolutionary, patriotic slogans to replace the old axioms of monarchical society. "With what good humor we still let ourselves be the dupes of words!" Robespierre lamented. "How the aristocrats and the moderates still rule us with the murderous maxims they gave us!" But the new revolutionary maxims would turn logic and language upside down, reversing meanings, transforming black into white. "To punish the oppressors of humanity is clemency," declared Robespierre. "To pardon them is barbarity."

Calling for new republican aphorisms to capture the Revolution's goals and consecrate its ideals, he tried his hand at formulating the essence of the revolutionary project. "Immorality is the foundation of despotism, just as virtue is the essence of a republic," Robespierre decreed. "The Revolution . . . is nothing more than the passing from the reign of crime to that of justice." Saint-Just also contributed to the canon, articulating the purpose of the Revolution. "Our aim is to create an order of things so that the universal inclination toward the good can be established, . . . so that a virile energy inclines the spirit of the nation toward justice. . . . Our aim is to establish a sincere government." If that description of the revolutionary enterprise was less than clear, he concluded with a lapidary axiom: "The republic is not a senate, it is virtue."

Some maxims elevated vengeance to a patriotic duty. "He who does not pursue crime cannot love virtue," Robespierre exclaimed. Other maxims warned against conciliation with the enemy. "Amnesty for perfidious deputies," Robespierre stated, "would mean the protection of crime, the suffocation of *virtue.*" For people who discerned more despotism than democracy in the Terror, there was also a slogan. "The Revolution is the despotism of liberty against tyranny," Robespierre asserted, ominously assimilating freedom and despotism, turning black into white.

Ultimately, revolutionary "maxims" were as impenetrable as they were illogical and hollow; they could hardly have been more different from the clear and simple phrases of the American founding documents.

But the French Revolution's most astonishing and ill-boding verbal sleight of hand was its malignant equation of virtue and terror. Virtue would be used to justify terror, but only after virtue had come to assume two different meanings. On the one hand, it signified virile energy, the tireless pursuit of justice, the relentless unmasking of enemies. On the other, it implied pity for the suffering masses of France. Cruelty and sentimentality were the two faces of the virtuous patriot.

Rousseau had taught the revolutionary generation that pity was the super-virtue, the source of all social virtues. "What is generosity, clemency, humanity," he asked, "if not pity applied to the weak, the guilty, the human species in general?" True patriots would know the pleasure of shedding tears for the people and communing with their suffering. Robespierre admitted that he himself delighted in "this tender, imperious, irresistibly delicious torment of magnanimous hearts, this profound horror for tyranny, this compassionate zeal for the oppressed, this sublime and holy love for humanity." He even proposed a touching new celebration, a national Festival of Unhappiness—"la Fête du Malheur"—which would honor unhappiness. The Revolution, he confessed, could not entirely banish unhappiness from the earth but it could comfort and console the wretched and abject people of France.

But Robespierre's ideal community of virtue, pity, and suffering was not an inclusive one. Though Rousseau had extolled pity, he had significantly added that "pity for the wicked is a great cruelty toward men." Similarly, for Robespierre and company, pity did not extend to the rich, to aristocrats, to traitors to the fatherland. Politicizing the "instinct" of pity, they reserved it for oppressed patriots and withheld it from all adversaries. Saint-Just alerted patriots that counterrevolutionaries would try to "stir up pity, . . . buy some tears, . . . touch our sympathies, . . . corrupt us." But virtuous citizens owed them nothing but inflexible justice and the blade of the guillotine—not misplaced sympathy.

Pity thus provided a foundation for exclusion rather than for solidarity. The political philosopher Hannah Arendt remarked that true human solidarity looks upon everyone—strong and weak, fortunate and unfortunate—with an equal eye; but pity, unlike solidarity, has a "vested interest in the existence of the weak." The Jacobin notion of community, based on the valorization of suffering and the cult of virtue and pity, required an anticommunity of oppressors and enemies. To be virtuous meant to weep for the people, to protect the innocent, to defend the nation, and to pursue energetically and punish fiercely the Revolution's enemies.

Virtue invoked violence. "Terror," Robespierre decided, "is nothing other than prompt, severe, inflexible justice. Hence terror is an emanation of virtue." A master in legerdemain, he asserted the interdependence of virtue and terror. "Terror without virtue is malignant," he decreed. "Virtue without terror is impotent."

It is a sad triumph over logic and rationality for a revolutionary regime, dedicated to freedom and justice, to justify oppression and tyranny. But the Jacobins' equation of virtue with energy and pity provided them with a powerful linguistic tool for claiming the morality of terror and for subordinating democracy and freedom to vengeance and violence. Several years of counterfeit virtue talk had prepared the terrain for this verbal transformation of violence into justice. In his great work on realpolitik, *The Prince*, Machiavelli had advised the prince not to deviate from what is good, but if necessary, to do evil. The Florentine diplomat never abolished the distinction between good and evil and never attempted to justify evil actions by calling them good. But the Jacobins went beyond Machiavelli, doing what he had never envisaged—that is, turning logic and morality upside down.

Mercy had become treason, energy had become vengeance, democracy had become tyranny. The Jacobins' rhetorical strategy vanquished not only civility and reason but also freedom, law, and justice. Revolutionary justice evidently required the suspension of the constitution, the suppression of all civil liberties, summary arrests, cruel imprisonments, hideous executions, and inhuman mass drownings. A few decades earlier, Montesquieu had perspicaciously wondered, "Is it not strange, though true, to say that virtue itself has need of limits?"

Hollow talk about aristocrats, traitors, conspiracies, virtue, and virile energy enervated speech as well as political thought. Ironically, the incendiary, energetic revolutionary language had devolved into a feeble, vacuous one that conveyed neither truth nor reason nor any meaningful political or moral insights. Indeed, no masterpieces of French literature were produced during the years of the Revolution. No gripping novels, no witty plays, no insightful essays, no great poetry. No French writers joined the ranks of Montaigne, Molière, Racine, La Fontaine, Pascal, La Rochefoucauld, Diderot, Voltaire, Marivaux, and so many others. The language itself seemed depleted.

The philosopher and writer Condorcet, himself condemned to death, believed that the revolutionaries' inability "to combine words," to articulate meaningful if not profound ideas had far-reaching political consequences. Trying to fathom the Terror, he argued that the Jacobin leaders, striving for greatness and historical immortality, had no choice but to resort to notorious *actions* as a way to compensate for their lame and shallow *words*. Condorcet was struggling to come to terms with the corruption of political speech in France and the relationship between speech and action, between the degradation of political discourse and violent repression.

Condorcet's thesis that radical leaders, realizing the insufficiency of their inept discourse, turned to violent deeds to make their splash in history stretches the imagination. But it may be fair to ask whether the Jacobins' numbing political discourse that fused virtue and denunciation was, as one historian believes, a "masterstroke" that enabled Robespierre to dominate the Assembly and conquer the Convention and the Committee of Public Safety. Or, on the contrary, whether the French Revolution's impoverished political language of suspicion and denunciation, a language as bereft of ideals and principles as it was of inspiration, was simply the product of its leaders' abysmal intellectual mediocrity. In either case or in both, as has happened innumerable times in history and politics, inflammatory, hyperbolic, polarizing political discourse took on a life of its own and propelled events toward violence. Two years before the Reign of Terror, Robespierre himself had marveled at the facility with which it was possible for some men to govern others with nothing but *words*.

THE STAGING OF CHARACTER

Jefferson commissioned the two greatest statues of George Washington—Houdon's statue for Richmond and Canova's statue for Raleigh; the massive Panthéon in Paris was redesigned to house the Revolution's outstanding heroes. The young sister republics needed heroes and role models, and revolutionary leaders obliged. Realizing that they were performers on the world stage, they wrote their scripts, designed costumes and even lighting to create public personae who would incarnate the values of their revolutionary movements.

In America, the founders self-consciously staged themselves as gentlemen-citizens, the embodiment of self-restraint and public service. In France, leaders wanted to appear, not as gentlemen who restrained their impulses, but instead as members of the *people*. They wished to be publicly identified with the primal energy, uninhibited honesty, patriotic fervor, and self-sacrifice supposedly belonging to revolutionary citizens. And whereas the American founders purposefully furnished their young country with models of altruistic national service, in France revolutionary leaders deliriously presented themselves as sacrificial offerings to the volatile, thirsty god of Revolution.

The American founders realized that they were living in a period that offered them the possibility of greatness and fame. "You and I, my dear friend, have been sent into life at a time when the greatest lawgivers of antiquity would have wished to live," wrote an exultant John Adams to Richard Henry Lee in 1777. "How few of the human race have ever enjoyed an opportunity of making election of government . . . for themselves or their children." The chance to participate in the creation of a world-historical experiment in democratic self-government held out the promise of *eternal* glory. And what more could a leader on the world stage aspire to than salvation—through immortal fame—from the oblivion that is man's fate? Men who will forever deserve the praise of historians, Machiavelli had remarked three hundred years earlier, are "those who establish republics or kingdoms."

What surer way to build a lasting monument to oneself and earn the perpetual admiration of posterity than to contribute to the founding and consolidation of the republic? Fame, Americans believed, would be awarded to those men who led lives of exemplary integrity and outstanding public service. "The love of honest and well-earned fame,"

James Wilson taught his students, "is deeply rooted in honest . . . minds," explaining that fame was all the more compelling a reward because "applause" was given only to men who held the most honorable principles and who engaged in the most consequential and meritorious public pursuits.

Here, again, Machiavelli had preceded the American founders, this time in linking fame and public service. He believed that good government in a republic depends on distinguished citizens, but, he added, distinction should be based solely on acts that are of benefit to the community. As if articulating the mentality and values of the founding fathers, the Florentine argued that "a well-regulated republic . . . should open the way to public honors to those who seek reputation by means that are conducive to the public good."

So interdependent were fame and a life of service to country for the American founders that any political leader who seemed unconcerned with applause was suspect—for such a person was probably motivated only by self-interest, unrestrained by a moral code. "Mr. Burr has never appeared solicitous for fame," commented Alexander Hamilton about his hated rival, "& that great Ambition unchecked by principle, or the love of Glory, is an unruly Tyrant who never can keep long in a course which good men will approve." Though self-interest could not be expected to vanish, the quest for glory and reputation, as Hamilton suggested, implied the fusion of personal ambition and public service. Love of fame, the historian Douglass Adair wrote, transformed the desire for self-aggrandizement and personal reward into a "golden concern" for public service.

People who pursued fame were motivated to be better—or at least to *appear* to be better—than they were. They could be expected to have disguised their own self-interest and to have channeled it into service to country. The authentic desires, drives, and emotions in one's heart were less important than one's mastery over them and one's ability to lead a life devoted to honorable, public pursuits. A social or political leader did not necessarily have to *be* disinterested, but he had to *appear* so and to *behave* in a disinterested, principled way, living a life committed to the public good.

The original master of the art of staging oneself for public consumption was Benjamin Franklin. "I cannot boast of much Success in acquiring the *Reality* of this Virtue [of humility]," admitted Franklin, "but I had a good deal with regard to the *Appearance* of it." Already as a young man, he skillfully set and even lighted the stage upon which he worked. Laboring in his printing shop late into the night, the lights inside all aglow, Franklin knew that he was being observed and that his perseverance was being applauded. "This Industry visible to our Neighbours," he wrote in his *Autobiography*, "began to give us Character and Credit." The comments of passersby gratified him. They marveled that Franklin's industriousness was superior to anything they had ever witnessed. "I see him still at work when I go home from Club," one man remarked, "and he is at Work again before his Neighbours are out of bed."

"First impressions are generally the most lasting," Washington wrote to his nephew, George Steptoe Washington. "It is therefore, absolutely necessary, if you mean to make any figure *upon the stage,* that you should take the first steps right." Washington offered "advisory hints" to his nephew, not on a career in the theater but on a life of service to his country. His letter to the young man contained one line on the acquisition of knowledge, one line on "moral virtues," one line on economy and frugality, twelve lines on friendship, and *thirty-four* lines on clothing. Thought must be given to costume. To play the part, one must look the part.

The audience for which men of the founders' social class performed was comprised of their peers, their social equals and superiors. One lived one's life under their gaze. What mattered, Washington emphasized to his nephew, was how one appeared "in the *eyes of judicious men.*" Alexander Hamilton similarly stressed the importance of earning "the esteem of the deserving." Thomas Jefferson, too, in his letters of advice to young relatives and friends, counseled that "a determination never to do what is wrong, prudence, and good humor will go far towards securing to you the *estimation of the world.*"

So crucial was the estimation of the world and so defining were the watchful, judgmental eyes of others that one learned to internalize their gaze and behave, even in private, as if one were performing in public—

or in a hall of mirrors. "Whenever you are to do a thing," Jefferson wrote to his nephew Peter Carr, "tho' it can never be known but to yourself, ask yourself how you would act if all the world were *looking at you* and act accordingly."

The Washington Family, by Edward Savage.
Washington, in military uniform, has before him a map
of the new District of Columbia. With Washington are Martha, her grandchildren
Nelly and Washington Custis, and a black servant

But how can a young man with no experience be sure to know how to behave well? How can he trust that his judgment is good? Jefferson knew that a young person could not be expected always to be wise and prudent, but he could learn from others how to play the part. By choosing exceptionally distinguished men as role models, one could pattern one's behavior after theirs and also imagine oneself performing before their judgmental eyes. "When I recollect that at 14. years of age, the whole care and direction of my self was thrown on my self entirely, without a relation or friend qualified to advise or guide me, and recollect the various sorts of bad company with which I associated from time to time,"

Jefferson confessed to his grandson, "I am astonished I did not turn off with some of them, & become as worthless to society as they were."

What saved Jefferson from a life of dereliction were several men "of very high standing" whom he knew and whom he wished to emulate. "Under temptations & difficulties, I would ask myself *what would Dr. Small, Mr. Wythe, Peyton Randolph do in this situation?* What course in it will insure me *their approbation? . . .* Knowing the *even & dignified* line they pursued, I could never doubt for a moment which of two courses would be in character for them." Jefferson passed on to his grandson the wisdom of this "self-cathechising habit," assuring the young man that it would lead him to the *"prudent selection & steady pursuits of what is right."* Ideally, the "role" one plays eventually becomes virtually indistinguishable from one's own moral character. "Politeness," Jefferson instructed his grandson, "is artificial good humor, it covers the natural want of it, & ends by rendering habitual a substitute nearly equivalent to the real virtue."

George Washington was the ultimate American role model, the incarnation, if ever there was one, of integrity and self-restraint. Washington was an ambitious man who disguised his appetite for power and glory with the appearance of magnanimous public service. The public image he created was that of a gentleman-farmer who yearned to leave the political arena to return to his land at Mount Vernon but who nevertheless was willing to sacrifice his personal happiness for the welfare of the nation by accepting important leadership roles. Indeed, again and again he acquired power by presenting himself as reluctant to exercise it and ready to relinquish it.

Washington's resignation speech as commander-in-chief of the revolutionary army, his announced reluctance to attend the Constitutional Convention, his imposing appearance—in his striking general's uniform—at that meeting followed by his *unanimous* election to the presidency of the Convention, his professed dismay at the offer of the presidency of the new federal union, his alarm at the prospect of a second term, his final Farewell Address—these were masterful performances that enabled Washington to wield power while professing to disregard it. He incarnated the legitimacy of the new nation because, as general and as President, he was willing to exercise power in the name of the people and equally willing to give up and transfer that power to another temporary custodian of the power that resided in the people. He was, in the words of Garry Wills, a "virtuoso of resignations."

Washington was not a charismatic leader. He was more.

The authority and prestige of a charismatic leader reside in his magnetic personality. His charisma, by definition, is not transferable. His power, founded on personality, disintegrates with his death or downfall. It cannot be transferred intact to a successor. But Washington's precious gift to his country was eminently transferable; it was character.

He was a school for character.

"When you Sit down, Keep your Feet firm and Even"; "Wear not your Cloths, foul, unript or Dusty"; "If you Soak bread in the Sauce let it be no more than what you put in your Mouth at a time"; "In the Presence of Others Sing not to yourself." At the young age of fifteen, a fastidious and enterprising George Washington, concentrating on making his way in the world, copied from a book a list of 110 exacting rules of conduct. Many of them would serve him for the rest of his life: "When you deliver a matter do it without Passion & with Discretion"; "Strive not with your Superiers in argument, but always Submit your Judgment to others with Modesty"; "Contradict not at every turn what others Say"; "When Another Speaks be attentive your Self"; "If two contend together take not the part of either unconstrained; and be not obstinate in your own Opinion, in Things indiferent be of the Major Side"; "Associate yourself with Men of good Quality if you Esteem your own Reputation."

The unusual self-restraint he self-consciously cultivated and exhibited at the age of fifteen fully anticipated the mature wisdom expressed by the Father of the Country at sixty-four. "Infallibility not being the attribute of Man," Washington wrote in the draft of his Farewell Address, "we ought to be cautious in censuring the opinions and conduct of one another."

The self-control, tolerance, and respect for others that Washington embodied could be codified, taught, and learned—but always with one sole purpose: public service. He instructed his young nephews that an honorable man would be both learned and virtuous, not merely because virtue is its own reward but rather because otherwise one can "never be qualified to render service to [his] country." A true leader, Washington encouraged people not merely to follow him but to surpass themselves. By establishing the first general decoration in the American army limited to non-officers, the Purple Heart, he demonstrated that great courage can be shown by men of any rank.

His lessons in character building and self-discipline were rigorous. When, at the Philadelphia Convention, Washington found a delegate's notes on Convention proceedings, a grave violation of the pledge of secrecy, the lecture he delivered was stern. "Gentlemen, I am sorry to find that some one member of this body has been so neglectful of the secrets of the Convention as to drop in the State House a copy of their proceedings," he scolded. "I must entreat gentlemen to be more careful. . . . I do not know whose paper it is, but there it is, let him who owns it take it." Washington bowed, picked up his hat, and left the room with a dignity so severe, commented William Pierce of Georgia, that every person seemed distressed. "For my part," Pierce recalled, "I was extremely [alarmed], for putting my hand in my pocket I missed my copy of the same paper, but advancing up to the table my fears soon dissipated. I found it to be in the handwriting of another person."

Even with members of his own family, Washington insisted that merit be displayed and respect earned. His affection was not unconditional. He warned his nephew that the young man would lose his place in his uncle's esteem as well as any hope for future assistance if any complaint about his behavior were ever made. "But if, on the contrary," added Washington, "your conduct is such as to merit my regard you may always depend upon the warmest attachment and sincere regard of Your affectionate friend and Uncle."

Reserve and self-restraint also implied a certain self-effacement and tolerance. Though the founders themselves held very definite views about government, order, liberty, and democracy, they displayed remarkable tolerance for the opinions of others. Unlike their counterparts in France, they explicitly disclaimed any monopoly on truth. Should he "set up [his] judgment as the standard of perfection?" Washington wondered in his draft notes for his first inaugural speech. "And shall I arrogantly pronounce that whosoever differs from me, must discern the subject through a distorting medium, or be influenced by some nefarious design?" His political position, he realized with self-awareness as impressive as it is rare, gave him no privileged access to truth or even to insight. Thomas Jefferson stressed similar tolerance to his grandson. Permit others to make errors of judgment, he counseled. "His error does me no injury, and shall I become a Don Quixot to bring all men by force of argument, to one opinion?"

The gifts the founders offered Americans were not just Declarations and Constitutions, Bills and Preambles, but the gift of character, their own exemplary lives of public service, self-restraint, integrity, and tolerance. They were living symbols of the principles and values of the republic. They *were* the republic.

The self-restraint exemplified by the American founders did not go unnoticed or unappreciated in France. The French recognized Washington's greatness of character, and yet his moderation appeared strangely beyond their grasp, as if it were suited for another planet. One French leader, who admired Washington, seemed not to comprehend Washington's perfect merging of character and democratic values. Nor did he understand that Washington did not crave power for its own sake but that he sought power only because it was a route to fame, glory, and the esteem of judicious men. "If Washington had been a Frenchman at a time when France was crumbling inside and invaded from outside," wrote Napoleon Bonaparte in his memoirs, "I would have dared him to be himself; or, if he had persisted in being himself, he would merely have been a fool. . . . As for me, I could only be a crowned Washington. And I could become that only at a congress of kings, surrounded by sovereigns whom I had either persuaded or mastered. Then, and then only, could I have possibly displayed Washington's moderation, disinterestedness, and wisdom. In all reasonableness, I could not attain this goal except by means of world dictatorship. I tried it. Can it be held against me?"

BRUTUS, ALIVE IN FRANCE

While the American founders emphasized appearances, French leaders insisted on stripping off all social masks. Political theater in France called for self-revelation.

"I will state frankly and with no pride what I have done," began Robespierre in a typical confessional speech. "I did not do all the good I would have liked nor all the good I might have done." Saint-Just too emphasized revolutionary honesty. Despising "false modesty," the true revolutionary patriot, according to Saint-Just, abjures "all deception, all affectation." Unlike the Americans who valued reserve and prudence, French leaders wished nothing more than to bare and unburden their souls and, in the Rousseauian confessional mode, reveal their innermost beings and authentic emotions. "I need to pour out my heart," confessed Robespierre in one speech, adding that his audience also needed to "hear the truth."

And what overwhelming emotion did they discover when they fathomed their hearts? Not surprisingly, love—love for the people of France. In their speeches they confessed over and over again their "sublime and tender" feelings for the people. "Only the people are good, just, magnanimous," exclaimed Robespierre.

But it was not just love that they felt for the virtuous people, but also complete identification. Though Robespierre, the middle-class lawyer, arguably had minimal knowledge of the "people," rarely coming into contact with the poor and uneducated masses of peasants and workers, he nevertheless contended that he was "neither a courtier, nor an advocate of caution, nor a tribune, nor a defender of the people. I am of the people myself." Saint-Just too claimed that he was one with the people. "I shall never place my personal will in opposition to the will of all," he maintained. "I shall desire what the people of France . . . may desire." Never voicing his own opinions or private interests, insisting that he belonged to no faction, he could be counted on, he proclaimed, to represent only the people's will.

The Jacobin leaders' public identification with the people placed them in an extremely powerful position. First of all, since the "people" were always defined as the locus of all political and moral virtue and all devotion to the Revolution, anyone who belonged to and spoke for them could also assert his virtue and selflessness.

Second, their love for the people enabled them to present themselves as the people's defenders. Jacobin leaders could justify their radical, violent deeds by claiming that their deep love for the people imposed upon them an obligation not only to nurse the people's wounds but to avenge the people and to restore to them their dignity. The incontestable truth and authenticity of their feelings for the people, the Jacobins asserted, overrode any legal constraints on their behavior. They were tied to the people's cause, Robespierre noted, "by bonds far stronger than all the cold formulae of oaths invented by laws." Jacobin leaders, loving the people, awarded themselves carte blanche to carry out acts of repression and unspeakable violence against citizens of France. "I have been accused over and over," Robespierre protested when he was criticized by moderate representatives, "of defending with too much fervor the cause of the weak, oppressed people against their powerful oppressors."

The Jacobin leaders' identification with the people of France gave them one other formidable tool for wielding power. By professing to know and mirror perfectly the people's General Will (which Rousseau had defined as infallible), Robespierre, Saint-Just, and other radical leaders could assert their privileged access to the "truth." "I have never taken any side other than that of *truth*," Saint-Just insisted.

These champions of the "truth" proceeded to conceive their role as the inquisitors of the nation. The inquisitor fought to unmask and punish all those who betrayed the will of the people—an ever-expanding fifth column of traitors. "I accuse all those perverted men whom I will unmask," declared Robespierre in a typical denunciation. Robespierre's inquisitorial speeches, endlessly repetitious, overflowing with insinuations and accusations, cast doubt on everyone and everything. Every citizen and politician came under suspicion, everything began to appear uncertain. Only Robespierre, as the historian Patrice Gueniffey remarked, could see what others wished to hide; only he knew the truth. There could be no debate, no contradiction.

Robespierre guillotining the executioner
after having guillotined all the French.
The obelisk reads "Here is buried all of France"

Armed with the "truth," Jacobins could brand any individuals who
dared to disagree with them traitors or fanatics. Any distinction between
their own political adversaries and the people's "enemies" was obliterated. By publicly staging themselves as defenders of the people and lead-

ers of the inquisition against traitors to the nation, the Jacobins laid the terrain for their license to carry out the Terror.

While George Washington's modest refusal to "set up [his] judgment as the standard of perfection" ensured tolerance if not respect for his political adversaries, radical leaders in France expressed no similar disavowal of omniscience. They rarely made public admissions of fallibility. And how could they have, given the dynamic they had created? Just as it was inconceivable for the virtuous, selfless, patriotic people to be in error, it was also logically impossible for the leaders who loved them and voiced their interests to be misguided.

And yet, although Robespierre occasionally proclaimed the triumph of the people over their enemies, as he did after the arrest of Danton, the process of ferreting out suspects and unmasking enemies and traitors was forever incomplete. New traitors—in greater and greater numbers—were always surfacing. Ultimately these men of virtue and violence felt incapable of defeating the forces of treason and corruption. The circle of virtuous citizens seemed to narrow, as more and more French men and women seemed to become the dupes of their enemies. In the Jacobins' paranoid imaginations, the legions of enemies could not be quelled.

Strange allusions to death and martyrdom began to creep into the Jacobins' public speeches, as these radicals grew more and more isolated, as their goal of a virtuous and unanimous people appeared ever more elusive. "Perhaps Heaven is calling me to shed my blood on the road that will lead my country to happiness and freedom," Robespierre declared as early as April 1792. "I accept with ecstasy this sweet and glorious destiny." "Great men do not die in their beds," divulged Saint-Just, bizarrely adding that Benjamin Franklin, who had passed away peacefully in 1790 at the age of eighty-four, had died—like Demosthenes, who committed suicide, and Marat, who was assassinated—a martyr's death.

Over and over we hear odes to death and offers of suicide. Saint-Just was morbidly fascinated with his own death, which he viewed as the natural and logical outcome of his own insufficiency—that is, his inability to wipe out all dissent and stamp out all "evil" in the world. "The day when I will become convinced that it is impossible to give the French people morals that are gentle, energetic, sensitive, and inexorable toward tyranny and injustice," Saint-Just wrote, "I will stab myself." "Certainly, I would be leaving very little," he bitterly remarked, "in leaving a life in which one has to be the accomplice or the mute witness of evil." Even stranger, though perhaps more revealing, was his admission of a deep need for violence, whether directed against others or against himself. "If Brutus does not kill others," Saint-Just observed, "he will kill himself."

Unable to annihilate their enemies, were Jacobin leaders, as scholar Carol Blum suggests, compelled to redirect their rage against themselves? Did they aspire to become revolutionary saints and holy martyrs? Or were their threats of suicide a way—albeit an infantile one—to exculpate themselves and deflect accusations of tyranny? "I, who do not in the least believe in the necessity for living, but only in virtue and in Providence, I find myself placed in the state where the assassins wished to put me," Robespierre defensively explained, offering himself as a sacrificial victim. "I feel myself more detached than ever from human wickedness. . . . We stand exposed before your homicidal daggers, chests bared, not wishing to be surrounded by guards. Strike, we await your blows." Robespierre defended himself by pointing to his enemies' hatred of him. "I sharpen the daggers against me," he admitted. Asserting that the greatest proof of virtue is to be murdered by the people's enemies, Robespierre proclaimed his willingness to die for the Revolution. "Let us rejoice and thank heaven," he exclaimed, "that we have served our fatherland well enough to have been found worthy of tyranny's daggers." The destiny of those who fight against tyranny, Robespierre declared, is "the grave and immortality."

The Revolution's fate was effectively sealed when leadership was eclipsed by talk of suicide, when the nation's principal politicians portrayed themselves not as representatives of the people but as martyrs. "For my part," Robespierre announced, "I consent gladly to be sacrificed. . . . How can you object to a man who is right and who can die for his country? I was born to combat crime, not to govern."

A martyr's death—not an exemplary life of public service, not the eternal praise of historians—towered as the statesman's highest calling. "The good and the bad all disappear from the earth," Robespierre sermonized. "Hear me, citizens: death is the beginning of immortality."

Washington and Jefferson were nostalgic for Virginia, not for death. When they spoke of leaving the political arena, they desired to return to independent, self-sufficient lives on their farms and estates, not to immolate themselves. And while little mattered more to them than their eternal reputations and the respect of judicious men, Robespierre asserted that he prized a few "honorable whispers" more than "shameful applause." His audience, he boasted, was "humanity," not the national legislature. As if distancing himself from the American founders' love of fame, he explicitly offered to give up his reputation along with his life. "Yes, there is another [sacrifice] that you can still demand of me . . . the sacrifice of my reputation. I hand it over to you; together you can all tear it to shreds." Insisting that he valued martyrdom more than fame, he disavowed any personal desire for honor or glory. "I wanted my reputation," Robespierre asserted, "only for the good of my country." Death alone seemed to arouse in him feelings of ecstasy. "O sublime people! receive the sacrifice of all my being," he rejoiced. "Happy is the man who is born in your midst! Even happier he who can die for your happiness!"

For all their talk of virtue and energy, the legacy left by Jacobin leaders was a barren one. Their public speeches contained no ringing, memorable tributes to freedom and justice, no insights into democracy. They abounded instead with illogical maxims, ferocious calls to love the people, paranoid denunciations, and delirious odes to suicide. The Jacobins bequeathed to France no exemplary models of courageous political leadership or creative, visionary intellectual leadership. Though in 1791 Robespierre announced his desire to leave "to posterity a spotless name and an example that all good people can imitate," he left the French a history stained by violence, lawlessness, and injustice. The Panthéon in Paris contains the tombs of only two minor revolutionary figures—the abbé Grégoire, the champion of Jewish emancipation, and the philosopher and educator Condorcet. This massive monument, redesigned to house the Revolution's heroes, has been sadly called "the Temple of Emptiness."

The fiery Edmund Burke summed it all up: "It is ordained in the eternal constitution of things," he wrote, "that men of intemperate minds cannot be free." Washington would have agreed.

★ 5 ★

Declaring—and Denying—Rights

homas Jefferson was displeased. No bill of rights! His disappointment and frustration boiled to the surface when he learned
in Paris that the recently drafted Constitution for the United
States had been approved without explicit guarantees of rights. "A bill
of rights," he lectured James Madison, "is what the people are entitled
to against every government on earth . . . & what no just government
should refuse." Even John Adams shared Jefferson's dismay. "What think
you of a Declaration of Rights?" he wrote to Jefferson from London.
"Should not such a Thing have preceded the Model?"

Indeed, the Constitution would contain no bill of rights until 1791.
Though the Bill of Rights has been the precious safeguard of the liber-
ties of Americans for two hundred years, arguably more crucial than the
Constitution itself, it came fifteen years after the Declaration of Inde-
pendence and the Revolutionary War, an addendum appended to the
Constitution of 1787.

The French Declaration of the Rights of Man and Citizen, on the
other hand, constituted the mythic founding document of the Revolution, born just a month after the storming of the Bastille. The French
jubilantly celebrated a Declaration of Rights that broke radically with

the past. Their Declaration, they exclaimed, was produced not by history but by Reason itself! Whereas the American Bill of Rights, summarizing what already existed in the bills of rights of the various states, was anchored in English and American tradition, the French congratulated themselves on inventing the credo of a new age.

Was the Americans' backward-looking respect for their own legal and constitutional antecedents less original, less revolutionary, less noteworthy than the daring French rupture with a thousand years of monarchical tradition? Perhaps. And yet, the value of experience and tradition must not be underestimated. With great pride and fanfare, the French neophytes exulted in proclaiming rights. But the Americans, experienced in writing state constitutions and bills of rights, knew how to guarantee them.

FIGHTING FOR RIGHTS

Profoundly disappointed over the absence of a bill of rights in the Constitution, Jefferson had it wrong. The prime purpose of the Constitutional Convention had been to create a strong central government. Reacting to Shays's Rebellion and to the virtually powerless government that existed under the Articles of Confederation, the Convention had concentrated on assuring national stability, security, and order—though many people assumed that guarantees of rights and freedoms would follow.

Even so, guarantees of individual rights mattered for some delegates as much as strong and stable government. Elbridge Gerry of Massachusetts, George Mason of Virginia, and others demanded that a charter of rights be inserted into the Constitution. When Gerry and Mason urged the adoption of statements of freedom of the press, freedom of religion, respect for writs of habeas corpus, and the right to jury trials, federalists rebuffed their efforts, claiming that "the representatives of the people may be safely trusted" in these matters and that no explicit guarantee of rights was necessary.

When deliberations on the Constitution ended in Philadelphia in September 1787, a frustrated and disappointed Gerry announced that he would "withhold his name." For George Mason too, the absence of a bill of rights constituted a "fatal objection." Mason left Philadelphia "in an exceeding ill humour indeed," Madison reported to Jefferson. Now antifederalists were returning to their states, armed with a potent argument for opposing the Constitution in their state ratifying conventions.

Alexander Hamilton tried to neutralize their objections. He argued, in *The Federalist* No. 84, that a bill of rights was not only unnecessary but "even dangerous." Bills of rights, he reminded his readers, were traditionally enacted to protect subjects from the power of kings. But in the new federal union no such protections against government were necessary, since the people themselves had framed the Constitution. The real security of the people, Hamilton maintained, hinged "on public opinion and on the general spirit of the people and of the government," not on definitions of rights that are inevitably open to evasion. Hamilton's essay, however, left supporters of rights unmoved, especially those who admired the long English tradition of protection of rights. Both the Magna Carta of 1215 and the bill of rights of 1689 had guarded subjects against abuses of power, although, as Hamilton pointed out, it was expected that any abuse of power would come from the king, not from the Parliament.

How deep was support for a bill of rights? Would antifederalists in Virginia succeed in adding a bill of rights to the Constitution and in correcting other flaws? From Paris, Thomas Jefferson suggested the Machiavellian strategy he would have adopted had he been present in Richmond. "Were I in America," he informed the son-in-law of John Adams, "I would advocate [the Constitution] warmly till nine should have adopted and then as warmly take the other side to convince the remaining four that they ought not to come into it till the declaration of rights is annexed to it."

Exceptionally talented men from all over Virginia poured into the New Academy Hall in Richmond to begin the debates on ratification. Supporters of the Constitution included such arresting figures as James Madison, John Marshall, Edmund Pendleton, and Henry Lee, while the antifederalists could count on George Mason, Richard Henry Lee, James Monroe, and especially Patrick Henry, the fiery orator and skilled lawyer. Leading the antifederalist opposition, Henry insisted on a Constitution that guaranteed liberty of the press, trial by jury, and other rights and also protected Virginia from overbearing Northern interests. For Henry, nothing mattered as much as liberty, "that precious jewel." Knowing that Jefferson strongly favored a bill of rights, he decided to speak for his fellow Virginian on the other side of the Atlantic. "Living in splendor and dissipation," Henry declared, "he thinks yet of bills of rights. . . . Let us follow the sage advice of this common friend of our happiness."

Federalists tried to seize the initiative. Since the states had their own bills of rights, they argued, a federal bill of rights was superfluous. The most famous Virginian of all, George Washington, maintained that a federal bill of rights might conflict with the various bills of the states. But Mason responded logically that "if federal law is to be supreme then the declarations of Rights, in the separate States, are no security." Ultimately federalists in Virginia were obliged to promise antifederalists that they would recommend the addition of a bill of rights to the Constitution. The final vote in Virginia was narrow: 89 voted for ratification, 79 against.

In Massachusetts too, delegates were troubled by the absence of a bill of rights. Histrionically raising the specter of the Spanish Inquisition, antifederalists ominously warned that nothing prevented the new Congress from instituting such frightening tribunals. Indeed, if the national Congress did not do so, it would be "owing entirely . . . to the goodness of the men, and not . . . the goodness of the Constitution." As in Virginia, Massachusetts federalists finally offered a compromise: Massachusetts would send a recommendation for amendments along with its decision to ratify the Constitution.

And at the New York ratifying convention, there was also pressure for a bill of rights. One representative overcame his reluctance to speak out and exclaimed that "our lives, our property, and our consciences, are left wholly at the mercy of the legislature. . . . Sir, in this Constitution we have not only neglected—we have done worse—we have openly violated . . . our public faith." The vote for ratification was alarmingly close: 30 to 27. While the prosperous seaboard cities of Boston, New

York, Philadelphia, Baltimore, and Alexandria supported the Constitution, pressure for a bill of rights was mounting among lower-income and lower-status citizens in the small inland towns.

Where did James Madison stand? On the question of a bill of rights, he had mastered the art of equivocation. In October 1788 he wrote to Jefferson that he himself had "always been in favor of a bill of rights." Still, he admitted, he had "not viewed it in an important light," and its absence from the Constitution hardly constituted a "material defect." Bills of rights, he mused, furnished little more than "parchment barriers" against infringements on citizens' rights, whereas the Constitution offered more effective protection to minorities through institutional structures designed to restrain an overbearing majority.

Thousands of miles from Virginia, Jefferson kept hammering away at Madison, stressing the paramount importance of a bill of rights. Such a bill might not offer complete protection, but, he noted with down-to-earth pragmatism, "half a loaf is better than no bread. If we cannot secure all our rights, let us secure what we can." Guarantees of rights might conceivably "cramp government," he allowed, but their absence, on the other hand, would have "permanent, affecting and irreparable" consequences.

When Jefferson wrote that letter in March 1789, he was unaware that Madison had already made a startling about-face.

Within months of expressing coolness toward a bill of rights, Madison metamorphosed into the passionate and skillful advocate of just such a bill. Had Jefferson's admonitions succeeded in changing his mind? Some historians attribute Madison's newfound commitment to a bill of rights less to Jefferson's efforts than to Madison's own political ambition. Anxious to represent Virginia in the new federal House of Representatives and defeat his close friend James Monroe, the candidate of the antifederalists, Madison needed to assure Virginia voters that, if elected, he would support a bill of rights. According to this scenario, after defeating Monroe, Madison faithfully kept his campaign promise.

But perhaps more convincing is the explanation that recognizes Madison's long-standing and consistent commitment to the protection of minorities. "The constants and continuities in his thinking about rights," notes historian Jack Rakove, "remain more striking than his adjustment to the hothouse politics of ratification." Madison championed a bill of rights in part because he felt that such a bill could educate American citizens and cement their commitment to the new government by incorporating the principles and "maxims" of free government into public awareness. In addition, he also came to agree with Jefferson that the judiciary should have a legal check over the legislature. As for the federalists' objection that any list of rights would relegate nonenumerated rights to inferior status, Madison solved that problem in the Ninth Amendment—"the enumeration in the Constitution, of certain rights, shall not be construed to deny or disparage others retained by the people."

"A few *milk-and-water* amendments," scoffed one representative at the first federal Congress taking place in New York in 1789, expressing his disdain for a bill of rights. Another ridiculed it as "an immense mass of sweet and other herbs and roots for a diet drink." Members of the House seemed more excited by discussions of taxes and tariffs than by the issue of citizens' rights. Again and again, Madison tried to raise the question of a bill of rights, only to be put off by representatives asserting that tedious money issues should be resolved first. "Without revenue the wheels of government cannot move," they evasively claimed. "I hope we shall be strong enough to postpone," wrote one forthright opponent. Others asked for a year's moratorium. Even antifederalists had lost their enthusiasm for a bill of rights.

But despite the lack of interest of some and the derision of others, a few farsighted representatives still appreciated the value of a bill of rights. "They will meliorate the government," wrote Tench Coxe to Madison, "by heightening and strengthening the barriers between necessary power and indispensable liberty."

Madison plunged ahead. In March 1789 he began sifting through the different state constitutions, looking for a consensus about fundamental rights and finally drafting some rights amendments. In June he formally moved that Congress take up the subject of the protection of rights, urging that the issue of rights be resolved before the end of the first congressional session. Continued delay and tiresome debates on procedure, he warned his fellow representatives, could arouse the suspicions of their constituents that their rights were not sufficiently protected. "We have . . . something to gain," Madison pragmatically exhorted the Congress, "and, if we proceed with caution, nothing to lose."

Finally Madison's perseverance was rewarded. By July the House had formed a committee to review Madison's draft, and by the end of August 1789 the Chamber had approved the amendments. The Senate followed suit the next month. Two years later, in 1791, three-quarters of the states had ratified the amendments, and the Bill of Rights became the law of the nation.

REVOLUTIONARY RIGHTS

Rights mania was sweeping Paris and the United States simultaneously. "All the world is occupied at present in framing, every one his own plan of a bill of rights," wrote Jefferson to a friend at the end of 1788, marveling at the new French vogue. The American minister in Paris was the living juncture at which the two rights movements crossed paths.

Jefferson seemed to be everywhere and to know everyone—almost at once giving interviews to the French about liberties in Virginia, translating into French his bill establishing religious freedom in his home state, expressing his doubts to his American friends about the French "ripeness" for freedom of the press, habeas corpus, and trial by jury, chiding Americans that the "enlightened part of Europe" was disappointed to see them give up so soon on a bill of rights, trying to galvanize a stalled James Madison by sending him a copy of Lafayette's draft of a bill of rights for France, composing his own version of a charter of rights for France and offering it to Lafayette "merely as a canvas . . . to work on." Buoyed by his own unshakable faith in the progress of humanity, Jefferson believed that a readiness for rights would evolve in France just as a bill of rights would ultimately be adopted in America.

While the French were stirred by the American guarantees of rights they found in Benjamin Franklin's French edition of American state constitutions and inspired by the draft of a charter of rights that Jefferson proposed to Lafayette, Americans, at the same time, were awakened by the French passion for rights and excited by their Declaration of Rights, printed in American newspapers in October 1789. Clearly, each nation had some impact on the other.

Still, neither country sought to mirror the other. They were rather both part of a "community of ideas," in the words of R. R. Palmer. And for all the cross-pollination of both declarations of rights, they remain strikingly different. The American Bill of Rights and the French Declaration were carefully tailored to suit their nations' ideals and fears.

In June 1789, just when Madison was presenting his draft for a bill of rights to the first American Congress, King Louis XVI in France was proposing his own version of a charter of rights to the Estates General. Sadly the hapless monarch, forever unable to grasp the meaning of events and seize the initiative, offered a bill that fell far short of the mark. Though he granted freedom of the press along with some mea-sure of equality to citizens, he preserved many of the feudal rights of his nobles. Ironically, two years earlier, Louis had supported the far more sweeping reforms advised by his finance minister Calonne. But a few weeks before the storming of the Bastille, the misguided, uncompre-hending king offered far too little and found himself bypassed by events. Within days, he was forced to recognize the authority of the new National Assembly.

What would come first, a constitution or a declaration of rights? The electrifying, transformational conquest of the Revolution, for the majority of representatives, lay in the guarantee of citizens' rights, free-doms, and equality before the law—not in a routine, technical descrip-tion of the structures and procedures of government. Indeed, a constitution would not be written until 1791.

American documents offered a useful model. Many French represen-tatives admitted finding strength and direction in the declarations of rights of Virginia, Massachusetts, and Pennsylvania. Even Robespierre praised the "energy of the American declarations." Still, the French were anxious to perfect and transcend the American model. Even Jefferson's friend Rabaut Saint-Etienne proclaimed that the Assembly "must not servilely follow the United States." Representatives on the left, enthralled by the idea of the "people's government," opposed the American concept of rights as protection *against* the power of the people's legislature. And those on the right favored coupling citizens' rights with their duties.

Throughout the summer of 1789, the more than one thousand representatives in the Assembly offered dozens of proposals for a declaration of rights. Lafayette, Sieyès, Mounier, and many others submitted their own drafts. In mid-August a committee sorted through the different proposals, and by the end of the month a declaration of rights was approved. Now France possessed, in the words of the representative Barnave, a "national catechism."

The Declaration of the Rights of Man and Citizen states citizens' rights and duties, but it does more than that too. The Declaration strikes unflinchingly at the heart and soul of monarchy, severing the nation irrevocably from its past. The Declaration ended the thousand-year-old mystique of monarchy by demoting the king to the mere executive of the people's will (Article 3, see Appendix). Indeed, the people's revolt against their king was justified since "resistance to oppression" is a "natural and imprescriptible" right of man (Article 2).

But the great triumph of the Declaration and its most enduring legacy lies in its assertion that citizens are equal before the law (Article 6). By recognizing the equality of all citizens, including in matters of taxation (Article 13), the Declaration dismantled all the hereditary distinctions and privileges that had buttressed monarchical society. The nature of sovereignty, the class structure of society, and the face of justice had been radically transformed forever.

RIGHTS AGAINST GOVERNMENT

"Congress *shall make no* law respecting an establishment of religion. The right . . . *shall not* be infringed. *No* soldier . . . *shall* be quartered in any house. The right of the people to be secure in their persons, houses . . . *shall not* be violated. *No* person *shall* be held . . . *Nor shall* [any person] be deprived of life, liberty or property, *without* due process of law. The right of trial by jury *shall be* preserved. Excessive bail *shall not be* required." The *limits* of governmental power, the lines it may *not* cross, are sharply drawn (see Appendix).

The American Bill of Rights declares citizens' freedom *against* government. Just as Jefferson had hoped, it guards "liberty against the legislative as well as executive branches of the government." Citizens' rights were recognized, and government was strictly prohibited from infringing upon those rights. Again and again the Congress is denied power, confirming that constitutional government is limited government.

"*No* law," "*no* person shall," "the right shall *not* . . ." The negatives abound. They are striking and straightforward—though, in light of the unfortunate challenges to the First Amendment, such as the Comstock Act of 1873 banning "indecent" and "immoral" publications and the "bad tendency test" of the early twentieth century that prohibited speech if it had a "tendency" to lead to a legal violation, one historian thinks that there should have been a separate section in the Bill of Rights reiterating that "no" means "no!"

Still, the Amendments are, as the historian William Lee Miller remarked, neither "speculative" nor "hortatory" but "mandatory." While the authors of the French Declaration of the Rights of Man and Citizen sought to proclaim revolutionary goals and enshrine the ideals of humanity, the framers of the Bill of Rights, experienced lawyers and legislators, had the more modest goal of formulating rights that would be enforceable in court.

Foremost in Madison's political thinking was his desire to protect individuals and minorities. This was his aim in drafting the Bill of Rights no less than in conceiving the Constitution. To understand the full intention of one, it is necessary to understand the other.

Madison feared the power of an oppressive majority. His plan for the new federal government called for curbs on the majority through fragmentation of power and checks and balances. Thus the minority opposition is allowed to play an active role in government, by capturing control of and taking refuge in one of the branches of government. Not only did Madison make it possible for the minority to have representation in the government, he even empowered the minority to block the majority.

The most potent protection for minorities, Madison was convinced, lay in such institutional mechanisms. But should a majority, acting through government, still seek to invade people's rights, a "parchment barrier" against the majority might finally be useful—the parchment of the Bill of Rights.

What makes the Bill of Rights an effective judicial check on the other two branches of government is the recognition of the "paramount" role of the Constitution. While ordinary legislation calls for only a transitory majority of the people's representatives, the entire people ("We the people . . .") is considered the author of the supreme law of the Constitution. Legislative power, Madison insisted in *The Federalist* No. 53, is subordinate to "the authority of a paramount Constitution." Thus the Bill of Rights offers the protection of the highest of standards. The crucial distinction Madison drew between "a Constitution established by the people and unalterable by the government and a law established by the government and alterable by the government" underscores his understanding of the principle of constitutional supremacy.

The big test came within that decade. Would the Bill of Rights be strong enough to protect a minority from an "oppressive majority"? Only seven years after ratification of the Bill of Rights, Federalists discovered a need not to protect a minority against government but rather to protect government against a minority. While they purported to support freedom of speech and freedom of the press, they claimed that such freedom should not be used to oppose constitutional government or disparage its officials.

"The freedom of the press was never understood to give the right of publishing falsehoods and slanders," asserted John Allen of Connecticut in 1798. Federalists were incensed at Republican attacks on them, at charges that President Adams was "a person without patriotism, without philosophy, and a mock monarch." "Can gentlemen hear these things and lie quietly on their pillows?" Allen demanded. "God deliver us from such liberty." Taking the offensive in Congress, Federalists passed the sweeping Sedition Law of 1798, making it illegal to say anything "false, scandalous, and malicious" against members of either house of Congress or the President, or to excite against them "the hatred of the good people of the United States." Of course, as the political historian James MacGregor Burns points out, there have been few governments or politicians who did not interpret criticism of them as defamatory slander or feel that such criticism was liable to arouse hatred against them. Still, Federalists associated criticism of them with an effort to subvert the whole government and the constitutional system.

Now prison sentences and fines could be imposed on political adversaries. One congressman from Vermont, "Spitting Matt" Lyon, was convicted of libeling the Federalist President, though he had also spat tobacco juice at a Republican on the floor of the House. Jailed for libel, "Spitting Matt" managed to win election to another term from his prison cell. Another case involved Luther Baldwin. In Newark, New Jersey, just after President and Mrs. Adams had driven down Broad Street, followed by the booms of cannon fire, someone said to Luther Baldwin, "There goes the President and they are firing at his a—." Baldwin replied that he didn't care if "they fired *through* his a—!" His feeble joke landed him in court, accused of sedition. He was tried, fined, and committed to jail until his fines were paid. A newspaper editor in Pennsylvania, Thomas Cooper, also provoked Federalists by calling President Adams a threat to liberty and the rights of man. After the jury deliberated for all of twenty minutes, he was convicted of "sedition." Opinions, jokes, and tobacco juice had become punishable acts.

The fears of the antifederalists had come true. Without an adequate check on the legislative and executive branches, the government could act arbitrarily and strip citizens of their constitutional rights. With Federalist judges controlling the courts and Republicans deprived of their right to defend themselves in the press, First Amendment rights came under a withering assault. Edward Livingston, Albert Gallatin, and others passionately defended the Bill of Rights, deriding Federalists for claiming that they were only "regulating" the First Amendment. Across the nation, citizens protested against the Alien and Sedition Acts. When Jefferson took over the presidency two years later, he let the Sedition Act die, but this dangerous foray into governmental repression testifies to the wisdom and foresight of the antifederalists who helped Americans secure their precious Bill of Rights.

And yet, some contemporary sociologists and legal scholars take a different view of rights. They want less emphasis on the rights of individuals and more emphasis on community. They stress the importance of conceiving rights not just in terms of minorities, interest groups, and individuals but rather in terms of the community as a whole and the common good. "The individualistic language of rights at the heart of the American legal tradition," comments sociologist Robert Bellah, "inadequately addresses the kind of interdependence that is crucial in modern society." By systematically protecting individual rights, Bellah argues, people are prevented from responding to increased social interdependence. The solutions to the grave problems facing American society, he contends, lie in conceiving rights less in terms of the individual and more in terms of the community. Legal scholar Mary Ann Glendon similarly criticizes "rights talk" for its "hyperindividualism, its insularity, and its silence with respect to personal, civic, and collective responsibilities."

Other scholars also maintain that it is incorrect to view our constitutional rights as "individualistic in nature." Legal historian Akhil Reed Amar, analyzing various rights such as those to assemble, possess firearms, and serve on juries, argues that these rights belong to us "less as private individuals entitled to be left alone" than as public citizens entitled to act together. For this scholar, the "main thrust" of the Bill of Rights was "not to impede popular majorities, but to empower them." In his opinion, the "essence" of the Bill of Rights was "majoritarian."

But Amar's collectivist interpretation of rights and Bellah's and Glendon's communitarian aspirations notwithstanding, the traditional individualistic view of rights still holds true. While some rights may indeed benefit the community as a whole, the framers conceived rights primarily as protection for individuals and minorities—not for the community as a collective entity. James Madison could hardly have been clearer. "In our Governments the real power lies in the majority of the Community," Madison reminded Jefferson, adding that "the invasion of private rights is *chiefly* to be apprehended . . . from acts in which the Government is the mere instrument of the major number of the constituents. This is a truth of great importance." A year later, addressing the First Congress, he again insisted that the greatest threat to rights came from the "community" acting through government. Though the

The Providential Detection.
This Federalist cartoon attacks Jefferson, who kneels
at the "Altar to Gallic Despotism." In Jefferson's right hand is a letter to Philip Mazzei,
the Italian radical to whom Jefferson confided his antipathy for the Federalists

Preamble to the Constitution recognizes the importance of the "General Welfare," both the pursuit of happiness and the "blessings of liberty" pertained to people in their singularity, not to the group.

For Jefferson, neither politics nor philosophy could be detached from the individual. In a memorable letter, he advised Lafayette that, if he wished to acquire knowledge of his own people and understand how laws and institutions really affect them, he should travel through his provinces incognito. "You must ferret the people out of their hovels as I have done," Jefferson recommended. "Look into their kettles, eat their bread, loll on their beds under pretence of resting yourself, but in fact to find if they are soft." Armed with such concrete knowledge of people's lives in all their particularity and misery, a politician could then proceed to try to improve their lives and aid them in their pursuit of happiness.

Does the founders' emphasis on the primacy of the individual diminish or preclude a sense of community? One can argue that, thanks to their First Amendment rights, citizens can speak out and express their views, publish and disseminate their opinions, assemble and form associations with others, thereby creating an informed, participatory political community. Jefferson even viewed the Seventh Amendment—the right to trial by jury—as the anchor of a community. For he saw the right to trial by jury benefiting not just the accused individual, but also the members of the jury who, by participating in the judicial process, become involved and responsible citizens. The jury system, Jefferson wrote to John Adams, presents a "*school* in which the people might begin to learn the exercise of civil duties as well as rights."

Rights that emphasize the sanctity of the individual can paradoxically contribute to the creation of a vital, democratic community. Still, many modern communitarians and legal historians would like to see more value attached to the rights of the community. Though these scholars are far tamer followers of Rousseau than were revolutionaries in France, a glimpse back into history, back to the French experiment with community rights during the French Revolution, may nevertheless serve us all as a cautionary tale.

LIBERTY BUT . . .

The reader of the Declaration of the Rights of Man and Citizen is thrilled by its ringing endorsement of the universal rights of man: "Men are born and remain free and equal in their rights" (Article 1). "The goal of all political associations is the preservation of the natural and imprescriptible rights of man. These rights are liberty, property, security and resistance to oppression" (Article 2). "No one may be disturbed for his opinions, not even for his opinions concerning religion" (Article 10).

"Free communication of thoughts and opinions is one of the most precious rights of man" (Article 11).

But reading a little closer, one discovers a troubling list of conditions, provisos, and exceptions to those rights: "Liberty consists in being able to do whatever does not harm *others*" (Article 4). "The law may rightfully prohibit only those actions that are *harmful to society*" (Article 5). "The exercise of the natural rights of each man has no limits *except* those that assure other members of society the enjoyment of those same rights" (Article 4). The freedom of "Man" may be unambiguous, but the freedom of the "Citizen" has many boundaries.

Why is there so much stress on restrictions on citizens' rights? The Preamble to the Declaration offers a clue. It explains that, as "members of the social body," individuals "at all times" must be aware of their rights and duties. Every right—whether freedom of speech, religion, press, or due process—is coupled with responsibilities to the community; every freedom is circumscribed by the possible effects it might have on other citizens and on the public order. Thus French citizens were accorded rights only insofar as they were cooperative, conforming members of the "social body," committed to the welfare of all.

The rights of the community took precedence. The emphasis that the Revolution always placed on the unity of the nation was translated into rights for the group as a unitary whole, not for autonomous, self-interested, or potentially disruptive individuals or minorities. Citizens could count on their "rights" only if they did not enter into conflict with the rest of society. Even in matters as sensitive as freedom of religion, the rights of the group outweighed the rights of individuals. "No one may be disturbed for his opinions, not even for his opinions concerning religion, *provided that* their expression does not disturb *public order* as established by law" (Article 10). Individuals and minority groups were free to worship in private but not to worship in public if their religion interfered with the state religion.

Rights were irreconcilable with the expression of opposition and conflict. Perhaps this is why the Declaration did not accord citizens the right to assemble peacefully, along with the rights it did bestow to speak, write, and print freely. The absence of freedom of assembly may betray the French apprehension that organized groups and factions would disrupt social order as well as the people's unity. And yet the ability of individuals and minorities to disrupt society is likely to be less formidable than the ability of society to repress its members.

Citizens were not free *from* government but they were free *to* participate in a communitarian society, one in which citizens are "at all times" aware of their social responsibilities. This was the concept of freedom that the French had inherited from Rousseau. In his *Social Contract,* Rousseau had described a form of freedom he considered superior to freedom *from* constraint—freedom *for* some higher good, for the enjoyment of the virtuous, moral life in a unitary, communitarian society. The more that individuals identify with the community, the "freer" they are and the more secure are their rights. They have the "right" to be part of the group.

While the American Bill of Rights sought to protect individuals and minorities from an oppressive majority, the French Declaration of the Rights of Man and Citizen was founded on the fear that self-interested individuals and "particularistic" minorities could disrupt the harmony and collective well-being of the nation. Indeed, in a country that had absorbed the Rousseauian doctrine of the General Will, minorities were anathema. Those who disagree with the General Will, Rousseau had argued, must be "forced to be free"—made to see the "light" and join the majority. "The emphasis is not on the rights of each against all," commented historian Tony Judt, "but rather the reverse."

Ultimately the French revolutionary belief system—the ideology of unity and the concomitant unwillingness to protect minorities—played a greater role in dooming rights in France than the language itself of the Declaration of Rights. Some very successful contemporary constitutions, such as those of Germany and Canada, contain similar language placing legal restrictions on citizens' rights. The German Constitution's bill of "basic rights," for example, stipulates that "everyone has the right to the free development of his personality insofar as he does not violate the rights of others or offend against the constitutional order or the moral code. . . . These rights may only be encroached upon pursuant to a law." The Canadian Charter of Rights and Freedoms also states that guarantees of rights and freedoms are subject to "such reasonable limits prescribed by law as can be demonstrably justified in a free and democratic society." But in modern Germany and Canada, unlike in revolutionary France, there is a genuine commitment to individual rights.

Madison himself recognized the limits of language. Even "absolute" restrictions on the government's power to infringe upon citizens' rights would ultimately matter less, he felt, than majority sentiment, "the decided sense of the public." Writing to Jefferson, he noted that if a rebellion were to break out in the United States, the federal government might be so alarmed as to suspend immediately habeas corpus rights, and "no written prohibitions on earth" would prevent them from doing so. Thus, just as important as the language of the Bill of Rights and Declaration of the Rights of Man and Citizen is what lies behind that language—a real commitment to protect individual and minority rights, or a cult of unity.

Whereas the French emphasized the primacy of "community," James Madison had viewed "community" as the primary danger to rights. The community, he judged, was more potentially destructive of rights and freedom than the government. In his famous address to the First Congress in June 1789, outlining his plan for rights amendments, Madison explicitly warned that abuse of power could occur in both the legislative and executive branches, but that the most menacing threat to freedom lay outside the government. "I confess that I do conceive," he said, "that . . . the great danger lies rather in the abuse of the community than in the legislative body, . . . in the body of the people, operating by the majority against the minority." The Bill of Rights was designed to protect the rights of individuals and minorities not so much against government per se as against an oppressive majority—the "community," the people themselves—acting through government and especially through its most powerful branch, the legislature.

In France, "society" had the final say on what rights individuals and minorities could enjoy. But in the United States, as the legal scholar Ronald Dworkin points out, "a right against the Government must be a right to do something even when the majority thinks it would be wrong to do it." If "society" has the right to do whatever is in the general benefit and can overrule the rights of individuals and minorities, then those rights are "annihilated." Individual rights, according to Dworkin, should compete with other individual rights, but not with "the 'rights' of the majority as such."

But unlike the Americans, who feared what Madison termed "legislative despotism," the French welcomed legislative sovereignty, in the name of "society." The French Assembly, after all, had been acclaimed as the voice of the nation and the General Will. It would have been illogical to restrain the people's government or to protect the people from it. The French Declaration of Rights bestowed on the legislature the potentially limitless authority to decide what rights the people could—and could not—enjoy, to circumscribe rights by reason of "public order" and "public necessity." The National Assembly was empowered to "rightfully prohibit . . . those actions that are harmful to society" (Article 5).

"Restrictions, precautions, and conditions," Mirabeau warned in vain in August 1789, "are replacing rights with duties . . . and will present man bound by the state and not the free man of nature." But the legislature had carte blanche. Ultimately, the law, not rights, was sacred.

In the United States, on the other hand, James Madison wanted to ensure that rights would be protected—and sometimes from the law itself. Thus in drafting the Bill of Rights, he took extreme care to choose words that would not empower the legislature. He knew well that each word, each phrase could have immense consequences. With what words would he conclude the Fifth Amendment, "no person shall be deprived of life, liberty, or property"? Would he decide to add "except by the *law of the land*," which was the language of the Tenth Article of the Virginia Declaration of Rights of 1776 as well as the language of most of the other state constitutions? Or would he write down "without due process of law," the innovative language of the New York State Constitution of 1787? As William Lee Miller points out, the phrase "the law of the land" would have left open the possibility that one could be deprived of life, liberty, or property simply by a legislative enactment: if a legislature passed it, then it would be "the law of the land." But, unlike the French, Madison conceived the Amendments as restraints upon government, and thus "due process" implied fair procedures of the courts.

One nation wanted to protect individuals and minorities from the majority. The other never doubted the majority's ability to legislate wisely. One nation wanted constitutional amendments, not to create rights but rather to guarantee them. The other was confident that its legislature could protect rights as well as simultaneously make laws concerning and circumscribing those rights.

So binding and incontestable were the laws enacted by the French National Assembly that the Declaration of Rights specifically prohibited any resistance to the law. "Any citizen summoned or seized by virtue of the law must obey *instantly:* he renders himself *guilty* if he resists" (Article 7). Although Article 2 of the Declaration states that one of the natural and imprescriptible rights of man is "resistance to oppression," that right seems to refer only to the events of the summer of 1789 and not to the rights of individuals in the future.

Was there no right of appeal against the law? Could individuals or minority groups not protest that their "natural and imprescriptible" rights were being violated? Both the sovereignty of the legislature and the doctrine of the General Will made any kind of appeal or judicial review illogical if not impossible. Because the legislature drafted laws and because the law was defined as "the expression of the general will" (Article 6), the legislature was assumed to have access to the General Will. There existed no standard, no immutable legal code, no constitution or other document higher than the General Will. Indeed, the Constitution of 1791 stipulated that "there is no authority in France higher than the Law."

And yet the "law" was forever changing. Its very essence was unstable as well as political. Revolutionaries like Condorcet saw the law as being essentially "revolutionary," which meant, as the historian Mona Ozouf explains, that its aim was to maintain the revolution in any ways it had to. The object of the law was less to assure social order and tranquillity than to thwart the resistance of counterrevolutionaries. "Everything must be allowed to those who are headed in the same direction as the Revolution," declared Saint-Just. Thus all forms of repression, persecution, and violence could hide behind the mask of revolutionary law.

"Illegality was necessarily consubstantial with the Revolution," concludes Ozouf. Judicial review was irrelevant.

Tocqueville pointed out that under the monarchy, the judiciary had not only preserved its independence but had regularly denounced—in the colorful, frank terms supplied by the Old French of the legal language—despotic or arbitrary acts of the royal government. But if any judicial tribunal in revolutionary France had similarly sought to contest legislative acts, it would have been seen as censuring the General Will and calling into question the sovereignty of the legislature and the very foundation of the nation.

The right of appeal or judicial review was all the more unlikely because the judiciary in revolutionary France was institutionally subordinate to the legislature. In 1790, the National Assembly prohibited judicial tribunals from interfering with the exercise of legislative power and from attempting to suspend the execution of the laws. The following year the Assembly decreed that the judiciary would have to report to it periodically. Montesquieu's great wisdom—that the separation of judicial power from legislative and executive power is a condition of freedom—was easily ignored. As Montesquieu had prophetically observed, when the judiciary is absorbed into the legislature, the legislature's power over citizens' lives and freedom becomes arbitrary.

The supremacy of the legislature and the emasculation of the judiciary sealed the fate of rights in revolutionary France. Nothing could protect citizens against the government's arbitrary decrees. Especially vulnerable were citizens accused of crimes. The American Bill of Rights is remarkable in the extensive protection it affords to accused citizens. Amendments Four, Five, Six, and Eight offered protection against unreasonable searches and seizures, double jeopardy, and cruel and unusual punishment, and provided guarantees of a speedy and public trial by jury, the right to have counsel, to be informed of charges and to confront accusers. But the Articles of the French Declaration offered no clear rights to accused citizens, neither trial by jury nor the right to counsel nor the right to a public trial. Articles 7 and 8 actually can withdraw any protection they seem to offer: "No man may be indicted, arrested or detained *except* in cases determined by law" (Article 7); "The law may establish only strictly and clearly necessary punishments" (Article 8).

The first law of the Terror, enacted in March 1793, called for indiscriminate arrest and summary justice. Individuals accused of infractions against the Revolution were assumed to be guilty and had to prove their innocence. They had no right to trial by jury and no right of appeal. But they were granted speedy trials! All those arrested had to be tried and executed within twenty-four hours. (In comparison to this terrifying legislative despotism, the old royal *lettres de cachet*, with which the king could arbitrarily imprison any of his subjects, seem almost benign.) Then came a string of even more arbitrary and ferocious laws: the hoarding of food became a capital offense, and in September 1793, the Law on Suspects made the mere suspicion of counter-revolutionary activities grounds for arrest. Revolutionary government used all its power to defend itself against those whom it suspected of opposition.

Finally, in December 1793, Robespierre announced the suspension of constitutional government and the simultaneous suspension of all individual rights. "Revolutionary government" had displaced constitutional government, and "public freedom" had eclipsed the freedom of the individual. "Under a constitutional regime," Robespierre explained, "it suffices to protect individuals against abuses by the public power; under a revolutionary regime, the public power itself is obliged to defend itself against all the factions that attack it."

"I shall rejoice," commented the great foe of the French Revolution, Edmund Burke, as he lamented the degradation of legal rights and the disappearance of justice across the Channel, "in seeing a judicial power established in France, . . . when they are not called upon to put any man to his trial upon undefined crimes of state, . . . when victims shall not be snatched from the fury of the people to be brought before a tribunal itself subject to the effects of the same fury, . . . I shall rejoice in seeing such a happy order established in France."

For his part, Tocqueville understood perfectly that the Revolution's suspension of individual and minority rights would have far more devastating consequences in history than its short-lived violence. The future, he predicted, would be colored not just by "contempt for individual rights and oppression of minorities" but by a new political doctrine legitimating such repression, asserting that individual rights did not exist—indeed that individuals themselves did not exist. The legacy that revolutionary France would bequeath to future generations, Tocqueville suggested, would be the idea of a "mass" existing in the place of individuals, a "mass" that can always do whatever it wants to achieve its ends. The history of the twentieth century has sadly confirmed Tocqueville's prediction.

TOWARD THE FUTURE

The French Revolution produced two Declarations of Rights. The second one is not well known, for it never went into effect. In 1792 and 1793, revolutionaries in France, Girondins and Jacobins together, composed a new version of a Declaration of Rights. But immediately after it was provisionally ratified, it was placed into "suspension," superseded by the reign of Terror. And yet so modern were its attempts to assure social and economic justice that even today not all democratic and progressive governments aspire to such an enlightened agenda.

Some historians contend that the Jacobins contributed to the draft of this Declaration merely to consolidate their power by winning the support of the sans-culottes and the peasants of France. Nonetheless, the Declaration of 1793 represents an undeniable step forward in the quest for equality, justice, and human rights. The historian Jules Michelet considered it the first truly humanitarian and philanthropic constitution—a breed apart, he wrote, from the "laissez-faire" school of Anglo-American constitutions.

This Declaration, the frontispiece to the Constitution of 1793, stresses once again communitarian values in its announcement that "the purpose of society is the collective happiness of all" (Article 1) and in its stipulation that the law can only prohibit actions that are "harmful" to society (Article 4). But it also strikes a new note when it suggests that any restrictions on individuals are embedded in the individual conscience—that is, in people's own moral judgment and ability to internalize the golden rule. "Freedom is the power that belongs to people to do whatever does not harm the rights of others," declared Article 6. "Its moral limit is in this maxim: 'Do not do to another what you do not wish to be done unto you.'"

And indeed, the enumeration of citizens' rights is no longer qualified by unspecified legal prohibitions. Citizens' rights to express their thoughts and opinions, "either by the press or any other means," are recognized and unrestricted. The right to assemble peacefully is now acknowledged, as is the free practice of religion (Article 7). As if nodding to the American Bill of Rights, the government is explicitly prohibited from infringing on individual rights: "The law must protect public and individual freedom from the oppression of those who govern" (Article 9).

Even more innovative and radical, however, is this Declaration's agenda for the economic and social transformation of France, in which "rights" and "claims" converged: people have a right to work. If there is no available work, they have a right to receive support from the government. "Society owes a livelihood to all unfortunate citizens, either by securing them work or by assuring some means of support to those unable to work" (Article 21). Citizens have a right to public education (Article 22). All forms of work and avenues of commerce must be open to all citizens (Article 17). Slavery is abolished: people may sell their work or their services but not their persons (Article 18). Citizens have the right to petition government (Article 32). And curiously they now have not the right but the duty to revolt against an oppressive government (Article 35). And if one hasn't grasped the full range of citizens' economic and social rights, they are summarized again at the end of the Constitution (Article 122).

Robespierre regretted that the Declaration of 1793 had not gone even further toward ensuring economic justice. He wanted limits on wealth and property. Why were restrictions placed on man's "eternal right" of freedom and not on the ownership of property, a mere social convention? Why was the country not doing more, he demanded, to alleviate the "extreme disproportion of wealth" in France? He proposed an article in the Declaration of Rights that mandated progressive taxation and that exempted poorer citizens from any tax burden whatsoever. And what about the Revolution's most far-reaching mission—the "universal revolution" and the fraternity of man? Robespierre suggested an alliance of all peoples against oppressors anywhere in the world. And, in a final ironic flourish, he demanded an article declaring that any law that violates the inalienable rights of man is unjust and tyrannical.

The visionary Declaration of 1793 predicted some of the economic reforms that would be made in France during the 1930s and after World War II. But it also anticipated Franklin Roosevelt's economic bill of rights: equality of opportunity for youth and for others; jobs for those who can work; security for those who need it; the ending of special privilege for the few; the preservation of civil liberties for all; the enjoyment of the fruits of scientific progress in a wider and constantly rising standard of living.

Roosevelt encapsulated his vision of a just world in his famous "Four Freedoms": freedom of speech and expression, freedom of religion, freedom from want, and freedom from fear. The Jacobins of 1793 had a not dissimilar dream of social and economic justice. They could not, however, have embraced Roosevelt's fourth freedom—freedom from fear—for they themselves incarnated what would become people's worst fear in the twentieth century: a totalitarian, repressive regime that stifles freedom and resorts to political purges and violence to achieve its ever elusive ends.

Though the Declaration of the Rights of Man and Citizen of 1789 played a more galvanizing role in the French Revolution and in French mythology than did the American Bill of Rights during and after the American Revolution, it was the leaders, legislators, and lawyers of the American Revolution who successfully placed individual and minority rights at the center of their revolutionary enterprise, guaranteeing their integrity for centuries to come. Still, the authors of the truly revolutionary French Declaration of Rights of 1793 gave the world a glimpse of a radically new agenda that linked economic justice to the pursuit of happiness. A century and a half later, their farsighted vision would begin to become law.

Enlightenment Legacies

The United States and France celebrate their nationhood on July 4 and July 14, dates that commemorate a revolutionary declaration of independence and the people's storming of a hated symbol of the *Ancien Régime,* the Bastille. On those summer days, red, white, and blue revolutionary flags fly gaily over American and French cities and villages. Colorful parades and fireworks, complemented by backyard barbecues and picnics, echo people's patriotic joy.

As American and French citizens jubilantly fete their love of country, are the courageous, violent revolutionary movements that accompanied their nations' births still remembered? July 4 and July 14 survive as summer festivals more than as historical commemorations, and people tend to forget the political audacity and courage of the men and women who fought to break with the past and transform their societies. So much so that during the nineteenth and twentieth centuries, the United Stales and France only rarely supported or encouraged other nations struggling for independence, liberty, and equality.

France fought, at a tremendous cost in lives and money, to retain her colonial outposts in Vietnam and Algeria and to deny their indigenous peoples' rights to independence and self-determination. The United

States has supported a plethora of dictators: Diem in South Vietnam, Batista in Cuba, Marcos in the Philippines, the Shah of Iran, Duvalier in Haiti, Pinochet in Chile. The list is disheartening. Only in March 1998 did the American Congress pass, by the smallest of margins, a bill allowing Puerto Ricans to vote on their own political status. France and the United States have become, as the historian David Brion Davis suggests, the world's leading adversaries of popular revolutions.

Thomas Jefferson would have been profoundly saddened, for his vision of the United States was inseparable from the idea of revolution. Whenever any form of government becomes destructive of "life, liberty and the pursuit of happiness," he wrote in the Declaration of Independence, "it is the right of the people to abolish it" and to institute a new government. Though Jefferson advised people to be prudent and not to engage in traumatic revolution for merely "transient causes," he nevertheless felt that when people are subject to a despotic regime, revolution is not only their right, "it is their duty."

Jefferson went even further, linking the survival of the young American republic to the success of revolutions abroad. A positive outcome of the French Revolution was crucial to prevent the young American nation from devolving into a conservative, English-style system. Successful foreign revolutions were essential, Jefferson wrote to George Mason, to further America's "liberating mission abroad" as well as "to protect liberty at home."

For Abraham Lincoln too, the meaning of the American Revolution was its universal, enduring promise of freedom and equality. After his election in 1860 Lincoln observed that the Revolution "was not the mere matter of separation of the colonies from the motherland" but rather the message contained in the Declaration of Independence "which gave liberty not alone to the people of this country, but hope to all the world, for all future time." The Declaration offered the hope that "in due time the weights would be lifted from the shoulders of all men, and that all should have an equal chance."

The French were no different: they had also believed in the universality of their revolution. The Declaration of 19 November 1792 promised fraternity with all oppressed people. It was France's sacred duty to help "all the peoples who wish to regain their freedom." But two restorations of the monarchy, two empires, and the pretensions and responsibilities of colonialism snuffed out most of France's revolutionary ardor, leaving her to draft a conservative, republican constitution in 1875.

Still, modern revolutionary leaders around the world have often turned to the two great sister revolutions for inspiration and guidance, finding in French and American foundational documents universal ideals of freedom and equality, a radiant Enlightenment promise of justice for all. American and French revolutionary institutions supplied models for the creation of democratic governments in other lands. The sister revolutions offered modern revolutionary leaders a script to follow—war of liberation, constitutional convention, bill of rights, the creation of political parties—and also warned of dangerous shoals to avoid—terror, extremism, reaction.

Revolutions, hypothesized the Spanish philosopher José Ortega y Gasset, "are not constituted by barricades, but by states of mind." Although a vast number of factors contribute to revolutionary momentum—from class conflict to famine—the intellectual, Ortega y Gasset insisted, "is always to be found in the center of the revolutionary stage." The intellectual, a student of history, never ignores the past. Indeed, for over two centuries, the sister revolutions provided a revolutionary tradition, a "usable past," and practical guideposts for modern insurgents. Over and over again, these modern revolutionaries conceived their own revolutionary projects within the frameworks of the sister revolutions.

SLAVERY AND REVOLUTION

"George Washington can never be claimed as a fanatic," wrote Frederick Douglass in 1857, a few years before the Civil War. Had Washington lived in the mid-nineteenth century, he continued, he would have been "a terror of the slaveholders." Douglass portrayed the nation's founders as good, beneficent fathers who wished for the freedom of all their "children"—white and black. America's most extraordinary abolitionist anchored his appeal for the emancipation of slaves in his praise for the American revolutionary tradition.

On the plantation, harvest season and planting season, not years or months, ordered the lives of slaves. Slaves did not have birthdays or even know how old they were. Douglass thought that he was born in 1817 or 1818. His mother, Harriet Bailey, a slave in Tuckahoe, Maryland, was hired out to a neighboring plantation. To see her son she had to travel all night on foot. Their meetings were rare, but all the more precious. "I was not only a child," he realized. "but *somebody's* child." On his mother's knee, he felt "prouder . . . than a king upon his throne."

Douglass's mother died when he was still young, leaving him with few "scanty" memories. But he learned that she was the only slave in Tuckahoe who could read, and this discovery whetted his desire for education, transforming his life. When he was eight, the wife of his master gave him a few reading lessons that were immediately halted when her husband objected. A slave, he reminded her, "should know nothing but the will of his master, and learn to obey it." From then on, Frederick was on his own—bribing his playmates with pieces of bread to teach him a few spelling and writing skills, intently watching carpenters etch letters onto pieces of wood, arduously copying letters and words from Webster's Spelling-Book. Douglass's intellectual awakening and moral outrage at his bondage eventually led him to escape, disguised as a sailor, to the North. "I am quite willing," he later wrote, "to attribute any love of letters I possess . . . to the native genius of my sable, unprotected, and uncultivated mother."

Douglass's father was probably Aaron Anthony, the white plantation superintendent for Colonel Edward Lloyd, a wealthy landowner and slaveholder in Maryland. Anthony, of course, never acknowledged his paternity. All the young Frederick ever received from him were several whippings and a few pats on the head. "I say nothing of *father*," he wrote. "He is shrouded in mystery." The laws of slavery reduced a child's identity to that of his mother. "Slavery," he explained, "does away with fathers, as it does away with families."

But in the nation's founders, Douglass discovered ideal father figures whose families all Americans could join. Indeed, there was only one family, he asserted, the human family. "I do now and always have attached more importance to manhood than to mere kinship or identity with one variety of the human family," he wrote. "Race . . . is narrow; humanity is broad." He conceived the abolitionist movement as the fulfillment of the founding fathers' promises of freedom and equality.

This was a switch. Before 1849, Douglass had criticized the American Revolution, condemning the Constitution for being a contradictory document, "at war with itself." The whole framework of the American government, he judged, was "radically at fault." It deceitfully enshrined liberty while brooking slavery. Thus, like the other followers of abolitionist William Lloyd Garrison, Douglass opposed any kind of political action to redress slavery, convinced that such action would be tantamount to an endorsement of an illegitimate government. Refusing even to vote, Garrisonians insisted on moral rather than political action.

But by 1855, Douglass had changed his strategy, breaking with Garrison and coming to the conclusion that political action to abolish slavery might indeed be more effective than mere moral suasion. He decided to praise rather than condemn the Constitution.

His new plan was to recognize the Declaration of Independence and the Constitution as the radical documents of a new, revolutionary order, and he challenged Americans to live up to their spirit and principles. "Stand by those principles, be true to them on all occasions," he declared, "in all places, against all foes, and at whatever cost." Southerners, he complained, tried to distort the nation's revolutionary past by reading the Constitution as a proslavery document. They claimed that slaveholding was a part of the Constitution, sanctioned by the founders, and that they even had the right to hunt down fugitive slaves.

Douglass angrily rejected such misrepresentations. The Constitution, he announced, was "a glorious liberty document." Not once, he insisted, did the word "slave," "slavery," or "slaveholder" appear in the Constitution. There was not a single principle in the Constitution that was not entirely hostile to the existence of slavery.

The founding fathers were not "impostors." On the contrary, they represented the epitome of rationality and morality. They were the "brains, heart and soul" of the republic, and they despised slavery. Washington, Douglass asserted, "desired to see Slavery abolished, and would gladly give his vote for such abolition"; Jefferson "trembled for his country when he reflected that God was just"; Franklin served as president of the first Abolition Society in America; and Madison utterly rejected the idea that human beings could constitute the property of others.

But Americans had betrayed their great revolutionary heritage. The Fourth of July, Douglass bitterly confessed, reminds the black man only of "the gross injustice and cruelty to which he is the constant victim. To him, your celebration is a sham . . . your denunciation of tyrants . . . your shouts of liberty . . . are . . . mere bombast, fraud, deception, impiety, and hypocrisy." "I am not included within the pale of this glorious anniversary," he bristled. "The rich inheritance of justice, liberty, prosperity and independence, bequeathed by your fathers, is shared by you, not by me. . . . This Fourth of July is *yours,* not *mine. You* may rejoice, *I* must mourn."

The future lay in a return to the nation's heritage, in a renewed commitment to America's founding principles. America, he warned, must not be "false to the past."

Violence, it could not be denied, belonged to that noble American tradition. Turning away from Garrison's philosophy of nonviolence and nonresistance, Douglass reminded his listeners that Americans had drenched the soil in blood merely to escape the payment of a three-penny tax upon tea! Why was it glorious, he asked, for Patrick Henry to shout "Give me liberty or give me death!" but a "crime" to save a black man, a fugitive slave, from bondage by shooting the "monster" who tracks him down to return him to slavery? Douglass recalled Jefferson's comment that one hour of bondage "is worse than ages of that which our fathers rose in rebellion to oppose."

But reserved, churchgoing Bostonians were shocked to hear Douglass defend violence. "I should welcome the intelligence tomorrow," he had told them, "that the slaves had risen in the South, and that the sable arms . . . were engaged in spreading death and devastation." Perceiving the alarm his remarks aroused, he chided his audience for greeting the news of foreign revolutions with joy but fearing similar upheaval and transformation at home. "You shed tears over fallen Hungary," he scolded. "You are all on fire at the mention of liberty for France or for Ireland; but are as cold as an iceberg at the thought of liberty for the enslaved of America." "Oh! that we had a little more of the manly indifference to death, which characterized the Heroes of the American revolution," he thundered.

When Lincoln finally delivered his Emancipation Proclamation, Douglass viewed it as a faithful return to the American revolutionary tradition. "We can scarcely conceive of a more complete revolution in the position of a nation," Douglass declared a few weeks later. "Mr. Lincoln has not exactly discovered a new truth," he said, "but has dared to apply an old truth, . . . a truth which carried the American people safely through the war for independence."

Douglass not only anchored the abolitionist movement in the American revolutionary tradition, he also transcended that tradition. Women were in a kind of slavery too. Whereas a founder like John Adams considered slavery "an evil of Colossal magnitude" and could envisage rights for black men, political rights for women always remained inconceivable to Adams. At most, the husband of the brilliant and talented Abigail countenanced women's authority in the private sphere of the home.

Douglass's support for women's rights broke new ground. Sexual equality—the emancipation of "half the human family"—would be "a revolution," he proclaimed, "the most strange, radical, and stupendous that the world has ever witnessed." The struggle for equal rights for women recognized the morality, dignity, and rationality of all citizens. Every able citizen would be an active and responsible member of the national political community. "No man should be excluded from the Government on account of his color, no woman on account of her sex," Douglass asserted. "There should be no shoulder that does not bear its burden of the Government." Once women were active in the public arena, society itself would be transformed by their intellect and "remarkable intuition" in public affairs. "Let women go to the polls and express their will, and we shall have different men and measures than we have now."

Douglass even surpassed the female leaders of the women's movement, for some of them, such as Elizabeth Cady Stanton, could not liberate themselves from their own retrograde racism. After ratification of the Fifteenth Amendment, guaranteeing black male suffrage, Stanton was outraged. Women were surely more qualified to vote than Negro men, she sputtered, classing them with "idiots and lunatics" and dismissing them as so many Sambos. It was Douglass who proved to be one of the truest revolutionaries of the nineteenth century, following the American revolutionary tradition and then forging ahead on his own.

ROBESPIERRE IN MOSCOW

For several months in 1918, Robespierre stood in the Kremlin. A likeness of the French revolutionary had been ordered personally by Lenin, the head of the new Russian government, to embellish the capital of the Soviet republic. But neither bronze nor marble had been available, for the October Revolution was also a time of civil war, foreign invasion, bread shortages, sacrifice, and suffering. The statue was sculpted in weak, temporary stone. Cracks soon formed and widened, and Robespierre eventually crumbled. The statue's collapse from within probably never caused Lenin to wonder about the fragility of the French model of revolution. On the contrary, he considered himself a Jacobin, like Robespierre, who would not recoil from the use of terror to achieve his ends.

The American Revolution never ignited Lenin's imagination. He would probably have viewed it as no more than an anticolonial revolt, too conservative to attempt any kind of radical social restructuring. Political power after the American Revolution remained in the hands of the same "bourgeois" interests who had possessed power during English colonial rule. Moreover, a constitution, parliament, and guarantees of civil liberties held no attraction for Lenin, as the historian Richard Pipes points out. Political liberalization, Lenin wrote in 1894, only fortifies the position of the bourgeoisie. The time had come, Lenin declared, to separate socialism from democracy.

But the French Revolution was Lenin's kind of meat. His manual for transforming Russian society was the French, not the American, Revolution. The events of 1789 and 1793 were his guidebook for eradicating a feudal past, eliminating political opposition, and institutionalizing terror. Its pages pointed out the three-star monuments to be revisited (the elimination of dissent, purges, and capital punishment), the tourist traps to be avoided (factions, the counterrevolution of Thermidor), and the shrines of heroes to be admired. Indeed, Robespierre and the Jacobins furnished Lenin with models of tough, forceful, and creative revolutionary leadership. "One cannot be a Marxist," he wrote in 1915, "without entertaining the deepest respect for the great bourgeois revolutionaries (Robespierre, Garibaldi, and others) . . . who roused tens of millions of people . . . in the struggle against feudalism."

"A real revolutionary Social Democrat," Lenin informed his friend Nikolay Vladislavovich Volsky in 1904, "must be a Jacobin." In those early days of revolutionary theorizing, the two men were living in Geneva, where they were members of the Russian community of political exiles. Together they strolled through the old streets of the town every afternoon, Lenin confiding in Volsky. "They charge us with Jacobinism," Lenin burst out one day, his cheeks flushed with rage. "These idiots, these Girondins, don't even understand that they are paying us a compliment by making such charges." He was indignant at the "spinelessness" of moderate Mensheviks who attributed "absolute value" to "democratic principles," recklessly undermining the idea of the dictatorship of the proletariat. Jacobin leaders, on the other hand, energetically defended the people while never shrinking from violence to realize their goals.

Stamping his foot, his eyes narrowing, Lenin proclaimed that Jacobinism signified "a struggle without kid gloves, without tenderness, without fear of resorting to the guillotine." The motor for political change and social transformation, he emphasized to Volsky, was violence. Jacobin violence and repression, he insisted over and over, were the necessary tools for a successful revolutionary movement. The peaceful streets and lovely lakeside promenades of Geneva provided an unlikely setting for Lenin's sanguinary visions of revolution.

Why was it "monstrous and criminal" for workers and peasants to use terror against the bourgeoisie? he demanded. When the British bourgeoisie used terror in 1649 and when the French bourgeoisie used it in 1793, it was considered "just and legitimate." If a bourgeois revolution like the one in France in 1793 had called for a Jacobin-style purge, Lenin remarked, then surely a Russian-style social revolution would require nothing less. "The dictatorship of the proletariat is an absolutely meaningless expression," he noted, "without Jacobin coercion." This ultimate goal could not be achieved without "the smashing and annihilation" of their enemies. Lenin did not view Jacobinism as a downward slide, but rather, as he wrote, "one of the highest pinnacles attained by the working class struggling for its emancipation."

Immediately after the Bolshevik Revolution in October 1917, Lenin briefly distanced himself from the French Revolution, expressing reluctance to use repressive or violent Jacobin measures. "We are reproached with using terror," he announced. "But such terror as was used by the French revolutionaries who guillotined unarmed people, we do not use and, I hope, shall not use." But Bolshevik theory called for the "one-party state," a centralized party structure, and strong party discipline. Within weeks Lenin decided that neither dissent nor pluralism could play a helpful role in the smashing of the old regime. Opposition would have to be eliminated—by violence and terror if necessary. The Jacobins were back.

The splendid, glittering reception halls of the Smolny Institute in St. Petersburg, once a finishing school for the daughters of the Russian aristocracy, were the setting for the first open sessions in December 1917 of the Central Executive Committee. There, during the revolution's earliest days, I. N. Steinberg, the newly appointed People's Commissar of Justice, witnessed the creation and organization of terror. He listened with horror as the revolution's leaders debated a decree demanding the arrest of the Kadets, the moderate Constitutional Democratic party. A few days earlier, the government had proclaimed them "enemies of the people." The Kadets had fought against tsarism and had held power briefly from February to October 1917. But after the Bolshevik Revolution in

October, some of their leaders had allied themselves with counterrevolutionary forces.

Would the new revolutionary parliament ratify the decree for their arrest? A victorious revolution, Steinberg protested, did not need to condemn its opponents with summary judgments. The order for their arrest en masse was not based on specific charges against them but merely on their being Kadets. If an individual Kadet was accused of conspiracy, he reasoned, he should be brought to trial and have the right to a defense. But an entire group should not be placed "outside the pale of human law."

The moderate Steinberg suddenly perceived the specter of the French Terror, the exclusion and the liquidation of all factions and opposition. "We dared not simply and blindly repeat the mistakes of the French Revolution," he wrote. A hundred years earlier the Girondin Vergniaud had prophetically warned the Convention that the exclusion of moderate factions was only the beginning of repression. Soon all citizens would come under suspicion. Now Steinberg echoed Vergniaud. "Withdraw legal protection from the liberals today, and the same is likely to happen to other political groups tomorrow."

Rising to answer Steinberg, a furious, contemptuous Trotsky icily remarked that people should be "grateful" to be thrown in jail, for in past revolutions "they would have been taken to the Palace Square and there made . . . a head shorter!" (Trotsky himself was ultimately made a head shorter when an assassin, wielding a pickax, struck him in the head.) Finally Lenin spoke, evoking the model of the French Revolution, declaring that criticism of the Russian Revolution would not be tolerated. "The great French Revolution," he recalled, "put the hostile parties outside the law."

The Bolsheviks won the vote—150 to 98—to arrest their opponents. But, surprisingly, the moderate Steinberg was not entirely displeased. He felt that terror had at least been brought into open debate. Still, he was forced to recognize that coercion had displaced persuasion. Free speech was muzzled, frozen into silence and obedience. Politics, he predicted, would be reduced to humiliation and slavery.

All who oppose government orders will be "destroyed on the spot," decreed Trotsky in a pamphlet he wrote in February 1918, in the wake of the attack of the German Army. The pamphlet, designed to awaken Russians' heroism and love for their country, concluded with this ominous threat of summary arrest and execution. Once again Steinberg strongly objected. At a meeting of the People's Commissars, he argued that this cruel threat undermined the "pathos" of Trotsky's manifesto. But Lenin, Steinberg later recalled in his memoirs, responded with derision, "Do you really believe that we can be victorious without the very cruelest revolutionary terror?" "Then why do we bother with a Commissariat of Justice?" Steinberg shouted. "Let's call it frankly the *Commissariat for Social Extermination* and be done with it!" Lenin's face suddenly brightened. "Well put," he replied. "That's exactly what it should be . . . but we can't say that."

The Bolsheviks, observed Steinberg, slavishly imitated the speech and behavior of the French Jacobins. "But," he added, "they forgot that the French Revolution itself was drowned in bloody defeat precisely because of its terrorism." Like their Girondin predecessors, Russian dissidents, including the revolution's own founders, Trotsky, Zinoviev, Kamenev, Bukharin, were later liquidated or exiled for their deviation from the party line.

Within a year, the Commissar of Justice had become one of the revolution's prisoners. Steinberg was arrested in February 1919, thrown into the Butyrki prison in Moscow. "How shall one relate the grim emotions of a revolutionist thrown into a prison of the revolution?" he wrote, trying to describe his sense of disbelief. Yet his weary mind grasped the parallel with the French Revolution when men similarly fell "from the height of power to the gates of prison." In prison, Steinberg requested Jean Jaurès's *Socialist History of the French Revolution*, seeking to put order and understanding into his thoughts.

Lenin never held the Jacobins or the Terror responsible for the downfall of the French Revolution. On the contrary, he believed that it was the Thermidorean reaction, not the Terror, that had spelled the end of the French Revolution. In Thermidor, July 1794, members of the French National Convention had risen up and revolted against Robespierre, shouting "Down with the tyrant!" The following day, Robespierre, Saint-Just, and their allies were arrested and guillotined. Lenin was determined to avoid the trap of a Thermidor. In other words, he was convinced that compromise with moderate elements might sometimes be necessary to avoid a counterrevolutionary movement.

In the winter of 1918, there was just such a movement for popular democracy, the counterrevolution that Lenin had feared. The sailors at the strategic naval base of Kronstadt, located on an island off Russia's Baltic coast, revolted. Deeply discontented with party policy, they demanded liberal concessions for workers and peasants—freedom for trade unions, the release of political prisoners, an end to official propaganda, free elections of Soviets, freedom of speech and freedom of the press. Instead of negotiating with the sailors, the Bolshevik government issued an ultimatum and prepared for an attack. Lenin and Trotsky, according to Victor Serge, demanded that the rebels surrender "or be shot down like rabbits." When they refused to capitulate, units of the Red Army trekked across the ice to assault Kronstadt and the battleships, frozen in the water. The ice cracked under the advancing soldiers' feet; the freezing water swallowed them. For several weeks in March both sides fought a ferocious battle, but the rebels were finally overpowered. Some escaped to Finland; the rest were shot in Petrograd.

"This is Thermidor," declared Lenin. "But we shan't let ourselves be guillotined. We shall make a Thermidor ourselves." Lenin's response to the idealistic counterrevolution of Kronstadt was his own "counterrevolutionary" liberal economic package. He announced that he was willing to make a moderate swing to the right. Indeed, his "New Economic Policy" granted peasants some control over their production, gave artisans more freedom in their trades, and permitted some private trade and private ownership. Lenin had backtracked, endorsing a "partial restoration of capitalism." It was a "retreat," he said, but "for a new attack." Political freedom, however, was not included in the Thermidorean bargain.

For Lenin, the French Revolution was not a failed movement but an unfinished one, a necessary stage in class history. He was convinced that the French Revolution, by furthering the rise of the bourgeoisie and the development of capitalism and by restructuring to a certain extent French society, had prepared the way for the eventual rise of the working class. The Russian Revolution would fulfill the promise of the French Revolution, finally inaugurating the reign of equality.

The Jacobins taught Lenin how to seize control of events, establish a disciplined ruling party, and steer the revolution ahead, following his ideological map. They also taught him not to concern himself with individual rights and liberties or with democracy, all of which had been left in the ditch. The Communist experiment in Russia lasted approximately seventy years. By the end of the twentieth century, Russian citizens and politicians recognized that Lenin's revolutionary project had failed economically, politically, and morally. When in 1989 Russians turned to a market economy, free elections, a multiparty system, political pluralism, and individual rights, were they not celebrating 1776 after all?

UNCLE HO

In September 1945, hundreds of thousands of people jammed the French-looking boulevards and streets of downtown Hanoi. They had traveled in oppressive heat from distant villages for the great day. Schools and offices were closed. Jubilant peasants wearing their black "pajamas" and straw hats, workers, mountain people, militia members carrying spears, Catholic priests in their black suits and Buddhist monks in their saffron robes all waited excitedly. Banners and flowers adorned the buildings; flags fluttered in the occasional warm breezes. All faces turned toward the platform erected in Ba Dinh Square, a large park near the French residential quarter.

A frail-looking wisp of a man advanced to the microphone. "All men are created equal," he declared, as all of Hanoi listened. "They are endowed by their Creator with certain unalienable Rights; among these are Life, Liberty, and the pursuit of Happiness." He paused and then elaborated. "This immortal statement," he explained, "was made in the Declaration of Independence of the United States of America in 1776. In a broader sense, this means: all the peoples on earth are equal from birth, all the peoples have a right to live, to be happy and free."

That was not all. Just as Jefferson's immortal vision of unalienable rights and freedoms was followed by a kind of legal brief that documented at length all the abuses committed by King George III and the English Parliament against their American subjects, Ho Chi Minh similarly outlined the grievances of the Vietnamese against France, their colonial master. As his listeners strained to hear him, he reminded them that France was still attempting to destroy Vietnamese unity by artificially dividing the nation into three separate political regions, Tonkin, Annam, and Cochin China. France burdened the Vietnamese with unjust taxes; France expropriated the people's land, rice fields, and forests; France ruled by decree and not by law; she built prisons instead of schools, and in Indochina's darkest hour, France abandoned her to the Japanese.

Jefferson, toward the end of his great document, had proclaimed that the Americans were simultaneously dissolving all political ties with Great Britain and declaring their independence. "We . . . the representatives of the United States of America, . . . do . . . solemnly publish and declare," he wrote, "that these united colonies are, and of right ought to be, free and independent states." Ho Chi Minh struggled to recall Jefferson's exact words. "We, the members of the provisional government of the democratic republic of Viet Nam proclaim solemnly to the entire world: Viet Nam has the right to be free and independent, and, in fact, has become a free and independent country."

The American Declaration of Independence ends with a pledge taken by all its signers. "And, for the support of this declaration, with a firm reliance on the protection of Divine Providence, we mutually pledge to each other our lives, our fortunes, and our sacred honor." Ho Chi Minh's version of the final pledge encompassed not just the signers but the whole Vietnamese people. "The entire people of Viet Nam," Ho declared, "are determined to mobilize all their spiritual and physical strength, to sacrifice their lives and property in order to safeguard their independence and liberty."

Days earlier, Ho Chi Minh and his advisers had been laboring to recall as much of Jefferson's language as they could. Ho had memorized the opening lines of the Declaration when he visited the United States as a menial laborer on a tramp steamer before World War I, but his memory had faded. He wondered if one of the American intelligence officers serving in Vietnam could help. During World War II, James Patti headed the Vietnam mission of the Office of Strategic Services, the OSS, the precursor of the CIA. During the summer and fall of 1945, Major Patti, along with Brigadier General Philip Gallagher and Captain Farris, observed Ho Chi Minh's Vietminh party. For Patti, Ho Chi Minh was a nationalist, not a "starry-eyed revolutionary or a flaming radical." "I felt he could be trusted as an ally against the Japanese," Patti recalled. "I saw that his ultimate goal was to attain American support for the cause of a free Viet Nam."

Ho explained to Patti that his draft of the Vietnamese declaration of independence needed polishing. Someone translated Ho's words as Patti listened carefully. Patti immediately realized that the translator was reading very familiar words. After the translator read a few sentences, Patti turned to Ho in amazement and asked if he really intended to use this text as his declaration of independence. "I don't know why it nettled me," Patti mused. "Perhaps a feeling of proprietary right, or something equally inane." Ho sat back in his chair, his palms together with fingertips touching his lips ever so lightly, as though meditating. "Should I not use it?" he asked. Patti was embarrassed. Why should Ho not use it? The translator started again: all men are endowed by their Creator with certain unalienable rights; among these are liberty, life, and the pursuit of happiness. "Life must come before liberty," Patti remarked. Ho snapped to the point. "Why, of course, there is no liberty without life." Ho pressed Patti for more, but that was all the American could remember.

For educated revolutionary leaders in Asia, American history had much to teach. In the 1920s, Sun Yat Sen, the Chinese revolutionary and republican, had written extensively on American history in his *Three Principles of the People*. This founder of modern China had studied in depth the two "finest" periods in American history, the American Revolution and the Civil War. Sun admired the Americans' revolt against their unequal treatment at the hands of the British, their willingness to endure eight years of war, and their creation of an independent state. The Civil War was another "shining" example of the struggle for equality. American history contained important lessons on revolution and democracy for the Chinese, although the Chinese, Sun noted, would eventually have to find their own formula for government.

Ho Chi Minh too turned to the United States for inspiration. Would he have borrowed Jefferson's words for the joyous celebration of Vietnamese independence if he had not understood and identified with the Americans' eighteenth-century anticolonial revolt, if he had not admired their revolutionary spirit? Perhaps there was a practical side to Ho's stratagem too. He might have felt that his use of Jefferson's Declaration would impart some legitimacy to his struggle, that it would be a signal to the Americans that he respected them, that he wanted their friendship as well as their support for his own sister revolution.

Indochinese independence had become a "near-obsession" for President Roosevelt during 1943 and 1944, and Ho's expectation that the United States would support his independence movement was entirely reasonable. Historians view Roosevelt's ideals as unquestionably anticolonial, though they note that he lacked a clear strategy for achieving these goals. To his Secretary of State, Cordell Hull, Roosevelt spoke frankly about Indochina. "France has milked Indo-China for one hundred years," Roosevelt wrote in a memo. "The people of Indo-China are entitled to something better than that." A month later at the Yalta Conference, where matters as consequential as the reconstitution and the future of Europe were decided, Roosevelt did not forget Indochina. He remarked to Stalin that "the Indochinese were people of small stature . . . and were not warlike. He added that France had done nothing to improve the natives since she had the colony."

Roosevelt's promise to grant independence to the Philippines buoyed Ho Chi Minh, for the American President had also urged the European colonial powers to grant independence to their own colonies. Ho hoped that his case for the independence of Vietnam would reach the attention of "the great president Roosevelt."

The situation changed somewhat, however, after de Gaulle's visit to America in the summer of 1944. The French leader proposed the idea of a French federation in which Indochina would have representation. As for the Vietnamese, they wanted Vietnamese unity and independence, not Indochinese citizenship within a "French Union." But Roosevelt wavered, finding it increasingly difficult to thwart the colonial claims of his close allies, England and the Free French.

After Roosevelt's death, America's diplomatic policy changed sharply. Only a few months after Ho's declaration of independence, the American State Department's Far Eastern Bureau declared that the United States would respect French sovereignty in Indochina. Roosevelt's anticolonialism was displaced by the Cold War's demands for an anti-Communist foreign policy. By 1946 all official American references to Ho in Washington were prefixed with the word "Communist." Dean Acheson, the Acting Secretary of State, branded Ho Chi Minh an "agent of international communism." Though the American OSS officers in Hanoi had liked and trusted Ho, even joining him in celebrating his Vietnamese "Fourth of July," by the end of the decade Ho had been transformed into a Communist enemy.

A State Department paper, written in 1949, "The Position of the United States with Respect to Indochina," announced that the new challenge facing the United States was to "prevent expansion of communist aggression in that area." China's and Russia's recent recognition of Ho's government worried the State Department. American analysts considered it likely that Thailand and Burma would fall under Communist domination if Indochina succumbed to Communist control. The conclusion reached in this paper came to be known as the "domino principle." "It is important to the United States security interests," the paper ended, "that all practical measures be taken to prevent further communist expansion in Southeast Asia."

Foreign policy was redesigned and tailored for the new Cold War environment. American anti-Communism seemed all the more urgent in the wake of several Communist "triumphs," such as Mao's victory in China in 1949, the confirmation of Soviet nuclear capability in 1949, as well as the surprise attack staged by North Korea against the South in 1950. The Truman government decided to back the French military effort to retain control over Vietnam, and in the early 1950s, the United States contributed hefty sums to the French military campaign to keep Indochina a French colony.

But the French and their American supporters underestimated the determination of the Vietminh. The dramatic battle of Dien Bien Phu was fought in a valley near the Laotian border. The French found themselves encircled by the revolutionary Vietnamese troops, "sitting ducks" for their fire. The French defeat was humiliating and definitive. At long last Ho Chi Minh's dream of a unified, independent Vietnam seemed within reach. The Geneva settlement in 1954 temporarily divided Vietnam along the seventeenth parallel, but stipulated that a Vietnam-wide election would take place in 1956 to decide the question of reunification. The United States refused to sign the Geneva accord, and the stipulated elections never took place.

Ho Chi Minh once again turned to American history—this time not for inspiration but rather to underline America's betrayal of her own revolutionary ideals. Pointing to George Washington, the military leader of the colonial revolt, to Lincoln, the courageous warrior for equality and national unity, and to the anticolonial Roosevelt, Ho composed an open letter to President Dwight Eisenhower. "You are, Mr. President, the inheritor of the great leaders of the United States," he wrote. "Washington, Lincoln or Roosevelt. . . . You speak often of peace and justice. . . . But, in your actions toward Viet Nam, your policy is the opposite." How different twentieth-century history might have been if Presidents Truman, Eisenhower, and Kennedy had understood the depth of the anticolonial aspirations in Vietnam. But Kennedy dismissed the warning of Charles de Gaulle, who cautioned the young American President not to become entrapped in the "bottomless military and political swamp" of Vietnam. An earlier American President too had been deaf to Vietnamese pleas for support for their independence.

That was in 1919.

The activity in Versailles was intense: diplomats and their assistants rushing around, dozens of typewriters pounding away, the monotone voices of translators echoing in the great mirrored halls. The Big Four, the victors of the war, held court. Woodrow Wilson, Lloyd George, Georges Clemenceau, and Vittorio Orlando, were setting the terms of the peace—and of the future.

T. E. Lawrence, garbed in his exotic Arab headcloth, his khaki uniform, and British badges, arrived with Prince Faisal to appeal for inde-

pendence for Syria and Mesopotamia. A less conspicuous and less celebrated petitioner than Lawrence of Arabia also appeared, desiring an
audience for his cause. He was a young, small man, uncomfortable in his
rented tuxedo. He was a Vietnamese—or an "Annamite," as the French
then said—named Nguyen Ai Quoc, one of the dozens of aliases of the
future Ho Chi Minh.

He had come to Versailles, inspired by President Wilson's Fourteen
Points, especially Wilson's recognition of the right of nations to self-
determination. Still, the program he hoped to present to President
Wilson in Versailles was a modest one. He was not asking for anything
so bold as independence for Vietnam. His "eight points" included equality before the law for Vietnamese as well as for French citizens in
Indochina, amnesty for political prisoners, government by law, not by
decree, a permanent delegation of Vietnamese representatives in the
French Parliament, and some civil rights—freedom of speech and freedom of the press.

He was totally ignored. When he tried to obtain a hearing, Wilson
neither received him nor acknowledged his appeal. Despite the American leader's principle of self-determination for all nations, Vietnam did
not exist. Wilson focused all of his energy on his political vision: the creation of a League of Nations. At such a critical moment, the American
President felt that he could not risk alienating his French allies by
undermining their colonial empire. Indeed, as the historian-statesman
Conor Cruise O'Brien noted, whereas underdeveloped countries would
eventually have an important voice in the United Nations, Wilson's
League of Nations represented the "haves of the world against the have-
nots."

On the one hand, Ho must have been disappointed to have his cause
rejected out of hand at the Peace Conference. On the other, the young
man had taken a chance and had traveled only a very short distance to
reach Versailles. In 1917, at the age of twenty-seven, he had moved to
Paris to study "what lay behind the words *liberté, égalité, fraternité.*"

When he was a young boy in Vietnam, he had seen the revolutionary
slogan inscribed in stone on public buildings. What did the words
mean? What did the French Revolution stand for? It was difficult to

come by answers. French authorities forbade the translation of Rousseau and Montesquieu into Vietnamese. In libraries in Vietnam, works on the French Revolution existed only in French and were inaccessible in Vietnamese.

After World War I, Paris was the exciting haven for scores of dissidents and revolutionaries from the French colonies and from the rest of Europe. Zhou Enlai and Deng Xiaoping lived there in the twenties as did one of the pioneers of Vietnamese nationalism, Phan Chu Trinh. Ho enjoyed wandering around the streets of Paris with his friends, discussing the future of Asia.

Though Woodrow Wilson had not even recognized Ho's presence, Ho attracted the attention of some of France's leading socialists, including Léon Blum. In Paris, Ho joined the French Socialist party. He later admitted that he joined the socialists because those "ladies and gentlemen . . . had shown sympathy toward me, toward the struggle of the oppressed people."

In Ho's first serious work of political propaganda, "French Colonization on Trial," he described the French colonial system, detailing its injustices along with the sadism of colonial rulers. The forced participation of colonized people in World War I especially enraged him. Suddenly second-class "dirty Negroes and dirty Annamese," he bitterly remarked, were promoted to the supreme rank of "defenders of law and liberty," forced to fight for rights and freedoms of which they themselves were deprived. They were obliged to leave their "rice fields, or their sheep, their children and their wives in order to cross oceans and go and rot on the battlefields of Europe."

The French colonial strategy, Ho explained, robbed the colonized people not only of independence but also of their sense of solidarity and nationhood. He accused the French of dividing each of their colonies into separate political entities, rupturing a people's sense of oneness, criticism a least partially unfair since some of these "divisions" had long existed along tribal lines and predated the arrival of the French. Also insidious, according to Ho, was the French strategy of turning one colonized people against another, forcing Algerians to fight in Vietnam and obliging the Vietnamese to fight for French interests in Africa. Brothers were turned against brothers.

France's revolutionary decree of November 1792 had memorably promised "fraternity and help to all the peoples who wish to regain their freedom." But the French had betrayed their revolutionary promise of fraternity with all oppressed peoples. In the twentieth century, Ho concluded, exploitation had replaced comradeship. Only in Russia, he believed, was fraternity alive and well.

Rebuffed at Versailles, Ho Chi Minh left Paris for Moscow. Lenin, he decided, was the "personification of universal fraternity," the inheritor of the French Revolution's oath of fraternity with all oppressed people. Lenin had not only liberated the men and women of his own country, Ho wrote, he showed the way to all the disinherited of the universe. He called Leninism "a compass" for the Vietnamese, "the radiant sun illuminating our path to final victory, to Socialism and Communism."

Ho Chi Minh returned to Vietnam in 1941—after an absence of thirty years. Was he a Communist, a socialist? Above all, he was a nationalist and a hard-nosed pragmatist who wanted independence for his nation—independence from the French and the Japanese. In later decades he demanded independence from the Americans no less than from the Chinese and Russians.

After World War II, Ho never ceased reminding the French and American invaders of their revolutionary traditions. As late as 1965, he told an American interviewer that "this aggressive war has . . . besmeared the good name of the United States, the country of Washington and Lincoln." To the French colonial masters, he called out, "Frenchmen in Indochina! It is now up to you to show that you are worthy children of the glorious heroes who struggled for liberty, equality and fraternity." But the French Revolution also taught Ho how to wield political power mercilessly. "The French Revolution sacrificed many people without flinching," he wrote. "If we want to wage revolution, we must not be afraid of sacrifices either." Ho will indeed be remembered not only for his single-minded nationalism but also for his ruthless land reforms in 1955, hideous massacres of civilians, and other atrocities.

Ho fought for fifty years against France and then against the United States, the two revolutionary nations that, at mid-century, had become fiercely antirevolutionary. And yet, though France and America refused to aid the Vietnamese in their quest for independence, their revolutions and ideals still emitted gleams of light, sporadically illuminating the revolutionary path.

THIRD WORLD EXPLOSIONS

In the closing decades of the twentieth century, new kinds of revolutionary movements have burst onto the world scene, movements that seem to have nothing in common with the sister revolutions of the eighteenth century. While the French and American Revolutions colored Ho Chi Minh's frame of reference even as he battled the French and the Americans, the leaders of these new insurgencies reject out of hand the rational and universalist values of the Enlightenment.

Algeria is an example. Though influenced for more than a century by French culture and language, revolutionary movements and regimes in Algeria have been laboring for decades to rid the land of all French and European baggage.

When Michel Debré, the Prime Minister of France and one of the principal architects of the Constitution of the Fifth Republic, adamantly refused to acknowledge the legitimacy of native Algerians' quest for some form of equality and independence, he consigned the French Revolution to irrelevance for Algerian revolutionaries. Justifying the entire colonialist project, Debré proclaimed in 1959 that "the authority of France in Algeria is a requirement of history, of nature, of morality." Not wanting to leave any doubt in the minds of his listeners, he added that "the truth is that Algeria is a land of French sovereignty." Algerians were all the more disappointed when one of France's greatest intellectuals, Albert Camus, a French-Algerian, hesitated to condemn colonialism and support the principle of self-determination for all nations.

Frantz Fanon was one of the leading intellectuals and "theorists" of the Algerian Revolution. Born on the French island of Martinique, he went to Algeria as a young psychiatrist to practice medicine. "The truth is," he wrote after having seen colonialism through the eyes and experiences of a psychiatrist, "that colonialism in its essence was already beginning to show itself as a great recruiter for the psychiatric hospitals." Though horrified by the massacres, terror, and torture inflicted by both sides, Fanon sympathized solely with the goals of Algerian nationalists. While Camus represented the point of view of European liberals sympathetic to the aspirations of the Algerian people, Fanon's point of view was simply that of the colonized and oppressed people themselves.

Fanon wished to see Algeria liberated not only from its colonial past but from all European frames of reference, an Algeria free to conceive fresh ideals and novel political structures. It was a weakness, he suggested, for Algeria to seek out "a model, . . . blueprints and examples." Explicitly dismissing the French revolutionary tradition, he proposed that Algerians "waste no time in . . . nauseating mimicry." The Algerian Revolution must not pay tribute to Europe by imitating her institutions and societies. "Humanity is waiting for something other from us. . . . Let us combine our muscles and our brains in a new direction. . . . It is a question of the Third World starting a new history of Man."

As if influenced by the lyrical, mystical vision of *négritude* of the great Martiniquais poet Aimé Césaire, Fanon wished to purge Algeria of all European influence so that a new society could be founded—not on European principles and concepts of "civilization," but rather on Algeria's own true soul. "For Europe, for ourselves and for humanity, comrades, we must turn over a new leaf, we must work out new concepts, and try to set afoot a new man."

But what were these new concepts? Fanon tried to develop a theory of violent revolution and rupture with Europe, but he had no clear vision for the political future of Algeria—aside from exhorting Algerians to "find something *different*." Violently expelling the colonialist regime was one thing—the easy part of revolution; constructing stable institutions or a free and open society another.

Ironically, though the Algerian anticolonial movement had repudiated all Western models, after the war of independence the Front for National Liberation (FLN) government incorporated the worst, most antidemocratic elements of the French revolutionary tradition. The FLN centralized the government *à la Révolution française,* excluding opposition parties, instituting a one-party government, and embracing violence. The FLN also found itself copying the Eastern European model of socialism and agricultural collectivism.

In 1989, Algeria was rocked by turmoil and massacres. This upheaval was the result of the growing frustrations of the majority of citizens who felt left out of the new prosperity ensured by Algeria's oil and gas reserves. Only then did the government agree to a multiparty system and to some other democratic reforms, but it is not clear to what extent these concessions represented a true commitment to a pluralist democracy rather than merely an attempt to appease dissidents.

In any case, it was too late. A second anti-Western insurgency had already begun—this time directed not against France but against the FLN itself. Indeed, the Islamic Salvation Front (FIS) takes much of its zeal from its anti-Western ideology. Frustrated by the growing gap between rich and poor, the flaunting of new wealth, the insufficient "Arabization" of Algerian society, the corruption introduced by Western social mores, and the lack of a collective national purpose, the FIS advocates a return to Islamic morality and to the nation's Arab-Islamic traditions—closure of stores during prayer hours, modest dress for women, etc. The goal is the installation of an "Islamic republic."

Not only did the FIS defeat the FLN two to one in municipal elections in 1990, but also the following year the FIS defeated the FLN in the first round of voting in a general election. The government promptly canceled the second round. A High Security Council proclaimed that it was taking charge, creating a High State Council to assume presidential power—an Algerian Comité du Salut Public.

But the widely popular Islamic insurgency could not be repressed, and far more radical and violent Islamist groups have emerged that are carrying out mass slaughters throughout the country.

Is the Islamist movement in Algeria an entirely new phenomenon, or should it be understood, as François Burgat argues, as a "third stage" in the process of decolonization? The first stage, according to Burgat, was the war for political independence; the second stage was economic independence. Islamism, "the rocket of the third stage," reflects the desire of a formerly colonized people to return to their cultural, traditional past, almost obliterated by colonial occupation.

On the one hand, the Islamist desire to purge Algeria of everything Western mirrors the anti-Westernism of Frantz Fanon. On the other hand, the FIS, like its adversary, the FLN, seems to embrace the exclusionary politics of the French Revolution.

It is not clear whether the FIS, should it come to power, would ban all non-Islamist parties or whether it would accept a multiparty, pluralist democracy. The FIS leader Abassi Madani pledged in 1994 to accept party pluralism and the free expression of opinion. The following year, at a conference in Rome, Madani's representative reaffirmed the FIS promise to abide by the principles of liberal democracy, renouncing violence as a way to achieve power. But the Algerian government rejected these promises, a move that seemed only to increase the power of the violent Islamist splinter groups.

At the century's end, Algeria is run by an authoritarian government that excludes its adversaries from the political arena and that resorts to violence and terror to maintain itself in power. Despite the Algerian anti-Western mantra, the French Revolution reigns.

THE UNUSUAL REVOLUTION

Must a revolution be violent to qualify for the title of revolution? Does the transformation of a society and a government require the suspension of constitutional law and individual rights and freedoms? Are political executions de rigueur?

The revolution that took place in South Africa in the early 1990s broke with the mold. "No models hold for us," wrote the South African newspaperman Denis Beckett in 1991. "We're entirely on our own."

He was right. For here was a revolution that transformed South African society but at the same time validated compromise and negotiation. It was a revolution that took place within the existing political framework. Instead of vengeance, there was a desire for reconciliation. Instead of purges, there was amnesty. The victors wanted apologies, not heads. The political losers, including embittered and recalcitrant ones, were tolerated, not outlawed, and they were included within the newly configured political arena. Throughout all the turmoil and dramatic change, there was never a large-scale resistance movement against majority black rule or a revolt in the security forces or in the military.

It was, moreover, a revolution conducted by black leaders who recognized the valuable economic leadership of the white settler minority and by pragmatic white leaders, like F. W. de Klerk, who preferred preserving capitalism to insisting on white political hegemony. Black revolutionary leaders never demanded or encouraged, as in Algeria, the expulsion of the colonial community from the country. They did not seek to eliminate, as in eighteenth-century France, an elite social class— or even to level society, despite the grinding poverty of the majority of citizens. Nelson Mandela always envisioned the two races eventually living together in harmony.

Even when, as a young man, Mandela was designing plans for sabotage of the South African infrastructure, his ultimate goal was reconciliation and coexistence with the white minority. The choices open to the ANC movement, Mandela explained in his autobiography, were open revolution, terrorism, guerrilla warfare, or sabotage. "It made sense," he wrote, "to start with the form of violence that inflicted the least harm against individuals: sabotage." Because it involved minimal loss of life, sabotage offered the best hope for eventual racial reconciliation. "We did not want to start a blood feud among the races," Mandela remarked.

Foreign governments also adopted a new attitude toward this particular revolution. The United States and France seemed suddenly to rediscover the morality of a revolutionary struggle for liberation. Only twenty years after their attempts to suppress movements for independence in Vietnam and Algeria, they denounced colonialism in South Africa, imposed economic sanctions, and supported boycotts against an illegitimate white minority government.

The revolution in South Africa began in 1989 when F. W. de Klerk released Nelson Mandela from prison. His reason? He needed someone with whom to negotiate. Everything had been going wrong in South Africa: decades of violent acts of terror and desperation on one side and brutal repression on the other; the ominous defeat of South African troops by Cuban troops in Angola; an untenable political and military situation in neighboring Namibia; growing white South African resistance to more (white) military casualties; general civil unrest; international economic pressure; the rise of a new generation of emboldened black South African radicals. Finally white South Africans made a calculated decision to enter into negotiations with moderate black South Africans. The bans on the African National Congress and the South African Communist Party were lifted.

After Mandela's liberation and after the white government's introduction of some insignificant token reforms that chipped away at apartheid, the last stage of the political and moral struggle against apartheid began. De Klerk, breaking with the traditional thinking in his party, came to realize that apartheid could not be "reformed," that there were no political solutions short of black enfranchisement, and that fortunately the ANC was a liberal democratic party that would protect political rights as well as private property. Thus, in this final stage, neither side propounded intransigent, ideological or extremist stands. On the contrary, both sides spoke of "democracy, rights, constitutionalism, the rule of law." The government as well as the opposition each made an effort to transcend their different concepts of nationhood. Both sides appeared willing to work for what each considered, in its own way, the "common good"—though the common good was conceived as continuing prosperity for the white minority and as redistribution of the wealth for the black majority.

To their great credit, de Klerk and Mandela proved Trotsky wrong. "History on the whole," the Russian had commented, "knows of no revolution that was accomplished in a democratic way. . . . Classes never consent to lose possessions, power and 'honour' by observing the rules of the game of 'democratic' parliamentarism." But in South Africa in the early 1990s, the established powers did not respond with violence to the movement to transform South African society.

The government instituted by the new South African Constitution of 1996 provides for a hybrid of majority rule, protection of minorities and individual rights, and a modified federal system. The black majority exercises its power. Minorities receive no extra representation in the legislature, no veto over legislation. No "super-majority" is required to pass legislation, something that would have empowered the minority to block the majority. But the Constitution's lengthy bill of rights, in addition to protecting individual rights, safeguards minority identities and the country's eleven official languages.

Although the African National Congress enjoys the support of an overwhelming majority of citizens, it neither crushes dissent nor excludes opposition parties. A "unity" government, led by Mandela and de Klerk, was tried but abandoned when de Klerk felt that he could exert more influence as the leader of a traditional opposition party.

Revolutionary politicians in South Africa seem to have followed the American revolutionary model rather than the French one. "As freedom fighters we could not have known of such men as George Washington, Abraham Lincoln, and Thomas Jefferson," said Nelson Mandela when he met with President George Bush, "and not been moved to act as they were moved to act."

Indeed, Mandela borrowed the best of that American tradition and incorporated it into his own unique revolutionary movement. And yet, despite an attempt to be inclusive and pluralist, South Africa, for all intents and purposes, is a one-party state. So entrenched is the black majority that the ANC seems likely to be the permanent party in power. In addition, party unity is extremely strong; voters vote for party lists, not for individual candidates, cementing the ANC's control of national politics. Still, minority parties are beginning to sprout; one promising new party is the multiracial United Democratic Movement, garnering, as of June 1998, 5 percent of the vote.

In a healthy democracy, the party in power and the opposition alternately govern; minorities and majorities alternate, and there is no disempowered "permanent" minority. Can a vital multiparty system exist and succeed in South Africa? Perhaps. Often, as history shows us, when there is an unchallenged majority party, that party eventually splits into different factions. This was the case in the United States after 1826, when the Jeffersonian Republicans, no longer facing a viable opposition from the Federalists, split into the Jacksonian "Democratic Republicans" and the "National Republicans," who by the mid-1830s became the

"Whigs." It is at least a possibility that internal dissension within the ANC may cause such fragmentation at some time to occur. But until then, there will be a permanent minority and a permanent majority, a situation that inevitably weakens the democratic spirit and "mores" of the nation. One observer urges white South Africans to find alternative power bases outside of politics—in the media, the arts, and the economic life of the country.

Can South African democracy survive without a vital two-party system? Can the nonvindictive republic survive the eventual death of the charismatic and conciliatory Nelson Mandela? For how long will political power compensate the majority for their lack of economic power? Will radical elements, inflamed by continuing economic inequality, fragment the ANC? And will the resulting fragmentation of the majority party threaten or strengthen this constitutional democracy?

The ringing phrases, the heroes, and the myths of the eighteenth-century sister revolutions have been passed down through the generations virtually intact. After two hundred years, "life, liberty and the pursuit of happiness" as well as *"liberté, égalité, fraternité"* still resonate around the world.

Curiously, for all its myriad complexities and failures, the appeal of the French Revolution is its *clarity*. For the French Revolution conceived itself in terms of a Manichaean struggle between good and evil—between patriots and traitors, believers and nonbelievers. The struggle between insiders and outsiders required the unity of those on the inside; and next to that ideal of unity, pluralism and the protection of individual and minority rights seemed counterrevolutionary. Lenin, like Robespierre himself, could justify his revolution's repressive features in the name of the unity of the people and their unrelenting battle against reaction and privilege.

Ambiguity, on the other hand, characterizes the American Revolution, making it a less popular model. For it evokes, not ideological clarity or a struggle against perfidious traitors, but rather conflicting interest groups and competing political parties—as well as the ultimate contradiction of slavery, the legal dehumanization of people in a nation founded on the conviction that "all men are created equal." For Frederick Douglass, this contradiction provided a fruitful challenge as well as a wealth of rhetorical material for his speeches. And perhaps even for Nelson Mandela, the American paradox of a revolutionary nation with a history of racial division could offer insight into the uncertainty of progress.

Tocqueville remarked that in America people's passion was for democratic ideas while in France their passion was for revolutionary ones. Is it possible to reconcile these two passions and offer modern revolutionary movements a third political model? The era of revolutions is not over, and future revolutionary movements might profit from a model that synthesizes the energy of the French Revolution with the stability of the American Revolution, that moderates revolutionary fervor with tolerance for ideological diversity, and, most of all, that can integrate the principle of the legitimacy of opposition into a political movement whose very essence may be a belief in its own holiness. Can there be a marriage of clarity and ambiguity, French lightning and American light?

★ 7 ★

On "Her Majesty's Loyal Opposition"

What if we took the best features of the American revolutionary political model, combined them with the best features of the French revolutionary political model, and tried to make them somehow converge? Could we invent a third kind of model that might provide guideposts for future revolutionary movements in search of a viable framework for democratic government?

Edmund Burke, for one, would not have approved. He abhorred the idea of inventing or importing ahistorical, abstract blueprints for a nation's government, insisting instead that institutions be the result of a people's traditions, "prejudices," and culture. *Prêt-à-porter* constitutions sold off the rack would not have been his cup of tea. Tocqueville too was convinced that a nation's democratic habits, nurtured and formed over time, are at least as important as its institutions.

Still, if one deplorable, repressive regime is not to replace another one, burgeoning nations (with histories that include, instead of bills of rights and democratically elected chambers, hereditary ruling elites and even postcolonial kleptocracies) might profit from some inspiration and political guidance. For they need institutions that can enable leaders to make sweeping changes while providing order, stability, justice, equality, and freedom.

Even the Americans and the French, as they enter the next century, might benefit from some critical distance from the political institutions that we not only take for granted but venerate as particularly enlightened.

THE PRICE OF STABILITY

Madison's constitutional plan for checks and balances has produced a workable, stable system that is reasonably democratic, that has allowed for progress and economic expansion, as well as for some measure of social and economic justice. Citizens value the Bill of Rights and have come to view their freedom in terms not only of freedom against government but also freedom through government. Jefferson's and Madison's contribution of a two-party political system injected into the political culture the recognition of the legitimacy of opposition along with a dose of creative energy. Together the constitutional and the party systems give representation, voice, and power to political minorities while also assuring remarkable political and social stability.

So successful has the American political system been that, during the more than two hundred years of the history of the union and the individual states, few major rebellions have broken out. With so many different governments at so many different levels and in so many places, shouldn't one expect, as Thomas Jefferson himself did, that people would find sufficient cause to revolt periodically against government?

The first rebellion against American government occurred during the winter of 1787, when farmers in western Massachusetts, taxed beyond their means, struggling against debt and foreclosure, spontaneously revolted against those in power—merchants, bankers, rich people. The aim of Shays's Rebellion was to close up the courts, free debtors from jail, and redress the farmers' grievances. Though most of the men were property owners and thus voters, the slow route of organizing an opposition political party evidently did not seem a viable option. "If you Dont lower the taxes we'll pull down the town house about you ears," wrote one anonymous rebel. "It shall not stand long then or else they shall be blood spilt. We country men will not be imposed on. We fought of our Libery as well as you did."

"For God's sake," George Washington beseeched a friend, "tell me what is the cause of all these commotions. Do they proceed from licentiousness . . . or real grievances which admit of redress." Citizens, Washington lamented, were "unsheathing the sword" to overturn the constitutions that they had freely established. Revolt against England was a right, but revolt against a constitutional system in which decisions are made by a majority of voters in free elections was most assuredly out of bounds. General William Shepherd and his militiamen vigorously stamped out Shays's Rebellion.

The second rebellion took place a few years later in Pennsylvania, after Congress imposed a small excise tax on the production of liquor. Antifederalist congressmen denounced the tax as "oppressive," and Pennsylvania farmers, who used whiskey instead of cash as currency, were incensed at the principle of an unjust tax. After mobs destroyed some excise offices, President Washington felt compelled to put down the uprising. Refusing to permit "a minority, a small one too [to] dictate to the majority," he called up thirteen thousand men to put down the small rebellion—which in truth consisted more of talk and whiskey than organized revolt. The two rebels who were convicted of treason were ultimately pardoned by the President.

The Southern rebellion, of course, was infinitely more devastating to the country, not only because it cost hundreds of thousands of lives but also because it demonstrated that in certain exceptional situations neither the two-party system nor attempts at conciliation and negotiation can work. This was the one period in American history when consensus—both constitutional consensus and political consensus—broke down entirely.

Prior to the Civil War, consensus on even incremental antislavery legislation had been impossible. The system that depended on brokerage, compromise, and the ballot box had resulted in deadlock. Not only was there no political consensus on slavery; soon there was not even a constitutional consensus on union. Violence, not politics, became the only option. Perhaps if Americans had been accustomed to a parliamentary-type majoritarian government instead of checks and balances, one progressive party might have been able to introduce over time significant changes, such as the transformation of slave labor into paid labor or the gradual "buying out" of slaveholders.

Still, what is most striking about the history of American rebellions is their paucity. Since the creation of the federal union, opportunities for dissent and opposition to the party in power have been so pervasive—especially after African-Americans and women secured the right to vote—that there have been startlingly few episodes of violent revolt. With the exception of the one-party South, a two-party system developed in most states, cities, and little towns, according citizens the formal capacity and channels to oppose government.

One of the greatest achievements of the American political system is the dog that did not bark—that is, the rebellions that did *not* take place. A free two-party system, in which virtually all citizens have come to enjoy the right to vote, has taken away any moral right to revolution. Not only is revolution in the United States morally wrong, it is politically superfluous. If there is to be a democratic revolution, it must take place at the polls.

And yet, despite the stability of the constitutional system and the inclusivity of the party system, citizens are often frustrated by the slow pace of progress and change. Indeed, James Madison's fear of an overbearing majority and antipathy for majoritarian politics bequeathed to subsequent generations a form of government that strikes many Americans as too stable, too safe, too paralyzed.

The system of checks and balances requires so many different and simultaneous presidential and congressional elections that our elected senators, representatives, and President ultimately represent different majorities—indeed, so many different majorities that it is impossible to judge if a particular branch of government represents the "government" and the will of the majority or the "opposition." "To say where 'the government' leaves off and 'the opposition' begins," remarks political scientist Robert Dahl, "is an exercise in metaphysics."

Our divided government also presents a problem of accountability. When policies fail, one branch of government blames the other; when policies succeed, everyone stampedes to take credit. Who is ultimately "in charge" and responsible? At whose desk does the buck stop?

But even more serious than the lack of accountability is deadlock. The "separation of powers" really means that veto power is distributed throughout the presidential-congressional system. Unless one party takes control of all branches of government, gridlock sets in. And even when one party seems to have control of the government, party rank and file can desert executive leadership, sometimes forming coalitions with the opposition. Thus, during FDR's second term, from 1936 to 1940, despite a top-heavy Democratic Congress from 1936 to 1938, with 75 Democrats to 17 Republicans in the Senate and 334 Democrats to 89 Republicans in the House, much of his progressive legislation was blocked, at first by conservative Southern Democrats and then, after 1938, by a coalition of Republicans and conservative Democrats. Later, during President John Kennedy's first two years in office, again despite a Democratic Congress, a conservative coalition of Northern Republicans and Southern Democrats voted together and defeated the President more than half the time in the Senate and two times out of three in the House. One can point to only a few periods in recent American history when politicians succeeded, in spite of checks and balances and party decentralization and fragmentation, in creating significant, sweeping change—perhaps only FDR's first term in office when he was able to pass important New Deal legislation and during LBJ's first years in office when the Congress passed his Great Society programs, in the wake of JFK's assassination.

The wheels of the legislative process turn at a snail's pace when the two opposing parties occupy the different branches of government. Then progress depends on both parties achieving a high level of consensus. The problem is that even when consensus can be reached, it is always located in the political center—making for unimaginative, marginal change that is always gradual and rarely significant, the inevitable product of negotiation and compromise. Madisonian government produces incremental change at best, deadlock at worst.

Just such deadlock took place in 1919 and 1920, when Woodrow Wilson fought to have the United States join the League of Nations.

Though majority opinion in the country wanted the League, though most newspapers endorsed it, though even Republicans such as the former President William Howard Taft wanted to join the League, Wilson was thwarted by Republican Senator Henry Cabot Lodge, the chairman of the Foreign Relations Committee, who, with his henchmen, succeeded in preventing the United States from joining the League. The final vote in the Senate was 49 in favor of the League, 35 against, still two votes short of the two-thirds majority necessary.

Years earlier, when he was a senior at Princeton in 1879, Wilson had sent an essay to the editor of the *International Review*. In it the young man argued against checks and balances, insisting that a responsible, effective American government called for the joining of the executive and the legislature. The decline in national leadership, he held, could be traced to the "degradation" of political parties and to the "absorption of all power by a legislature which is practically irresponsible for its acts." The editor of the *International Review*, Henry Cabot Lodge, then twenty-nine and himself a (Republican) party man, accepted and published the article. Four decades later, Lodge and Wilson would act out precisely the kind of institutional deadlock that Wilson had warned against.

During periods when people clamor for meaningful if not radical change, for truly innovative legislation, the separation of powers, disunited, heterogeneous parties, and a relatively weak executive undermine the possibility of such sweeping change. Even bold and visionary presidents, engaged in brokering an endless series of deals, find themselves locked into transactional, not transformational, national leadership.

Checks and balances are written into a Constitution as enduring as stone. Still, Thomas Jefferson himself would never have felt eternally bound to an institutional blueprint more than two centuries old. This believer in the "sovereignty" of the living generation was convinced that "no society can make a perpetual constitution" and that constitutions and laws "naturally expire" at the end of a generation. Jefferson might well be astonished that Americans intend to enter a new millennium with a horse-and-buggy Constitution. Will the tortoiselike pace of our constitutional government be able to keep up with the rapid acceleration of social change, with the new needs of citizens in the twenty-first century, and with, as Arthur Schlesinger, Jr., remarked, the increasing velocity of history itself?

PROSPERITY VS. DEMOCRACY

Political life in contemporary France is just as problematic and complex. Indeed, the problems of both countries are ultimately strikingly similar and call for transfusions of ideas and imagination.

Revolutionary France galvanized the world with her electrifying energy—the popular will to overhaul the nation and enact immediate, radical, transforming measures. The French wanted, above all, the vigor and impact that result from the clear and unchecked rule of the "people." The downside was that politicians were intellectually as well as tactically opposed to securing a legitimate place within the political system for dissidents. In the decades following the Revolution, the notion of a legitimate opposition continued to puzzle people in France, striking them as mysterious and foreign. "An opposition, as in England, is that it?" asked Napoleon as he soaked in his bathtub. "I haven't been able to understand yet what good there is in an opposition."

In the wake of the Revolution and the Empire, political parties slowly crystallized and gained legitimacy. Still, when people did summon the courage to oppose government, they were often contesting not merely the government's policies but its very legitimacy. Since the Revolution, the legitimacy of virtually every government has been challenged—the Revolution and the Empire by monarchists, the Third Republic by many Catholics and workers, Vichy by Charles de Gaulle and other resistance groups, the Fourth Republic by leftists opposed to the European Defense Community and by rightists opposed to abandoning control over Indochina and Algeria.

Charles de Gaulle wanted to restore unquestioned legitimacy to French government by drafting a constitution for France's Fifth Republic that would reconcile the various opposing trends in French history— the Old Regime vs. the Revolution, the sovereignty of a strong charismatic leader vs. the sovereignty of a representative legislature. De Gaulle sought a constitutional marriage of a strong, "monarchical" President and a parliamentary "revolutionary" system of representation.

And yet, despite this blueprint for strong executive leadership, France, like the United States, suffers from divided government. The victory of the Socialist party and the appointment of a Socialist Prime Minister in 1997 compromised the authority of the Gaullist President. Those elections marked the third time that a President of the Fifth Republic had to share executive responsibilities with the leader of the opposition. Though the areas of the President's authority do not overlap with those of the Prime Minister, the ideological split at the heart of the government surely undermines de Gaulle's vision of a powerful executive.

But, surprisingly, cohabitation and the sharing of the government by two adversarial parties have not paralyzed French government. On the contrary, France, according to innumerable commentators, suffers from an overload of consensus.

A chorus of critics complains that ideological debate and contention in France are disappearing. In a country that, since the Revolution, has prided itself on being oppositional and on valuing critical Cartesian thinking and intellectual individualism, many people are alarmed at the eclipse of the ideological conflicts that have long nourished French politics.

The French are wasting time, these critics contend, fruitlessly contesting the legitimacy of the constitutional system instead of energizing the political life of the nation with adversarial party conflict. "The paradox is that the French confront one another in a domain where there should be consensus," writes political scientist Pierre Rosanvallon, "and they feign consensus in the domain where there should be debate. The big loser in this system is democratic deliberation."

Why are political debate and contention in decline in France? Many political analysts agree that the collapse of the Soviet Union dealt crippling blows to the political left as well as to the political right in France. When the potent Communist experiment failed, unable to compete with capitalist individualism, the revolutionary left lost its polestar while the right lost its best foil and its most effective argument for itself. Where passionate ideological contention once took place, there is now a vacuum.

A vacuum or a new kind of consensus? For many, the two are one and the same. The French seem to be reaching a new consensus in the political center, but that consensus is based not on political principles or passions but only on the new global religion: prosperity. Concerns about jobs, security, industrial and technological development have eclipsed debate on political ideas. French Socialists find themselves embracing policies that are not substantively different from those of the center-right.

One symptom of the displacement of politics by economics is, according to one French analyst, "the frightening emptiness of contemporary political discourse." Under the Third Republic, recalls one historian, Parliament was the place par excellence where people could propound and defend their ideas. Political orators fearlessly examined fundamental questions. But at the end of the twentieth century, the lack of clear, imaginative ideological alternatives and the displacement of politics by economics together create a sense that "politics is becoming empty of meaning."

But ideological debate is not the only casualty. So is citizens' participation in the political arena. Consumers have replaced active citizens. As we "rush to acquire private wealth or the benefits of the welfare state," as we focus on consumption and pleasure, we leave the responsibilities of citizenship—concern for the public good, for democratic ideas, for freedom—in the dust.

The words "education" and "seduction" share the same Latin root. To educate derives from the Latin *ex-ducere*, to lead out, to develop one's faculties. The derivation of the verb "seduce" is *se-ducere*, to lead one astray. Citizens' involvement in self-government, in juries, in various associations, Thomas Jefferson argued, constitutes a vital education in democracy. But citizens' preoccupation with their own narrow self-interest, their obsession with acquisition and accumulation, seduce them and lead them astray—away from participation in self-government and in a dynamic political community.

"If citizens continue to close themselves off more and more narrowly in the circle of their own domestic interests," warned Tocqueville, "it is reasonable to fear that ultimately they will shut the door on the great and powerful public emotions that cause turmoil within nations but also help them evolve and renew themselves." Tocqueville lucidly predicted that man's love of wealth and property would seduce him, turning him inward, away from a vital engagement in society.

On both sides of the Atlantic, there now exists a kind of apolitical consensus on prosperity aggravated by the weakening of political parties and the absence of galvanizing party platforms. Politically apathetic citizens and political parties mired in intellectual stagnation lounge at the threshold of the new millennium.

BILL CLINTON OR TONY BLAIR?

Two hundred years after the sister revolutions, France and the United States are unquestionably committed to democracy yet suffer from centrist leadership, a contentless consensus, and an enervated electorate.

What happened to the dynamic, courageous, populist leadership of the French Revolution? What happened to the substantive ideological contention that took place among the founding fathers and between Federalists and Republicans? Political parties used to be a defining feature of American politics; they are that no longer.

Can we reasonably expect our societies to continue to progress without meaningful adversarial conflict? Leaders of the House of Representatives aspire to mold the Congress into "a more civil, respectful and consensual body." The buzzwords "moderate," "mainstream," and "middle of the road" accompany the scramble to the insipid center.

A fresh political model may be seasonable not only for emerging nations but also for the United States and France themselves. Emerging nations must found institutions, but established democracies must renew and reenergize their own. Especially if we wish to offer new states something more inspiring than techniques for industrialization and production and something more idealistic than an obsession with consumption and wealth, we need to consider revitalizing our own institutions and our commitment to democracy.

What essential features should a model democracy possess?

A civilized state requires, first and foremost, order. Without order and stability, no social or economic life is possible. Without order, neither a legal system nor freedom nor even life itself is secure. But though order is the sine qua non of civilization, it should be not only an end, as dictators erroneously believe, but also a means. A means to what? To an open, egalitarian society and a lively, inclusive political culture in which diverse individuals are free to govern themselves, fulfill themselves, and pursue their own happiness.

This kind of society will offer individuals and groups opportunities to participate in the contentious ideological debate that alone produces the creativity necessary for progress and renewal. There will be majoritarian rule and respect for minorities. Leadership will be dynamic, bold, imaginative.

In short, a healthy society requires order but thrives on ideas, vision, and conflict. Just as Niccolò Machiavelli discovered five centuries ago, conflict and tumult paradoxically promote stability and order. James Madison also recognized that conflict would always be part of political life. But for Madison, conflict seemed an inescapable, disagreeable defect, "sown in the nature of man," rather than the greatest single source of fresh, innovative visions for change and progress.

Is there one political model that best combines order and conflict? And is it possible to wed the energetic populist leadership of the French Revolution with an adversarial two-party system while also protecting individual rights?

Yes. The wedding already took place. In Great Britain.

"Whether we speak of differences in opinion or differences in interest," remarked Daniel Defoe, the author of *Robinson Crusoe*, in 1701, "we must own we are the most divided, quarrelsome nation under the sun." England's affinity for political quarrels has produced the longest-lasting and arguably most vital democracy on the planet.

The dominant features of the modern English model of parliamentary democracy are two distinct, competitive parties that alternate in power, a strong elected executive, and—as far as the executive and legislature are concerned—no marked constitutional separation of powers. After a political party in Great Britain wins a national election, the party leader becomes the country's Prime Minister. There are no formal limits to the power of the Prime Minister's government, as long as it retains its parliamentary majority. The party is free to enact policies and programs, thus assuring clear majoritarian rule.

Still, the losing party does not disappear from the scene, for the opposition constitutes an integral, essential part of the constitutional system. "Her Majesty's Opposition" has the duty to criticize the party in power and is as much a part of the polity as the administration itself. Its prime responsibility is not to fell the government in power but rather to offer an alternative government and to present positive—not just oppositional—policies. In addition to these responsibilities, the opposition has rights too—for example, it selects topics of parliamentary debate. A forceful and effective opposition constantly reminds leaders and citizens of a clear alternative to the majority government's policies, yet the majority may continue to enact its policies unimpeded.

Together "Her Majesty's Government" and "Her Majesty's Opposition" make up the two halves of the constitutional system. One Prime Minister, in the 1930s, tried to form a unity government, but government without opposition proved to be a dismal failure. During World War II, a wartime coalition successfully governed, but as soon as the war was over, national elections threw Churchill's government out of power, returning party conflict to Parliament.

Peaceful political conflict and institutionalized opposition depend on rules—rules of decorum, language, and behavior. During the seventeenth and early eighteenth centuries such rules crystallized. Limits applied not only to language but also to how a defeated or unpopular political leader could be treated—politicians could not give free rein to their desires for vengeance against their political enemies. The English system functions smoothly, according to one historian, because of limits on verbal abuse, limits on the penalties for defeat, and limits on the abuse of power by any one political body.

Paradoxically, adversarial party politics requires consensus—sometimes a high level of consensus, sometimes a minimal level. First of all, there must exist a fundamental consensus in the nation as to the constitutional system itself as well as to citizens' rights and freedoms. Second, though the system depends on ideological conflict, there must not be too much conflict—or too little. If criticism of government is too severe, if the different parties are too polarized, and if conflict is so intense as to eliminate the "mediating center," the social fabric of the society may suffer. Still, too little conflict means that the government is immune from healthy criticism and that significant alternative policies are not being offered. A delicate balancing act is required to produce, in the words of Robert Dahl, "a society where dissent is low enough to encourage a relatively calm and objective appraisal of alternatives, and yet sufficient to make sure that radical alternatives will not be ignored or suppressed."

Are English institutions superior to others? The very thought insults the collective narcissism of the French and the Americans—though Hamilton, Adams, and other founders were themselves ardent Anglophiles and though a president like Woodrow Wilson always wanted to see American institutions more closely mirror English ones. In any case, the United States and France cannot be expected to toss out their political institutions and set up new ones along English lines. Even Edmund Burke advised against making the British Constitution a model "for any people scrvilely to copy." But Burke did recommend that people study "the *principles* from which it has grown."

For the past two centuries, the English and American democracies have accepted the *principle* of conflict and learned to exploit it. They have integrated conflict into their institutions, they have normalized it and ritualized it and thus tamed it, they have created rules and procedures for defanging and resolving it. And not only have both political systems thrived on conflict, they have also been remarkably able to weather a variety of other storms—from horrific world wars to violent social upheaval.

Indeed, the United States and England (and her Canadian and Australian offspring) are virtually alone among nations in having been able to withstand all the catastrophes of the twentieth century—two world wars, fascism, Stalinism, a devastating economic depression. Those governments remained stable and intact throughout the century, persevering in their careful, orderly ways while the rest of the world reeled. And that resilience is due—at least in part—to their ability to tolerate, defang, and absorb conflict.

But at the dawn of a new century, can the United States and France still boast vibrant political arenas? Do we continue to value political conflict or are we more interested in conflict resolution, more drawn to the center, to consensus and unity? A host of politicians and commentators bombard Americans with appeals for an end to "party politics as usual." Their assumption seems to be that, since the founders built conflict into the very structure of government, the best strategy for governing is to rise above conflict. And perhaps an even more basic assumption is that consensus and unity are somehow healthier, more noble, less disruptive and destructive than partisan conflict. And yet, the sister revolutions teach us that a democracy achieves political stability not by valorizing concord but rather by encouraging competing interests and opposing ideologies.

Are there remedies for our political ailments? One possible solution—a booster shot for parties. For while bland consensus and mainstream leaders starve people for bold ideas and political passion, party conflict energizes citizens (and increases voter turnout) with substantive ideas, new alternatives, meaningful choices, and visionary leadership. Party politics stands at the very heart of a democratic system, and battles between parties and candidates should be clear-cut, honest, visible, and responsible.

In addition to strengthening political parties and making them more disciplined and more ideological, we might also begin to consider making some reforms in our quasi-sacred Constitution: lengthening terms for members of the House of Representatives and shortening terms for senators so that they all coincide with the four-year presidential term.

Senators, representatives, and President would serve concurrently, thereby moving American government a step closer to majoritarian parliamentary democracy. Presidential, congressional, and senatorial candidates of the same party would run essentially on the same party team, collectively sharing responsibility for the policies of their party. There would be a strong, dynamic majoritarian government and a minority opposition that would try to regain power in the next election.

Countries—from China to Cuba, Singapore to Iran—can profit from the historical and political examples of the sister revolutions. The French and American experiments in revolution can teach them that tumult and conflict, civil political discourse, and guarantees of individual and minority rights are the necessary ingredients in a healthy political culture. Simple lessons on the proven importance of a legitimate opposition and adversarial political parties could surely assist a host of nations far more than vague lectures about "human rights"—for it costs dictators less to pay lip service to human rights than to permit citizens to form viable opposition parties that can legitimately challenge their monopoly on power.

As for France and the United States, do they need to repeat the eighteenth-century exercise in revolution?

Few events can be more traumatic for a nation than revolution—for revolution means the total political, social, and intellectual transformation of a country. But perhaps more damaging to a nation is stagnation, the fear of change, the timorous flight from experiment. Between revolution and stasis lies a third path, that of renewal and renovation. Jefferson himself, though a starry-eyed lover of revolutions, felt that nations could avoid such turbulent upheaval by continually renewing themselves and energetically keeping pace with the times.

If the United States and France wish to ensure the renewal and health of their societies, they might do well to recall that revolution means return. As we enter the third millennium, let us return to the wisdom and insights into democracy of some of our greatest political thinkers—

Machiavelli, Jefferson, Madison, and Tocqueville—who meditated on conflict, tumult, and renovation.

But revolution also entails audacity. As we contemplate fresh solutions to fresh problems, let us audaciously hurl a few experimental bolts of lightning into our sky of eighteenth-century light.

Appendix

The Bill of Rights

[The first ten amendments to the American Constitution were ratified on December 15, 1791, and form what is known as the Bill of Rights.]

AMENDMENT 1. RELIGION, SPEECH, ASSEMBLY, AND POLITICS

Congress shall make no law respecting an establishment of religion, or prohibiting the free exercise thereof: or abridging the freedom of speech, or of the press; or the right of the people peaceably to assemble, and to petition the government for a redress of grievances.

AMENDMENT 2. MILITIA AND THE RIGHT TO BEAR ARMS

A well regulated Militia, being necessary to the security of a free State, the right of the people to keep and bear Arms, shall not be infringed.

AMENDMENT 3. QUARTERING OF SOLDIERS

No Soldier shall, in time of peace be quartered in any house, without the consent of the Owner, nor in time of war, but in manner to be prescribed by law.

AMENDMENT 4. SEARCHES AND SEIZURES

The right of the people to be secure in their persons, houses, papers, and effects, against unreasonable searches and seizures, shall not be violated, and no Warrants shall issue, but upon probable cause, supported by Oath or affirmation, and particularly describing the place to be searched, and the persons or things to be seized.

AMENDMENT 5. GRAND JURIES, SELF-INCRIMINATION, DOUBLE JEOPARDY, DUE PROCESS, AND EMINENT DOMAIN

No person shall be held to answer for a capital, or otherwise infamous crime, unless on a presentment or indictment of a Grand Jury, except in cases arising in the land or naval forces, or in the Militia, when in actual service in time of War or public danger; nor shall any person be subject for the same offense to be twice put in jeopardy of life or limb; nor shall be compelled in any criminal case to be a witness against himself, nor be deprived of life, liberty, or property, without due process of law; nor shall private property be taken for public use, without just compensation.

AMENDMENT 6. CRIMINAL COURT PROCEDURES

In all criminal prosecutions, the accused shall enjoy the right to a speedy and public trial, by an impartial jury of the State and district wherein the crime shall have been committed, which district shall have been previously ascertained by law, and to be informed of the nature and cause of the accusation; to be confronted with the witnesses against him; to have compulsory process for obtaining Witnesses in his favor, and to have the Assistance of Counsel for his defense.

AMENDMENT 7. TRIAL BY JURY IN COMMON LAW CASES

In Suits at common law, where the value in controversy shall exceed twenty dollars, the right of trial by jury shall be preserved, and no fact tried by a jury shall be otherwise re-examined in any Court of the United States, than according to the rules of the common law.

AMENDMENT 8. BAIL, CRUEL AND UNUSUAL PUNISHMENT

Excessive bail shall not be required, nor excessive fines imposed, nor cruel and unusual punishments inflicted.

AMENDMENT 9. RIGHTS RETAINED BY THE PEOPLE

The enumeration in the Constitution, of certain rights, shall not be construed to deny or disparage others retained by the people.

AMENDMENT 10. RESERVED POWERS OF THE STATES

The powers not delegated to the United States by the Constitution, nor prohibited by it to the States, are reserved to the States respectively, or to the people.

Declaration of the Rights of Man and Citizen

[*The following is the text of the Declaration of the Rights of Man and Citizen adopted on August 26, 1789.*]

The representatives of the French people, constituting the National Assembly, believing that ignorance, disregard or contempt for the rights of man are the sole causes of public ills and governmental corruption, have resolved to set forth, in a solemn declaration, the natural, inalienable and sacred rights of man, so that this declaration, always present in the minds of all the members of the social body, can remind them at all times of their rights and their duties; so that the acts of the legislative power and the executive power, open at every instant to comparison with the goals of all political institutions, may be all the more respected; so that the demands of citizens, founded henceforth on simple and incontestable principles, always correspond to the preservation of the constitution and the happiness of all. Thus the Assembly recognizes and declares, in the presence and under the auspices of the Supreme Being, the following rights of man and citizen:

1. Men are born and remain free and equal in their rights. Social distinctions can be founded only on what is useful to all.

2. The goal of all political associations is the preservation of the natural and imprescriptible rights of man. These rights are liberty, property, security, and resistance to oppression.

3. The principle of sovereignty resides essentially in the nation. No body, no individual may claim any authority that does not emanate explicitly from the nation.

4. Liberty consists in being able to do whatever does not harm others. Thus the exercise of the natural rights of each man has no limits except those that assure other members of society the enjoyment of those same rights. Only the law can determine what these limits are.

5. The law may rightfully prohibit only those actions that are harmful to society. Whatever is not forbidden by the law cannot be prohibited, and no one can be forced to do what the law does not require.

6. The law is the expression of the general will. All citizens have the right to take part, in person or through their representatives, in its creation. It must be the same for all, whether it protects or punishes. All citizens being equal in its eyes are equally eligible for all honors, offices, and public employment, according to their abilities, and with no criteria other than their virtues and talents.

7. No man may be indicted, arrested or detained except in cases determined by law and according to the procedures that it has stipulated. Those who instigate, expedite, execute or cause to be executed arbitrary orders must be punished; but any citizen summoned or seized by virtue of the law must obey instantly: he renders himself guilty if he resists.

8. The law may establish only strictly and clearly necessary punishments, and no one may be punished except under a law established and promulgated before the time of the infraction and legally applied.

9. Inasmuch as every man is presumed innocent until he is judged guilty, if it is deemed indispensable to keep him under arrest, all measures not necessary for securing his person should be severely limited by law.

10. No one may be disturbed for his opinions, not even for his opinions concerning religion, provided that their expression does not disturb public order as established by law.

11. The free communication of thoughts and opinions is one of the most precious rights of man: every citizen may therefore speak, write and print freely, but he is liable for abuse of this freedom in cases determined by the law.

12. The guarantee of the rights of man and citizen requires the existence of public forces. These forces are therefore instituted for the protection of all, not for the private benefit of those to whom they are entrusted.

13. For the upkeep of such public forces and for the costs of administration, common taxation is necessary: it should be apportioned equally among all citizens according to their ability to pay.

14. All citizens have the right, by themselves or through their representatives, to have demonstrated to them the necessity of public taxes, to consent to them freely, to supervise the use made of the proceeds and to determine the shares to be paid, the means of assessment and collection and the duration.

15. Society has the right to hold accountable every public agent of its administration.

16. Any society in which the guarantee of rights is not assured or in which the separation of powers is not determined, has no constitution.

17. Inasmuch as property is an inviolable and sacred right, no one may be deprived of it, except for an obvious requirement of public necessity, legally construed, and then only on condition of a fair compensation in advance.

[Translated by Susan Dunn]

Notes

1. SISTER REVOLUTIONS

3 **On Lafayette's life:** See Lafayette, *Memoirs of General Lafayette*, trans. B. Sarrans (New York: Harper, 1833); Lafayette, Gilbert du Motier, marquis de, *Lafayette in the Age of the American Revolution: Selected Letters and Papers, 1776–1790*, ed. Stanley J. Idzerda, 4 vols. (Ithaca: Cornell University Press, 1980); Stanley J. Idzerda, Anne C. Loveland, and Marc H. Miller, *Lafayette, Hero of Two Worlds: The Art and Pageantry of His Farewell Tour of America, 1824–25* (Hanover, N.H.: University Press of New England for The Queens Museum, 1989); Charlemagne Tower, Jr., *The Marquis de La Fayette in the American Revolution* (Philadelphia: J. B. Lippincott Company, 1895); Peter Buckman, *Lafayette: A Biography* (London: Paddington Press, 1977); Olivier Bernier, *Lafayette, Hero of Two Worlds* (New York: Dutton, 1983); James MacGregor Burns, *The Vineyard of Liberty* (New York: Random House, 1982).

4 **"Dear Heart . . .":** Lafayette to Adrienne, 30 May 1777, in Lafayette, *Lafayette in the Age of the American Revolution: Selected Letters and Papers*, ed. Idzerda, 1:56.

4 **On Washington and Lafayette:** See Lloyd Kramer, *Lafayette in Two Worlds* (Chapel Hill: University of North Carolina Press, 1996), 19 and 21.

5 **"I do most devoutly wish . . .":** Washington to Gouverneur Morris, 24 July 1778, in *The Writings of George Washington*, ed. W. C. Ford (New York: G. P. Putnam's Sons, 1890), 7:118.

5 **Washington confided to friends:** Memoirs of Brissot, in Gilbert Chinard, ed., *George Washington as the French Knew Him* (Princeton: Princeton University Press, 1940), 87.

5 **They cheered at American victories:** Comtesse de Fars-Fausselandry, quoted by Simon Schama, *Citizens: A Chronicle of the French Revolution* (New York: Knopf, 1989), 49.

5 **A new vocabulary:** Dutens, *Mémoires d'un voyageur qui se repose,* quoted in Lewis Rosenthal, *America and France: The Influence of the United States on France in the XVIII Century* (New York: Henry Holt & Co., 1882), 68.

6 **Franklin in Paris:** See Claude-Anne Lopez, *Mon Cher Papa: Franklin and the Ladies of Paris* (New Haven, Conn.: Yale University Press, 1990), 232.

6 **Grave risk for an absolute monarch:** Malouet, *Mémoires sur l'administration des colonies,* quoted in Rosenthal, *America and France,* 18.

6 **The anguished king admitted . . . :** Louis XVI, quoted in Louis Gottschalk, "The Place of the American Revolution in the Causal Pattern of the French Revolution," in *The Making of Modern Europe,* ed. Herman Ausubel (New York: The Dryden Press, 1951), 510.

7 **Washington's address and a sermon dedicated to Lafayette:** See Louis Gottschalk, *Lafayette and the Close of the American Revolution* (Chicago: University of Chicago Press, 1942), 326–327.

7 **"The play is over":** Lafayette to the Comte de Maurepas, 20 October 1781, in Lafayette, *Lafayette in the Age of the American Revolution,* ed. Idzerda, 4:422.

7 **The Marquis de Ségur showered him with compliments:** The Marquis de Ségur to Lafayette, ca. 5 December 1781 and 5 December 1781, in *Lafayette in the Age of the American Revolution,* ed. Idzerda, 4:447 and 448.

8 **"Monsieur de La Fayette . . . we prepared our own":** Cerutti to Noailles, 4 August 1789, in Rosenthal, *America and France,* 181.

8 **Chastellux's observations about America:** Chastellux, *Travels in North America,* ed. Howard Rice, 2 vols. (Chapel Hill: University of North Carolina Press for the Institute of Early American History and Culture, 1963), 2:535.

9 **People applauded the Revolution as the most important event:** Lacretelle, 1785, *Mercure de France,* 23 May 1789, quoted in Rosenthal, *America and France,* 142 note.

9 **"sublime exposition of sacred rights . . .":** Condorcet, quoted in Rosenthal, *America and France,* 144.

9 **France "has been awaked . . .":** Jefferson to Washington, 4 December 1788, in *The Papers of Thomas Jefferson,* ed. Julian P. Boyd (Princeton, N.J.: Princeton University Press, 1958), 14:331.

11 **"hopelessly different":** Stanley Elkins and Eric McKitrick, *The Age of Federalism* (Oxford: Oxford University Press, 1993), 312.

11 **Jefferson and Madison admitted that a few seats:** John Dalberg-Acton, *Lectures on the French Revolution,* ed. John Neville Figgis (London: Macmillan, 1916), 26.

12 **"I [took] the opportunity to tell him . . . must inevitably fail":** *A Diary of the French Revolution by Gouverneur Morris,* ed. Beatrix Davenport, 2 vols. (Boston: Houghton Mifflin, 1939), 23 June 1789, 1:121.

13 **Lafayette brought his friends to Jefferson's town house:** Jefferson, *Autobiography,* in Jefferson, *Writings,* ed. Merrill Peterson (The Library of America, 1984), 97.

13 **"I have never feared . . . years of confusion & anarchy":** Jefferson to Lafayette, 2 April 1790, in Boyd, ed., *Jefferson Papers,* 16:293.

13 **Lafayette's "canine" appetite for popularity:** Jefferson to James Madison, 30 January 1787, in Jefferson, *Writings,* ed. Peterson, 885.

13 **Jefferson congratulated himself on having slept quietly:** Jefferson to Diodati, 3 August 1789, in Boyd, ed., *Jefferson Papers,* 15:325.

13 "So far it seemed that your revolution . . . liberty in a feather-bed": Jefferson to Lafayette, 2 April 1790, in Boyd, ed., *Jefferson Papers*, 16:293.

14–15 **Lafayette and the National Guard, and subsequent events:** See Kramer, *Lafayette in Two Worlds*, 43, 40, 44.

15 "I verily believe . . . no populace in America": Morris to Washington, 1 August 1792, in Morris, *A Diary of the French Revolution*, ed. Davenport, 2:483.

16 **Washington instructed Morris to express the sentiments of this country regarding Lafayette:** Washington to Jefferson, 13 March 1793, in Ford, ed., *Writings of George Washington*, 12:269.

18 **Lanjuinais mocked "the Anglo-American Mr. Adams":** Lanjuinais, Session of 7 September 1789, quoted in Rosenthal, *America and France*, 196.

18 **Montmorency acknowledged that Americans had created a worthy precedent:** Montmorency, session of 1 August 1789, quoted in Rosenthal, *America and France*, 184.

18 **For Condorcet, the American Revolution had merely paved the way:** Antoine-Nicolas de Condorcet, *Sketch for an Historical Picture of the Progress of the Human Mind*, trans. June Barraclough (Westport, Conn.: Greenwood Press, 1979), 56, 58.

18 "O nation of France, you are not made to receive an example": Rabaut de Saint-Etienne, 23 August 1789, quoted in Rosenthal, *America and France*, 208.

18 **Saint-Just pitied the American "federal" nation:** Saint-Just, 15 May 1793, in Saint-Just, *Oeuvres complètes*, ed. M. Duval (Paris: Gérard Lebovici, 1984), 444.

19 **Cloots divulged that the Americans were secretly envious:** Session of 30 April 1793, quoted in Rosenthal, *America and France*, 280.

19 "consider[ed] the establishment and success of the [French] government": Jefferson to George Mason, 4 February 1791, in Jefferson, *Writings*, ed. Peterson, 971.

19 "And you, brave Americans, . . . your enemy!": Robespierre, Speech of 20 November 1793, quoted in Rosenthal, *America and France*, 293 note.

19 "what the French took from the Americans . . . sewing": John Dalberg-Acton, *Lectures on the French Revolution*, ed. Figgis, 32.

20 **Cooper, remarking that Lafayette now stood alone:** James Fenimore Cooper, *Notions of the Americans: Picked Up by a Traveling Bachelor*, quoted by Anne C. Loveland, *Emblem of Liberty: The Image of Lafayette in the American Mind* (Baton Rouge: Louisiana State University Press, 1971), 7.

20 **Citizens . . . were simply thrown into "delirium":** Jefferson to Richard Rush, 13 October 1824, in *The Writings of Thomas Jefferson*, ed. Paul Leicester Ford (New York: G. P. Putnam's Sons, 1899), 10:322.

20 **Lafayette's reunion with Jefferson:** J. Bennett Nolan, *Lafayette in America, Day by Day* (Baltimore: The Johns Hopkins Press, 1934), 257.

20 **Madison joined them for dessert:** James MacGregor Burns, *The Vineyard of Liberty*, 255.

20 **Lafayette appeared in fine health; Lafayette at the University of Virginia and at Montpellier:** James Morton Smith, ed., *The Republic of Letters: The Correspondence Between Thomas Jefferson and James Madison 1776–1826*, 3 vols. (New York: W. W. Norton, 1995), 3:1889.

20 "beloved General": Lafayette to Washington, 21 December 1781, in Idzerda, ed., *Lafayette in the Age of the American Revolution*, 4:450.

22 **Cooper observed that "at the public dinners . . .":** James Fenimore Cooper, quoted in Loveland, *Emblem of Liberty*, 75.

22 **Another observer agreed that the only surviving general . . .:** George Ticknor, quoted in Kramer, *Lafayette in Two Worlds*, 194.

22 **Lafayette "rall[ied] us together":** Jefferson to Richard Rush, 13 October 1824, in Ford, ed., *Writings of Thomas Jefferson*, 10:322.

22 **Lafayette too spoke of the feelings of fellowship his visit had engendered:** Lafayette, quoted in Loveland, *Emblem of Liberty*, 76.

24–25 **de Gaulle's speeches:** Speech in Vincennes, 3 October 1947, and Speech in Marseille, 10 November 1961, in *De Gaulle a dit* (Paris: Plon, 1989), 41 and 55.

25 **Jefferson vs. Hamilton, Lincoln vs. Douglas, Roosevelt vs. Hoover:** Edmund S. Morgan, "Conflict and Consensus in the American Revolution," in *Essays on the American Revolution*, ed. Stephen G. Kurtz and James H. Hutson (Chapel Hill: University of North Carolina Press for the Institute of Early American History and Culture, 1973), 309.

25–26 **"Basically, only affairs of our own times"; "the long drama of the French Revolution":** Tocqueville to Louis de Kergorlay, 15 December 1850, in Tocqueville, *Selected Letters on Politics and Society*, ed. Roger Boesche, trans. James Toupin and Roger Boesche (Berkeley: University of California Press, 1985), 254–255.

26 **"reflect . . . unceasingly on themselves . . . from this end":** Tocqueville to Claude-François de Corcelle, 17 September 1853, in Tocqueville, *Selected Letters on Politics and Society*, ed. Boesche, 294.

2. REVOLUTIONARY LEADERSHIP

28 **Tocqueville on competition for a constitution:** *L'Ancien Régime et la Révolution: Fragments et Notes inédites sur la Révolution*, ed. André Jardin, vol. 2, pt. 2, of Tocqueville, *Oeuvres complètes*, ed. J.-P. Mayer (Paris: Gallimard, 1953), 2:104–105. All translations from the French are my own.

29 **Hofstadter on Constitutional Convention:** Richard Hofstadter, *Anti-intellectualism in American Life* (New York: Alfred A. Knopf, 1962), 145.

29 **Educational backgrounds of members of Constitutional Convention:** Merle Curti, *American Paradox: The Conflict of Thought and Action* (New Brunswick, N.J.: Rutgers University Press, 1956), 15–16.

29 **"reflection and choice":** Alexander Hamilton, *The Federalist* (New York: The Modern Library, n.d.), No. 1, 3.

29 **"Otherwise they would never . . . institutions":** Bruce Ackerman, *We the People* (Cambridge, Mass.: The Belknap Press of Harvard University Press, 1991), 1:20.

29–30 **"the most powerful apostle":** Tocqueville, *De la Démocratie en Amérique* [1832] (Paris: Flammarion, 1981), Bk. 1, pt. 2, ch. 7, 1:360. All translations from the French are my own.

30 **Gladstone on American Constitution:** See John Bartlett, *Familiar Quotations* (New York: Little, Brown, 1943), 450.

30 **Wood on exceptional leadership in the American Revolution:** Gordon Wood, "The Democratization of Mind in the American Revolution," in *Leadership in the American Revolution* (Washington, D.C.: Library of Congress, 1974), 67 and 64.

31 **Tocqueville on widespread dissatisfaction with the status quo and "internal force of energy"**: Tocqueville, *Fragments et Notes,* 2:35, n. 3, and 2:45, emphasis added.

31 **entrenched system . . . reshaping the country**: Tocqueville, *L'Ancien Régime et la Révolution* [1856], vol. 2, pt. 1, of Tocqueville, *Oeuvres complètes,* ed. J.-P. Mayer (Paris, 1952), 1:195.

31–32 **They could not see "where . . . dark"**: Tocqueville, *Fragments et Notes,* 2:59–60.

32 **"only the interplay . . . their art"**: Tocqueville, *L'Ancien Régime et la Révolution,* 1:198, emphasis added.

33 **"it is less important . . . the dreamers"**: Tocqueville, *Fragments et Notes,* 2:35–36, 114–115, and 36, emphasis added.

33 **"simple and elementary rules"**: Tocqueville, *L'Ancien Régime et la Révolution,* 1:194.

33 **brutal and violent character of this "necessary destruction"**: Tocqueville to Gustave de Beaumont, 24 April 1856, in Tocqueville, *Selected Letters on Politics and Society,* ed. R. Boesche (Berkeley: University of California Press, 1985), 330.

33–35 **Tocqueville on men of letters in the period**: Tocqueville, *L'Ancien Régime et la Révolution,* Bk. 3, ch. 1, 1:195–200.

35 **"The Convention . . . of the human mind"**: Tocqueville, *Fragments et Notes,* 2:255, 337, 228.

36 **Tocqueville on political panorama in America**: Tocqueville, *De la Démocratie en Amérique,* Bk. 2, pt. 1, ch. 1, 2:13 and ch. 4, 2:28.

36 **giving the "substance of reality" to French dreams**: Tocqueville, *L'Ancien Régime et la Révolution,* 1:199.

36 **political philosophy had led . . . new forms of servitude**: Tocqueville, *L'Ancien Régime et la Révolution,* 1:306 notes.

37 **Rossiter on political experience of American founders**: Clinton Rossiter, *1787: The Grand Convention* (New York: Macmillan, 1966), ch. 8.

37 **"when . . . the researches of the human mind . . . forms of Government"**: Washington, Circular to the States, 8 June 1783, in *The Writings of George Washington from the Original Manuscript Sources, 1745–1799,* ed. John C. Fitzpatrick (Washington, D.C.: U.S. Government Printing Office, 1938), 26:485.

38 **"I dread the reveries"**: Alexander Hamilton to Lafayette, 6 October 1789, in Harold C. Syrett, ed., *The Papers of Alexander Hamilton* (New York: Columbia University Press, 1962), 5:425.

38 **"reflection and choice"**: Hamilton, *Federalist* No. 1, 3.

38 **Hamilton's wariness of visionary men**: Hamilton, *Federalist* No. 6, 29.

38 **Hamilton on "prodigious innovations" in France**: Hamilton to Washington, 15 September 1790, in Syrett, ed., *Hamilton Papers,* 7:51.

38 **"experience" was "the least fallible guide"**: Hamilton, *Federalist* No. 6, 30.

39 **Morris's enjoyment of social life in Paris**: Morris, Letter to Comte de Moustier, 23 February 1789, and diary entry of 1 March 1789, in Morris, *A Diary of the French Revolution,* ed. Davenport, 1:xli and 1.

39 **Morris unimpressed by French "Leaders of Liberty"**: Morris, diary entry of Friday, 12 June 1789, in *A Diary of the French Revolution,* ed. Davenport, 1:113.

39 **"the best heads . . . Judgment or Reflection":** Morris, Letter to George Washington, 31 July 1789, in *A Diary of the French Revolution,* ed. Davenport, 1:171, emphasis added.

39 **the French "have taken Genius . . . Lightning to Light":** Morris, Letter to William Short, 18 September 1790, in *A Diary of the French Revolution,* ed. Davenport, 1:594, emphasis added.

39 **"The Men who live in the World . . .":** Morris, Letter to Washington, 24 January 1790, in *A Diary of the French Revolution,* ed. Davenport, 1:381.

39 **From books emerged . . . traditions and history:** Morris, in *A Diary of the French Revolution,* ed. Davenport, 1:104.

39 **the same "Roman standard":** Morris, Letter to Carmichael, 4 July 1789, in *A Diary of the French Revolution,* ed. Davenport, 1:136.

39 **"metaphysic" theories of government:** Morris, Letter to Jefferson, 23 October 1792, in *A Diary of the French Revolution,* ed. Davenport, 2:564.

40 ***"Experience* is a safe pilot":** Noah Webster, "An Oration Pronounced Before the Citizens of New Haven, 4 July 1798," quoted in Linda Kerber, *Federalists in Dissent: Imagery and Ideology in Jeffersonian America* (Ithaca, N.Y.: Cornell University Press, 1970), 21.

40–42 **Adams on the *philosophes:*** Zoltan Haraszti, *John Adams and the Prophets of Progress* (Cambridge, Mass.: Harvard University Press, 1952), 21 and 241.

41 **Adams on Turgot:** John Adams to Jefferson, 13 July 1813, in Lester J. Cappon, ed., *The Adams-Jefferson Letters,* 2 vols. (Chapel Hill: The University of North Carolina Press, 1959), 2:356.

41 **Adams on Condorcet:** Haraszti, *John Adams and the Prophets of Progress,* 241, 242, and 256.

41 **Adams on Lafayette:** Adams to Jefferson, 13 July 1813, in Cappon, ed., *Adams-Jefferson Letters,* 2:355.

41 ***philosophes* set history on a backward course:** Adams to Jefferson, 2 March 1816, in Cappon, ed., *Adams-Jefferson Letters,* 2:464.

42 **"They rent and tore the whole garment":** Adams, *Discourses on Davila: A Series of Papers on Political History,* in Charles Francis Adams, ed., *The Works of John Adams* (Boston: Little and Brown, 1851), 6:276; Adams, 1811, quoted in Haraszti, *John Adams and the Prophets of Progress,* 258.

42 **"I was determined . . . foulness":** Adams to Jefferson, 13 July 1813, in Cappon, ed., *Adams-Jefferson Letters,* 2:356.

42 **"the wisest and happiest" government:** John Adams, *Thoughts on Government,* quoted in Bernard Bailyn, *The Ideological Origins of the American Revolution,* rev. ed. (Cambridge, Mass.: The Belknap Press of Harvard University Press, 1967), 272–273.

42 **"I dread the Spirit of Innovation":** Adams to Benjamin Hichborn, 29 May 1776, in Robert J. Taylor, ed., *Papers of John Adams* (Cambridge, Mass.: The Belknap Press of Harvard University Press, 1979), 4:218.

42 **"many heads and many hands":** Madison, Letter of 1834, quoted in Irving Brant, *James Madison, Father of the Constitution* (New York: Bobbs-Merrill, 1950), 3:154–155.

42 **"the profound politician with the scholar":** William Pierce, quoted in Max Farrand, *The Framing of the Constitution* (New Haven, Conn.: Yale University Press, 1930), 17.

43 **"theoretic politicians":** Madison, *Federalist* No. 10, 58.

43 **"in a man's closet":** Madison, *Federalist* No. 53, 352.

43 **limits of human sagacity:** Madison, *Federalist* No. 37, 229.

43 **"Much is to be hoped . . . ought to be tried":** James Madison, "For the *National Gazette*, 31 Jan. 1792," in Robert A. Rutland et al., eds., *The Papers of James Madison* (Charlottesville: University Press of Virginia, 1983), 14:207.

43 **Madison on Montesquieu:** Madison, "For the *National Gazette*, 18 Feb. 1792," in Rutland et al., eds., *Madison Papers*, 14:233.

43 **fallibility and flaws in all facets of human understanding:** Madison, *Federalist* No. 37, 229–230.

43 **"experience is the oracle of truth":** Madison, *Federalist* No. 20, 124.

43 **They "furnish no other light . . . pursued":** Madison, *Federalist* No. 37, 226.

44 **"no parallel in the annals":** Madison, *Federalist* No. 14, 85.

44 **"the creation of the world":** Madison in Jonathan Elliot, ed. *The Debates of the Several State Conventions on the Adoption of the Federalist Constitution* (Philadelphia: J. B. Lippincott, 1937), 3:616.

44 **"Is it not agreed . . . an experiment?":** James Madison, in Elliot, ed., *Debates in the Several State Conventions*, 3:394 and 399.

44 **"The class of literati . . . means of happiness":** James Madison, "Notes for the *National Gazette* Essays, ca. 19 Dec. 1791–3 March 1792," in Rutland et al., eds., *Madison Papers*, 14:168.

44 **America's "glory be completed . . . purity of the *theory*":** James Madison, "For the *National Gazette*, 18 Feb. 1792," in Rutland et al., eds., *Madison Papers*, 14:234, emphasis added.

44 **"the most rational government . . . on its side":** Madison, *Federalist* No. 29, 329.

45 **"mobish insurgents":** Abigail Adams to Jefferson, 29 January 1787, in Cappon, ed., *The Adams-Jefferson Letters*, 1:168.

45 **"I like a little rebellion . . . Atmosphere":** Jefferson to Abigail Adams, 22 February 1787, in Cappon, ed., *The Adams-Jefferson Letters*, 1:173.

45 **"pray that heaven send them good kings":** Jefferson to Abigail Adams, 22 February 1787, in Cappon, ed., *The Adams-Jefferson Letters*, 1:173.

45 **more serious awareness of politics:** Jefferson to David Humphreys, 18 March 1789, in Boyd, ed., *Jefferson Papers*, 14:676.

45 **Those who had leisure to think:** Jefferson to Richard Price, 8 January 1789, in Boyd, ed., *Jefferson Papers*, 14:421.

45 **Jefferson's belief in the power of reason to shape history:** See Jefferson to Diodati, 3 August 1789, in Boyd, ed., *Jefferson Papers*, 15:326; and Jefferson to George Mason, 4 February 1791, in Jefferson, *Writings*, ed. Peterson, 972.

45 **"a full scope to reason . . . channel":** Jefferson to David Humphreys, 18 March 1789, in Boyd, ed., *Jefferson Papers*, 14:677.

45 **French intellectuals, versed only in theory and new in the practice of government:** Jefferson to Madison, 28 August 1789, in Boyd, ed., *Jefferson Papers*, 15:365.

45 **Jefferson counseled Lafayette to proceed step by step:** Jefferson to Lafayette, 28 February 1787, in Boyd, ed., *Jefferson Papers*, 11:186.

45–46 **Should the French attempt more . . . realization of their goals:** Jefferson to Madame de Tessé, 20 March 1787, in Boyd, ed., *Jefferson Papers*, 11:228, n. 8.

47 **improvements should "follow from the nature of things":** Jefferson to Washington, 4 November 1788, in Boyd, ed., *Jefferson Papers*, 14:330.

47 **"We must be contented . . . step by step":** Jefferson to Moustier, 17 May 1788, in Boyd, ed., *Jefferson Papers*, 13:174.

47 **"no just government should refuse":** Jefferson to Madison, 20 December 1787, in Jefferson, *Writings*, ed. Peterson, 916.

47 **"We must be contented with the ground . . . amiss in it":** Jefferson to Moustier, 17 May 1788, in Boyd, ed., *Jefferson Papers*, 13:174.

47 **"through every stage of these transactions . . . a total change of government":** Jefferson to Thomas Paine, 11 July 1789, in Boyd, ed., *Jefferson Papers*, 15:268.

48 **"an Adam and an Eve left in every country . . .":** Jefferson to William Short, 3 January 1793, in Boyd, ed., *Jefferson Papers*, 25:14.

48 **goals "worth rivers of blood . . .":** Jefferson to John Adams, 4 September 1823, in Jefferson, *Writings*, ed. Peterson, 1478.

48 **"freshness and boldness in the tone of the eighties . . .":** Bernard Bailyn, "The Central Themes of the American Revolution: An Interpretation," in *Essays on the American Revolution*, ed. Stephen G. Kurtz and James H. Hutson (Chapel Hill: The University of North Carolina Press for the Institute of Early American History and Culture, 1973), 19–20.

48 **"the earth belongs always to the living generation":** Jefferson to Madison, 6 September 1789, in Boyd, ed., *Jefferson Papers*, 15:395–396.

48 **Machiavelli on *rinnovazione:*** Machiavelli, *The Discourses*, Bk. 3, ch. 1.

48 **Jefferson similarly favored "tumult":** Jefferson to Edward Carrington, 16 January 1787, in Boyd, ed., *Jefferson Papers*, 11:49.

48–49 **On Lincoln:** See Ralph Lerner, *Revolutions Revisited: Two Faces of the Politics of Enlightenment* (Chapel Hill: The University Press of North Carolina, 1994), 88–111.

49 **Madison attempted to calm his fellow Virginian:** Madison to Jefferson, 4 February 1790, in Rutland et al., eds., *Madison Papers*, 13:19–20.

49 **"utterly defective":** Elliot, ed., *Debates in the Several State Conventions*, 3:98.

49 **"experiments are of too ticklish a nature . . . multiplied":** Madison, *Federalist* No. 49, 329.

49 **periodic, nonviolent constitutional revision instead of periodic revolution:** Jefferson to Samuel Kercheval, 12 July 1816, in Jefferson, *Writings*, ed. Peterson, 1402.

49 **Jefferson's bold and resilient faith in the future:** See Jefferson to John Adams, 8 April 1816, in Cappon, ed., *Adams-Jefferson Letters*, 2:466.

49–50 **"Our Revolution . . . our former education":** Jefferson to Major John Cartwright, 5 June 1824, in Jefferson, *Writings*, ed. Peterson, 1491. Emphasis added.

50 **"Lightning to Light":** Morris to William Short, 18 September 1790, in Morris, *A Diary of the French Revolution*, ed. Davenport, 1:594.

50 **"My theory . . . gloom of despair":** Jefferson to François de Marbois, 14 June 1817, in Jefferson, *Writings*, ed. Peterson, 1411, emphasis added.

51 **"gradual change of circumstances . . . ruinous innovations":** Jefferson to Samuel Kercheval, 12 July 1816, in Jefferson, *Writings*, ed. Peterson, 1401.

52 **"The dread of innovation . . . spirit of improvement":** Jefferson to John Waldo, 16 August 1813, in Jefferson, *Writings*, ed. Peterson, 1295 and 1299.

52 **"I cannot help fearing . . . progress no farther":** Tocqueville, *De la Démocratie en Amérique* Bk. 2, pt. 3, ch. 21, 2:324.

3. CONFLICT OR CONSENSUS?

53–54 **"a deep conviction . . . public good":** James Madison on the Philadelphia Convention, *The Federalist* (New York: The Modern Library, n.d.), No. 37, 231–232.

54 **some extreme crisis:** See Drew McCoy, *The Last of the Fathers: James Madison and the Republican Legacy* (Cambridge: Cambridge University Press, 1989), 63.

54 **"an invitation to conflict":** Edmund S. Morgan, "Conflict and Consensus in the American Revolution," in *Essays on the American Revolution*, ed. Stephen G. Kurtz and James H. Hutson (Chapel Hill: The University of North Carolina Press for the Institute of Early American History and Culture, 1973), 307.

55 **"one homogeneous mass":** Madison, in Max Farrand, ed., *The Records of the Federal Convention of 1787* (New Haven, Conn.: Yale University Press, 1911), 1:422.

55 **Madison on reason and on factions:** *Federalist* No. 10, 55.

56 **no such "perfect homogeneousness of interests":** Madison, 1833, draft of a letter on majority governments, in *The Mind of the Founder: Sources of the Political Thought of James Madison*, ed. Marvin Meyers (Hanover, N.H.: University Press of New England, 1981), 415.

56 **"the latent causes of faction . . .":** Madison, *Federalist* No. 10, 55.

56–57 **Machiavelli on conflict and tumult:** See Machiavelli, *The Discourses*, Bk. I, ch. 4, 5, 6.

57 **Divisions among a variety of religious groups:** William Miller, *The Business of May Next: James Madison and the Founding* (Charlotte: University Press of Virginia, 1992), 13.

57 **"social and political equilibrium":** Richard K. Matthews, *If Men Were Angels: James Madison and the Heartless Empire of Reason* (Lawrence: University of Kansas Press, 1995), 85.

58 **"the combinations of the majority":** Madison, *Federalist* No. 51, 339.

58 **institutionally split "between different bodies of men . . .":** Madison, quoted in Jonathan Elliot, ed., *Debates in the Several State Conventions*, 5:242.

58 **appearance of political pamphlet:** See Jean-Denis Bredin, *Sieyès: La clé de la Révolution française* (Paris: Editions de Fallois, 1988), 79.

59 **The nation and the Third Estate were one and the same:** Sieyès, Speech of 20–21 July 1789, in *Orateurs de la Révolution française*, ed. François Furet and Ran Halévi (Paris: Gallimard, 1989), 1:1015.

59 **The aristocracy were "enemies" and "traitors":** Emmanuel Sieyès, *Qu'est-ce que le tiers état?*, ed. Roberto Zapperi (Geneva: Droz, 1970), 123, 140.

59 **"war cry"**: Tocqueville, *L'Ancien Régime et la Révolution: Fragments et Notes inédites*, 2:139.

59–60 **Sieyès on the first two orders:** *Qu'est-ce que le tiers état?*, ed. Zapperi, ch. 6, 194; ch. 1, 124; ch. 6, 217–218.

61 **"It is through union and concord . . . slave"**: Representative Maure, quoted by Roland Debbasch, *Le Principe d'unité et d'indivisibilité de la République* (Paris: Economica, 1988), 128.

61 **Sieyès on the unity of the Third Estate:** *Qu'est-ce que le tiers état?*, ed. Zapperi, ch. 6, 198–199 and 208.

61 **"Theoretic politicians . . . their passions"**: Madison, *Federalist* No. 10, 58–59.

62 **General Will not equivalent to will of all, or even majority:** Though Rousseau explicitly wrote that often there can be a great difference between the will of all and the General Will (*Social Contract*, Bk. 2, ch. 3), wanting it both ways, he also stated that "all the characteristics of the General Will" are found in the will of the plurality (Bk. 4. ch. 2).

62 **"always constant, unalterable, and pure"**: Rousseau, *The Social Contract*, Bk. 1, ch. 4.

62 **On the nature of the General Will:** See *The Social Contract*, Bk. 2, ch. 1–4.

63 **a radically original society, geared not to individuals interested in maximizing private interests:** Furet, "Rousseau and the French Revolution," in *The Legacy of Rousseau*, ed. Clifford Orwin and Nathan Tarcov (Chicago: University of Chicago Press, 1997), 181.

64 **"Whoever refuses to obey the general will . . . forced to be free"**: Rousseau, *The Social Contract*, Bk. 1, ch. 7.

64 **Any individual who "exits from the common quality of citizen . . ."**: Sieyès, *Qu'est-ce que le tiers état?*, ed. Zapperi, ch. 6, 211–212.

64 **no legitimate role for dissent:** Sieyès, *Vues sur les moyens d'exécution dont les représentans de la France pourront disposer*, quoted in Introduction, Zapperi, ed. *Qu'est-ce que le tiers état?*, 76.

64 **minority faction has no right to oppose the majority:** See Zapperi, Introduction, *Qu'est-ce que le tiers état?*, 75.

66 **"there is no point in trying to reason with him"**: Sieyès, *Qu'est-ce que le tiers état?*, ed. Zapperi, ch. 5, 189.

66 **"Everyone must forget his own interest . . . through the public good"**: Saint-Just, Speech of 28 January 1793, in Saint-Just, *Oeuvres complètes*, ed. M. Duval (Paris: Lebovici, 1984), 408.

66 **"The social union has as its object . . . freedom of all"**: Sieyès, Speech of 20–21 July 1789, in Furet et al., eds., *Orateurs de la Révolution française*, 1010.

67 **Jefferson on Descartes:** quoted in Conor Cruise O'Brien, *The Long Affair: Thomas Jefferson and the French Revolution, 1785–1800* (Chicago: The University of Chicago Press, 1996), 10.

67 **"My own personal role . . . no doubt"**: Sieyès on reason, *Qu'est-ce que le tiers état?*, ed. Zapperi, ch. 6, 214 and 212.

68 **Bossuet on the unity of France:** Bossuet, *Politique tirée des propres paroles de l'écriture sainte* (Geneva: Droz, 1967), Bk. 2, 54.

68 **"one must conceive the nations of the earth as individuals"**: Sieyès, *Qu'est-ce que le tiers état?*, ed. Zapperi, ch. 5, 183.

69 **exchange between Sieyès and Paine:** Sieyès, text 30, Letter from Thomas Paine to Sieyès, 8 July 1791, and Sieyès's answer, excerpts from *Moniteur*, 16 July 1791, in *Oeuvres de Sieyès*, ed. Marcel Dorigny (Paris: EDHIS, 1989), vol. 2.

69 **"If the horses are of equal strength . . . torn to pieces"**: Benjamin Franklin, quoted by Thomas Paine in "Constitutional Reform," in Thomas Paine, *The Complete Writings of Thomas Paine*, ed. Philip S. Foner, 2 vols. (New York: The Citadel Press, 1945), 2:1006.

71 **"What are the different classes of legislators . . . they determine?"**: Madison, *Federalist* No. 10, 56.

71 **hopes for such a neutral referee were vain:** Madison, Letter of 16 April 1787, in Rutland et al., eds., *Madison Papers*, 9:384.

71 **patience of the French "worn threadbare"**: Jefferson to John Jay, 19 September 1789, in Boyd, ed., *Jefferson Papers*, 15:458.

71 **local governments were overthrown:** See Albert Soboul, *La Révolution française*, 2 vols. (Paris: Idées Gallimard, 1962), 1:159–163.

72 **"The will of one cannot outweigh the General Will of all"**: Sieyès, quoted by Albert Soboul, *La Révolution française*, 1:174.

73 **no need for a balance of powers in a classless republic:** Turgot to Dr. Richard Price, 22 March 1778, in *Life and Writings of Turgot*, ed. W. Walker Stephens (London: Longmans, Green & Co., 1895), 299.

73 **outcome of vote on proposal for a single legislative chamber:** R. R. Palmer, *The Age of Democratic Revolution*, 2 vols. (Princeton, N.J.: Princeton University Press, 1959), 1:497.

73 **Adams on the "blind love" of French revolutionary leaders for "the Constitution of Mr. Franklin":** Adams to Perley, 19 June 1809. Mentioned in Alfred Aldridge, *Franklin and His French Contemporaries* (New York: New York University Press, 1957), 88.

73 **"this question of two chambers is the question of *freedom*"**: Tocqueville, "Draft of speech," in *Ecrits et discours politiques*, ed. André Jardin in *Oeuvres complètes*, ed. J.-P. Mayer (Paris: Gallimard, 1990), 3:206.

74 **"Would to God I believed more in the omnipotence . . . no such thing"**: Tocqueville to Claude-François de Corcelle, 17 September 1853, in Tocqueville, *Selected Letters on Politics and Society*, ed. R. Boesche (Berkeley: University of California Press, 1985), 294.

74 **Condorcet criticizing the American system of checks and balances:** See Patrice Higonnet, *Sister Republics: The Origins of French and American Republicanism* (Cambridge, Mass.: Harvard University Press, 1988), 251.

74 **After winning presidential election in New York City, Jefferson called on President John Adams:** Jefferson to Dr. Benjamin Rush, 16 January 1811, in Jefferson, *Writings*, ed. Peterson, 1237.

75 **Energy, through conflict, . . . returned to government:** Jefferson to John Dickinson, 6 March 1801, in Jefferson, *Writings*, ed. Peterson, 1084.

75 **"as real a revolution in the principles ... form":** Jefferson to Judge Spencer Roane, 6 September 1819, in Jefferson, *Writings*, ed. Peterson, 1425.

75 **evolution of parties shaped far more by events than by design:** Burns, *The Vineyard of Liberty*, 91.

76 **Burke on men acting in concert with one another:** Edmund Burke, *Thoughts on the Cause of the Present Discontents*, in *The Writings and Speeches of the Right Honourable Edmund Burke* (Boston: Little, Brown, Beaconsfield Edition, 1901), 1:529 and 533–534.

76 **"an obstinate adherence to party":** Hamilton, *Federalist* No. 85, 570.

76 **Hamilton on the value of consensus in a young society:** See Gerald Stourzh, *Alexander Hamilton and the Idea of Republican Government* (Stanford, Calif.: Stanford University Press, 1970), 114.

76 **"a division of the republic ... under our Constitution":** John Adams, quoted by Richard Hofstadter, *The Idea of a Party System* (Berkeley: University of California Press, 1969), 2.

76 **"If I could not go to heaven ... there at all":** Jefferson, quoted in James MacGregor Burns, *The Deadlock of Democracy* (Englewood Cliffs, N.J.: Prentice Hall, 1963), 27.

76 **"I was no party man myself ... reconcile them":** Washington to Jefferson, 6 July 1796, in Washington, *Writings*, ed. John Rhodehamel (New York: The Library of America, 1997), 952.

76 **parties "render alien to each other ... affection":** Washington, Farewell Address, in Washington, *Writings*, ed. Rhodehamel, 967.

77 **When a policy of his was challenged ... also constituted a party:** Hofstadter, *The Idea of a Party System*, 91.

77 **Washington and other leaders shaping embryonic political parties:** See Burns, *The Vineyard of Liberty*, 91.

77 **"internal dissensions" were "harrowing our vitals":** Washington to Jefferson, 23 August 1792, and to Hamilton, 26 August 1792, in Washington, *Writings*, ed. Rhodehamel, 817 and 819.

77 **"the baneful effects of the Spirit of Party":** Washington, Farewell Address, in Washington, *Writings*, ed. Rhodehamel, 969.

78 **Ezra Stiles on the news of the execution of the king:** R. R. Palmer, *The Age of the Democratic Revolution* (Princeton, N.J.: Princeton University Press, 1964), 2:540.

78 **On the stated purpose of the Sedition Act:** See Burns, *The Vineyard of Liberty*, 126.

79 **Sedition Act came spectacularly close to the kind of repression practiced by the Jacobins:** See R. R. Palmer, *The Age of Democratic Revolution*, 2:538.

79 **trials "travesties of justice ...":** See Richard Hofstadter, Willam Miller, and Daniel Aaron, *The American Republic* (Englewood Cliffs, N.J.: Prentice Hall, 1959), 331–332.

79 **people could be educated and persuaded to resist "dupery":** Jefferson to Edmund Pendleton, 29 January 1799, in Paul L. Ford, ed., *Writings of Thomas Jefferson* (New York: G. P. Putnam's Sons, 1896), 7:338.

80 **majority rule, as a "fundamental law of nature":** Jefferson to John Breckinridge, 29 January 1800, in Jefferson, *Writings*, ed. Peterson, 1074.

80 **"As there will always be an opposition . . . republicans"**: Jefferson to Elbridge Gerry, 3 March 1804, in Ford, ed., *Writings of Thomas Jefferson*, 8:297.

80 **It should not be a "general prosecution . . ."**: Jefferson to Thomas McKean, 19 February 1803, in Ford, ed., *Writings of Thomas Jefferson*, 8:218–219. See also Leonard Levy, *Legacy of Suppression: Freedom of Speech and Press in Early American History* (Cambridge, Mass.: The Belknap Press of Harvard University Press, 1960), 300.

80 **"sink federalism into an abyss . . . no resurrection for it"**: Thomas Jefferson to the Attorney General, Levi Lincoln, 25 October 1802, in Ford, ed., *Writings of Thomas Jefferson*, 8:176.

80 **"I wish nothing but their eternal hatred"**: Jefferson, quoted in Hofstadter, *The Idea of a Party System*, 165.

80–81 **"from the fangs of *Jefferson?*"**: Alexander Hamilton to Theodore Sedgwick, 4 May 1800, in *The Works of Alexander Hamilton*, ed. Henry Cabot Lodge (New York: Putnam, 1903), 10:371.

81–82 **Hamilton on blocking Jefferson's election:** Letter to John Jay, 7 May 1800, in Lodge, ed., *Works of Alexander Hamilton*, 10:371–373.

82 **Hamilton's ambivalence toward Adams:** Hamilton to Charles Carroll, 1 July 1800, in Lodge, ed., *Works of Alexander Hamilton*, 10:380.

82 **Hamilton's antipathy to Burr:** Hamilton to Oliver Wolcott, 16 December 1800, in Lodge, ed., *Works of Alexander Hamilton*, 10:392.

82 **Hamilton's support of Jefferson over Burr and rejection of any attempt to thwart the election:** Hamilton to Morris, 9 January 1801, in Lodge, ed., *Works of Alexander Hamilton*, 10:407.

82 **"Mr. Jefferson's character . . . violent system"**: Hamilton to Bayard, 16 January 1801, quoted by Hofstadter, *The Idea of a Party System*, 137.

82 **"Nil desperandum . . . abuse of power"**: Gouverneur Morris, *Diary and Letters of Gouverneur Morris*, ed. Anne Cary Morris (New York: Charles Scribner's Sons, 1888), 2:383, 415.

82 **Fisher Ames on being the opposition party:** Fisher Ames, quoted in Hofstadter, *The Idea of a Party System*, 145.

83 **"strange hybrid"**: Burns, *The Deadlock of Democracy*, 46.

84 **David's plans for the Fête de la Réunion:** Jacques-Louis David, Speech of 11 July 1793, *Archives parlementaires*, First Series, 1789–1799, edited in 1875–1877, 68:565.

84 **Billaud-Varenne demanded the punishment of the citizens of Toulouse:** Speech of Billaud-Varenne, 11 July 1793, *Archives parlementaires*, 68:564.

85 **"Trapped by the spirit of harmony . . . resolve their differences"**: Tocqueville, *Fragments et Notes*, 2:133.

85 **"The psychology of purging . . . cohesion"**: R. R. Palmer, *Twelve Who Ruled* (Princeton, N.J.: Princeton University Press, 1973), 324.

86 **"to uncover, thwart, and punish . . . misery of the people"**: Barère, Speech of 19 June 1789, *Archives parlementaires*, First Series, 1789–1799, edited in 1875–1877, 8:136.

86 **"the most fatal conspiracy . . . punish the guilty!"**: Robespierre, Speech of 27 July 1789, *Archives parlementaires*, 8:279.

86 **"Let the people be certain . . . vengeance of the law!"**: Robespierre, Speech of 31 July 1789, *Archives parlementaires*, 8:312–313.

86 Mirabeau tried to be a calming voice of reason: Mirabeau, Speech of 24 June 1789, *Archives parlementaires*, 8:167.

86 "It is necessary for us to know . . . our enemies": Sieyès, "Déclaration volontaire proposée aux patriotes," 17 June 1791, in Dorigny, ed., *Oeuvres de Sieyès*, 2:5.

86 "everything that is opposed . . . is the enemy": Saint-Just, Speech of 19th day of first month of the Year II, in Saint-Just, *Oeuvres complètes*, ed. Duval, 521.

86 "only two parties . . . evil ones": Robespierre, Speech of 26 July 1794 (8 Thermidor Year II), in Charles Vellay, ed., *Discours et Rapports de Robespierre* (Paris: Charpentier et Fasquelle, 1908), 391.

87–88 Woloch on political clubs: Isser Woloch, *Jacobin Legacy, The Democratic Movement Under the Directory* (Princeton, N.J.: Princeton University Press, 1970), 4–8.

88 Factions "create the most fearsome public enemies": Sieyès, *Qu'est-ce que le tiers état?*, ed. Zapperi, ch. 6, 206.

88 "No one knows better . . . all factions": Mirabeau, Speech of 2 October 1790 about the October Days 1789, in François Furet et al., eds., *Orateurs de la Révolution française*, 787.

88 "I abhor . . . factious men": Robespierre, 14 July 1791, quoted by Debbasch, *Le Principe révolutionnaire*, 109.

88 "We will not permit . . . Republic": Garnier, Meeting of Jacobin Club, 16 Germinal Year II, quoted in Raoul Girardet, *Mythes et mythologies politiques* (Paris: Seuil, 1986), 147.

88 "Factions are a *malady* . . .": Morisson, Speech of 13 November 1792, in Michael Walzer, ed., *Regicide and Revolution: Speeches at the Trial of Louis XVI*, trans. Marian Rothstein (Cambridge: Cambridge University Press, 1974), 119, emphasis added.

88 "factions are the most terrible *poison*": Saint-Just, Speech of 9 Thermidor Year II (27 July 1794), in Saint-Just, *Oeuvres complètes*, ed. Duval, 911, emphasis added.

88 "You must absorb . . . define its path": Danton, Speech of 29 October 1792, in H. Morse Stephens, ed., *The Principal Speeches of the Statesmen and Orators of the French Revolution*, 2 vols. (Oxford: Clarendon Press, 1892), 2:180 and 181.

89 People like Mirabeau who advocated federalism . . . Parisian populace: John Dalberg-Acton, *Lectures on the French Revolution*, ed. Figgis, 37.

89 "Some day one state . . . against another": Saint-Just, Speech of 15 May 1793, in Saint-Just, *Oeuvres complètes*, ed. Duval, 444.

89 Girondins also proclaimed fidelity to god of unity: Debbasch, *Le Principe révolutionnaire*, 236.

90 Michelet on the trial of the Girondins: Jules Michelet, *Histoire de la Révolution française*, 2 vols. (Paris: Gallimard, 1952), Bk. 13, ch. 9, 2:614.

90 Reactions of the Girondins to the verdict: Alphonse de Lamartine, *Histoire des Girondins*, ed. J.-P. Jacques (Paris: Plon, 1984), 2:529.

90 The improbable argument was made . . . elected officials: Debbasch, *Le Principe révolutionnaire*, 238–239.

90 "Let us examine . . . wherever they may be": Marat, quoted by Debbasch, *Le Principe révolutionnaire*, 235.

90 "at a time when freedom . . . accusations have been made": Biroteau, quoted by Debbasch, *Le Principe révolutionnaire*, 235.

90 **A few lone, defensive voices:** Cambon and Barère, quoted in Michelet, *Histoire de la Révolution française*, Bk. 10, ch. 11, 2:380.

91 **"what constitutes a republic . . . opposition to it":** Saint-Just, Rapport du Comité de Salut Public, 8 Ventôse Year II, in Saint-Just, *Oeuvres complètes*, ed. Duval, 700.

91 **"vomit out":** Desmoulins, quoted by Debbasch, *Le Principe révolutionnaire*, 238.

91 **he woefully regretted his incendiary words:** Michelet, *Histoire de la Révolution française*, Bk. 13, ch. 9, 2:617.

92 **estimates of people executed during the Terror:** Marc Bouloiseau, *La République jacobine* (Paris: Seuil, 1972), 233, 235.

92 **Robespierre demanded that the Tribunal be unhampered:** Robespierre, Speech of 25 August 1793, in Vellay, ed., *Discours et Rapports de Robespierre*, 320–321.

92 **"There can be no prosperity . . . except the guillotine":** Saint-Just, Rapport fait au nom du comité de salut public, 19th day of the first month of the Year II, in Saint-Just, *Oeuvres complètes*, ed. Duval, 521.

93 **"unmask the charlatans . . . hearts and minds":** Barère, 2 Germinal Year II, quoted by Debbasch, *Le Principe révolutionnaire*, 286.

93 **"I would rather let 25 million . . . indivisible Republic":** Hydens, quoted by Debbasch, *Le Principe révolutionnaire*, 203.

93 **"far from claiming . . . foreign intrigue has triumphed!":** Robespierre, Speech of 8 Thermidor Year II, in Vellay, ed., *Discours et Rapports*, 418–419.

93 **France's enemies established within France a rival government:** Robespierre, Speech of 25 December 1793, in Vellay, ed., *Discours et Rapports*, 317–318.

93 **"This conspiracy owes . . . decimate all factions!":** Robespierre, Speech of 8 Thermidor Year II (26 July 1794), in Vellay, ed., *Discours et Rapports*, emphasis added.

95 **Furet points out . . . reached its apogee:** François Furet, "Terror," in François Furet and Mona Ozouf, eds., *A Critical Dictionary of the French Revolution*, trans. Arthur Goldhammer (Cambridge, Mass.: The Belknap Press of Harvard University Press, 1989), 143.

96 **no political trials ending in a death sentence in revolutionary America:** Patrice Higonnet, "Le Sens de la terreur dans la Révolution française," *Commentaire*, 35 (1986), 439.

96 **"can tolerate opponents . . . own existence":** R. R. Palmer, *The Age of Democratic Revolution*, 2:522.

96 **"right of organized opposition to those who govern":** See Robert A. Dahl, ed., "Preface," *Political Oppositions in Western Democracies* (New Haven, Conn.: Yale University Press, 1966), xviii.

96 **The distinction between democracy and dictatorship:** E. E. Schattschneider, *Party Government* (New York: Farrar and Rinehart, 1942), 1.

96 **"constitutional consensus":** Hofstadter, *The Idea of a Party System*, 4.

96 **Rosanvallon on "democratic consensus":** Pierre Rosanvallon, in Furet, Rosanvallon, Julliard, eds., *La République du centre* (Paris: Calmann-Levy, 1988), 168–169.

97 **"agglomeration of hostile individuals . . . benefit":** Gordon Wood, *The Creation of the American Republic* (Chapel Hill: University of North Carolina Press for the Institute of Early American History and Culture, 1969), 607.

97 **"Madison cannot envision . . . three individuals . . . but no community":** Matthews, *If Men Were Angels*, 67–68 and 278.

97 **Hartz on "peculiar sense of community" in Madison's America:** Louis Hartz, *The Liberal Tradition in America: An Interpretation of American Political Thought Since the Revolution* (New York: Harcourt, Brace & World, 1955), 55.

98 **unusually rich, diversified, and inclusive political community . . . national community:** Burns, *The Deadlock of Democracy,* 22.

99 **Tocqueville on citizens' engagement in their community:** Tocqueville, *De la Démocratie en Amérique,* vol. 1, pt. 2, ch. 6, 1:338–339.

99 **"Freedom of association . . . strengthens the polity":** Tocqueville, *De la Démocratie en Amérique,* vol. 2, pt. 2, ch. 7, 2:150.

99 **"Without this mutual disposition . . . not a society":** Jefferson to John Dickinson, 23 July 1801, in Ford, ed., *Writings of Thomas Jefferson,* 8:76.

99 **"The happiness of society . . . amalgamated":** Jefferson to William Claiborne, 23 July 1801, in Ford, ed., *Writings of Thomas Jefferson,* 8:72.

99 **"The greatest good . . . shade of his own":** Jefferson to John Dickinson, 23 July 1801, in Ford, ed., *Writings of Thomas Jefferson,* 8:77.

99–100 **Jefferson on the "ward republic":** Jefferson to Kercheval, 12 July 1816, in Jefferson, *Writings,* ed. Peterson, 1399.

100 **The Alien and Sedition Acts as well as Jefferson's forays into suppression of criticism:** See Levy, *Legacy of Suppression,* 297ff.

4. REVOLUTIONARY TALK, REVOLUTIONARY STAGE

102 **"When I hear another . . . especially on politics":** Jefferson to Thomas Jefferson Randolph, 24 November 1808, in Jefferson, *Writings,* ed. Peterson, 1195–1196.

102 **"Be courteous to all . . . your confidence":** Washington to Bushrod Washington, 15 January 1783, in Washington, *Writings,* ed. Rhodehamel, 483.

102–3 **Washington's most distinctive characteristic . . . excitable disposition:** Jefferson to Dr. Walter Jones, 2 January 1814, in Ford, ed., *Writings of Thomas Jefferson,* 9:448.

103 **"Never to speak ill of any body":** John Adams, *Diary of John Adams,* in L. H. Butterfield, ed., *Diary and Autobiography of John Adams* (Cambridge, Mass.: The Belknap Press of Harvard University Press, 1961), 1771–1781, 2:72.

103 **In old age . . . "humble and mortify him":** Adams, *Diary and Autobiography,* 3:336.

103 **"eternal taciturnity":** Adams, quoted in Joseph J. Ellis, *Passionate Sage: The Character and Legacy of John Adams* (New York: W. W. Norton, 1993), 64.

103 **"If I do not subscribe . . . ingenuity":** Jefferson, "Opinion on the Treaties with France," 1793, in Boyd, ed., *Jefferson Papers,* 25:608.

104 **"the vigorous accent of freedom and equality":** Barère, Speech of 8 Pluviôse 1794, in Stephens, ed. *Principal Speeches of the Statesmen and Orators of the French Revolution,* 2:40–50.

105–7 **Philadelphia Convention:** Pinckney, 11 August 1787, in Farrand, ed., *Records of the Federal Convention,* 2:263; Morris, 23 August 1787, 2:391; Morris, 9 August 1787, 2:237; Hamilton, 18 June 1787, 1:288; Williamson, 12 September 1787, 2:585; Franklin, 17 September 1787, 2:642–643, emphasis added.

107 In his *Autobiography* . . . provocation and opposition: Benjamin Franklin, *The Autobiography of Benjamin Franklin*, ed. Leonard W. Labaree, Ralph L. Ketcham, Helen Boatfield, and Helene Fineman (New Haven, Conn.: Yale University Press, 1964), 65–66.

107 Gouverneur Morris admitted . . . "go with the stream": Morris, 17 September 1787, and Mercer, 7 August 1787, in Farrand, ed., *Records of the Federal Convention*, 2:645 and 2:212.

107–8 "If, then, gentlemen, . . .'; "perilous" and "destructive": Patrick Henry, quoted in Elliot, ed., *Debates in the Several State Conventions*, 3:50.

108 "only the rational and enlightened part": Gordon S. Wood, "The Democratization of Mind in the American Revolution," in *Leadership in the American Revolution*, 67.

108 "sooner chop off his right hand": Mason, 31 August 1787, in Farrand, ed., *Records of the Federal Convention*, 2:479.

108 Mr. King commented that . . . "on the score of passion": King, 30 June 1787, in Farrand, ed., *Records of the Federal Convention*, 1:493, emphasis added.

108 "suspicion is a virtue . . . that jewel": Patrick Henry, quoted in Elliot, ed., *Debates in the Several State Conventions*, 3:45, emphasis added.

108–9 "I confess that a certain degree . . . *disturb a community*": Governor Randolph, quoted in Elliot, ed., *Debates in the Several State Conventions*, 3:70, emphasis added.

109 "you can run no hazard . . . proceedings of its citizens": Washington to Morris, 22 December 1795, in Washington, *Writings*, ed. Rhodehamel, 928.

109 "I did not believe until lately . . . common pick-pocket": Washington to Jefferson, 6 July 1796, in Washington, *Writings*, ed. Rhodehamel, 952.

109–10 Federalists branded Republicans "atheists" and "tyrants": Andrew W. Robertson, *The Language of Democracy: Political Rhetoric in the United States and Britain, 1790–1900* (Ithaca, N.Y.: Cornell University Press, 1995), 34.

110 Callender's attacks on Washington and Adams: Michael Durey, *"With the Hammer of Truth": James Thomson Callender and America's Early National Heroes* (Charlottesville: University Press of Virginia, 1990), 72 and 181.

110 Hofstadter on paranoid beliefs about conspiracies: Richard Hofstadter, *The Paranoid Style in American Politics* (New York: Alfred A. Knopf, 1965), 39.

110 Federalists were not willing to block Jefferson's ascension to the presidency: Hofstadter, *The Idea of a Party System*, 138–139.

110 "It is a fact that he is . . . self command": Hamilton quoted in Ellis, *Passionate Sage: The Character and Legacy of John Adams*, 22.

111 "act of political suicide": Ellis, *Passionate Sage: The Character and Legacy of John Adams*, 23.

111 Madison on Addison: See Ralph Ketcham, *James Madison: A Biography* (Charlottesville: University Press of Virginia, 1990), 40–41.

111 "Who can love the fatherland coldly?": Robespierre, Speech of 5 Nivôse Year II, quoted in Vellay, ed., *Discours et Rapports*, 315.

111 People were not permitted . . . wanted to express: Tocqueville, *Fragments et Notes*, 2:81.

111 **"The French people are two thousand years ... a different species"**: Robespierre, Speech of 18 Floréal Year II, in Vellay, ed., *Discours et Rapports*, 350.

111 **"The French are the first people ... a true democracy"**: Robespierre, Speech of 18 Pluviôse Year II, in Vellay, ed., *Discours et Rapports*, 328.

112 **Michelet on Marat**: Michelet, *Histoire de la Révolution française*, 1:517.

112 **a member had once proposed a rule ... four members speaking at once**: Romilly, quoted in Stephens, ed., *Principal Speeches*, 1:15.

112 **Tocqueville on the language of male frankness in the old French Parliament**: Tocqueville, *Fragments et Notes*, 2:56–57.

112 **But what happens, Tocqueville asked, ... but a revolution**: Tocqueville, *Fragments et Notes*, 2:80.

112–13 **"We do not need to protect ... weakness"**: Robespierre, Rapport de 18 Pluviôse Year II, in Vellay, ed., *Discours et Rapports*, 329.

113 **"show a *firm*, patriotic ... character"**: Robespierre, Speech of 27 April 1792, in Vellay, ed., *Discours et Rapports*, 173.

113 **"Do not for a second hesitate ... cadaver"**: Robespierre, Speech of 5 Nivôse Year II, in Vellay, ed., *Discours et Rapports*, 314.

113 **"The most perilous shoal ... own courage"**: Robespierre, Speech of 18 Pluviôse Year II, in Vellay, ed., *Discours et Rapports*, 329.

113 **"The cause of our ills ... idiotic confidence"**: Robespierre, Address to the French, summer 1791, in Robespierre, *Ecrits*, ed. Claude Mazauric (Messidor/Editions Sociales, 1989), 135.

113 **"We must be prepared ... terrifying punishments"**: Danton, Speech of 6 Frimaire Year II, in Stephens, ed., *Principal Speeches of the Statesmen and Orators of the French Revolution*, 2:267–269.

113 **"Crime has a softer voice ... truth"**: Saint-Just, Fragments d'un manuscrit, in Saint-Just, *Oeuvres complètes*, ed. Duval, 451.

113 **"recourse of despair"**: Mirabeau, Speech of 15 June 1789, in Stephens, ed., *Principal Speeches*, 1:62.

113–14 **a chastened Danton tried to defend ... no longer necessary**: Danton, Speech of 14 Pluviôse 1794, in Stephens, ed., *Principal Speeches*, 2:280.

114 **"a want of *firmness*"; "*strong* and *manly* features"**: *Gazette of the United States*, 24 September 1796, quoted in Robertson, *The Language of Democracy*, 30–31, emphasis added.

114 **"*Christian* Sparta"**: Samuel Adams, quoted in Gordon Wood, *The Creation of the American Republic* (Chapel Hill: University of North Carolina Press for the Institute of Early American History and Culture, 1969), 118.

115 **"We invoke forms ... we lack *energy*"**: Robespierre, Speech of 3 December 1792, in Walzer, ed., *Regicide and Revolution: Speeches at the Trial of Louis XVI*, 133, emphasis added.

115 **"fear that later they will suffer ... that *soaring vigor* of which we have such need"**: Saint-Just, Speech of 13 November 1792, in Walzer, ed., *Regicide and Revolution*, 122, emphasis added.

115–16 **"A people does not judge ... justice of courts"**: Robespierre, Speech of 3 December 1792, in Walzer, ed., *Regicide and Revolution*, 133, emphasis added.

115 **"Some day men will be astonished . . . Brutus had over Caesar"**: Saint-Just, Speech of 13 November 1792, in Walzer, ed., *Regicide and Revolution*, 122 and 126, emphasis added.

115 **Marat . . . shouted out . . . botched:** David P. Jordan, *The King's Trial* (Berkeley: University of California Press, 1979), 197.

115 **"treason, wickedness, and perfidy"**: Marat, Speech of 27 December 1792, in Walzer, ed., *Regicide and Revolution*, 166.

115 **"less to persuade you . . . corrupt your *energy*"**: Saint-Just, Speech of 27 December 1792, in Walzer, ed., *Regicide and Revolution*, 168, emphasis added.

116 **"What scruple . . . *zeal*?"**: Robespierre, Speech of 28 December 1792, in Walzer, ed., *Regicide and Revolution*, 179, emphasis added.

116 **"the false veil of politeness"**: Rousseau, *Discourse on the Sciences and Arts* (1750), in Rousseau, *The First and Second Discourses*, ed. Roger D. Masters (New York: St. Martin's Press, 1964), 38.

116 **"the plain and emotive effusions . . . insecure demonstrations of politeness"**: Rousseau, *La Nouvelle Héloïse* (Paris: Garnier, 1960), pt. 2, Letter 14, 207.

116 **self-mastery and self-repression in Rousseau:** See Rousseau, *The Social Contract*, Bk. 2, ch. 4.

116 **"Let us be bold . . . bold forever!"**: Danton, Speech of 2 September 1792, in Stephens, ed., *Principal Speeches*, 2:170.

117 **"the language of Republicans . . . frankness"**: Abbé Grégoire, quoted in Peter France, "'L'éloquence revolutionnaire," *Saggi e richerche*, 1985, 54.

117 **Danton's ad hominem attacks:** Speech of 29 October 1792, in Stephens, ed., *Principal Speeches*, 2:179, emphasis added; Danton, Speech of 21 January 1793, 2:184–185; Danton, Speech of 14 June 1793, 2:244.

117 **Lasource also claimed that *frankness* . . . feelings about Danton:** Lasource, intervention in Danton's speech of 1 April 1793, in Stephens, ed., *Principal Speeches*, 2:214, emphasis added.

117 **Unable to find a book of rules for Mirabeau . . . prevailed in the Assembly:** *Memoirs of Sir Samuel Romilly, written by himself,* 1840, quoted in Introduction, Stephens, ed., *Principal Speeches*, 1:15.

117 **"I don't like this new science . . . legislative assemblies"**: Robespierre, Speech of 16 May 1791, in Vellay, ed., *Discours et Rapports*, 48, emphasis added.

118 **"To punish the oppressors . . . barbarity"**: Robespierre, Speech of 18 Pluviôse Year II, in Vellay, ed., *Discours et Rapports*, 335.

118 **"Immorality is the foundation . . . reign of crime to that of justice"**: Robespierre, Speech of 18 Floréal Year II, in Vellay, ed., *Discours et Rapports*, 354.

118 **"Our aim is to create . . . it is virtue"**: Saint-Just, Speech of 8 Ventôse Year II, in Saint-Just, *Oeuvres complètes*, ed. Duval, 702–703.

118 **"He who does not pursue crime . . . virtue"**: Robespierre, Speech 18 Pluviôse Year II, in Vellay, ed., *Discours et Rapports*, 333.

118 **"Amnesty for perfidious deputies . . . *virtue*"**: Robespierre, final speech, 8 Thermidor Year II, in Vellay, ed., *Discours et Rapports*, 424.

118 **"The Revolution is the despotism of liberty against tyranny"**: Robespierre, Speech of 18 Pluviôse Year II, in Vellay, ed., *Discours et Rapports*, 333.

119 **"What is generosity... human species in general?"**: Rousseau, *Second Discourse on the Origins of Inequality,* Preface.

119 **"this tender, imperious... holy love for humanity"**: Robespierre, Speech of 8 Thermidor 1794, in Vellay, ed., *Discours et Rapports,* 396.

119 **"la Fête du Malheur"**: Robespierre, Speech of 18 Floréal Year II, in Vellay, ed., *Discours et Rapports,* 373.

119 **"pity for the wicked is a great cruelty toward men"**: Rousseau, quoted by Carol Blum, *Rousseau and the Republic of Virtue* (Ithaca, N.Y.: Cornell University Press, 1986), 178.

119 **"stir up pity... corrupt us"**: Saint-Just, Speech of 13 November 1792, in Walzer, ed., *Regicide and Revolution,* 127.

119 **pity has a "vested interest in... the weak"**: Hannah Arendt, *On Revolution* (New York: The Viking Press, 1974), 84.

120 **"Terror without virtue... is impotent"**: Robespierre, Speech of 18 Pluviôse Year II, in Vellay, ed., *Discours et Rapports,* 332.

120 **Montesquieu on limits of virtue:** Montesquieu, *De l'esprit des lois,* Bk. 11, ch 4.

121 **Condorcet on Jacobins' inability "to combine words"**: See Carol Blum, *Rousseau and the Republic of Virtue,* 234–235.

121 **"masterstroke"**: Patrice Gueniffey, "Robespierre," in Furet et al., eds., *A Critical Dictionary of the French Revolution,* 302.

121 **Robespierre himself had marveled... nothing but words:** Robespierre, Speech of 11 August 1791, in Vellay, ed., *Discours et Rapports,* 91.

122 **"How few of the human race... children"**: John Adams, quoted by Douglass Adair, in "Fame and the Founding Fathers," in *Fame and the Founding Fathers: Essays by Douglass Adair,* ed. Trevor Colbourn (New York: W. W. Norton, 1974), 21.

122 **Machiavelli on men who deserve the praise of historians:** Machiavelli, *The Discourses,* Bk. 1, ch. 10.

122 **"The love of honest and well-earned fame"... public pursuits:** James Wilson, quoted in Garry Wills, *Cincinnatus: George Washington and the Enlightenment* (Garden City, N.Y.: Doubleday, 1984), 129.

123 **"a well-regulated republic... public good"**: Machiavelli, *The Discourses,* Bk. 3, ch. 28.

123 **"Mr. Burr has never appeared... good men will approve"**: Alexander Hamilton, quoted in Wills, *Cincinnatus,* 128.

123 **a "golden concern" for public service:** Adair, "Fame and the Founding Fathers," 24.

124 **"I cannot boast... *Appearance* of it"**: Franklin, *The Autobiography of Benjamin Franklin,* ed. Labaree et al., 159, Franklin's emphasis.

124 **Franklin working at night in his printing shop:** Franklin, *The Autobiography of Benjamin Franklin,* ed. Labaree et al., 119 and 125.

124 **"First impressions are generally the most lasting"**: Washington to George Steptoe Washington, 23 March 1789, in Washington, *Writings,* ed. Rhodehamel, 720.

124 **"in the *eyes of judicious men*"**: Washington to George Steptoe Washington, 23 March 1789, in Washington, *Writings,* ed. Rhodehamel, 721, emphasis added.

124 **"the esteem of the deserving"**: Hamilton, quoted by Wills, *Cincinnatus,* 102.

125 **"Whenever you are to do a thing . . . act accordingly":** Jefferson to Peter Carr, 19 August 1785, in Jefferson, *Writings*, ed. Peterson, 815.

125–26 **"When I recollect that at 14. years of age . . . nearly equivalent to the real virtue":** Jefferson to Thomas Jefferson Randolph, 24 November 1808, in Jefferson, *Writings*, Peterson, ed., 1194–1195, emphasis added.

127 a **"virtuoso of resignations":** On Washington ready to relinquish power, see Wills, *Cincinnatus*, 23 and 3.

127 **"When you Sit down . . . if you Esteem your own Reputation":** Washington, "Rules of Civility & Decent Behavior in Company and Conversation," copied from Francis Hawkins's *Youths Behavior* (1646), a translation of a 1595 Jesuit treatise, "Bienséance de la Conversation entre les Hommes," in Washington, *Writings*, ed. Rhodehamel, 3–10.

127 **"Infallibility not being . . . conduct of one another":** Washington, Draft of Farewell Address, in Washington, *Writings*, ed. Rhodehamel, 947.

127–28 **He instructed his young nephews that . . . "render service to [his] country":** Washington to George Steptoe Washington, 5 December 1790, in W. C. Ford, ed., *The Writings of George Washington* (New York: G. P. Putnam's Sons, 1891), 11:509–510.

128 **Washington and the Purple Heart:** Wills, *Cincinnatus*, 198.

128 **"Gentlemen, I am sorry . . . handwriting of another person":** William Pierce, quoted in Wills, *Cincinnatus*, 107.

128 **"But if, on the contrary, . . . friend and Uncle":** Washington to George Steptoe Washington, 23 March 1789, in Washington, *Writings*, ed. Rhodehamel, 722.

129 **"And shall I arrogantly pronounce . . . nefarious design?":** Washington, Draft of First Inaugural, in Washington, *Writings*, ed. Rhodehamel, 707.

129 **"His error does me no injury . . . one opinion?":** Jefferson to Thomas Jefferson Randolph, 24 November 1808, in Jefferson, *Writings*, ed. Peterson, 1195.

129 **"I would have dared him . . . held against me?":** Napoleon, quoted in J. Christopher Herold, *The Age of Napoleon* (Boston: Houghton Mifflin, 1963), 123.

130 **"I will state frankly . . . good I might have done":** Robespierre, Speech of 27 April 1792, in Vellay, ed., *Discours et Rapports*, 161ff.

130 **Despising "false modesty . . . all affectation":** Saint-Just, Speech of 26 Germinal Year II, in Saint-Just, *Oeuvres complètes*, ed. Duval, 809.

130 **"I need to pour out my heart"; "hear the truth":** Robespierre, Speech of 8 Thermidor Year II, in Vellay, ed., *Discours et Rapports*, 384.

130 **"sublime and tender" feelings:** Robespierre, Speech of 27 April 1792, in Vellay, ed., *Discours et Rapports*, 161–163.

130 **"neither a courtier . . . of the people myself":** Robespierre, Speech of 27 April 1792, in Vellay, ed., *Discours et Rapports*, 167.

130 **"I shall never place . . . may desire":** Saint-Just, Speech of 13 November 1792, in Walzer, ed., *Regicide and Revolution*, 126.

131 **"by bonds far stronger . . . invented by laws":** Robespierre, Speech of 27 April 1792, in Vellay, ed., *Discours et Rapports*, 163.

131 **"I have never taken . . . than that of *truth*":** Saint-Just, Speech of 9 Thermidor Year II, in Saint-Just, *Oeuvres complètes*, ed. Duval, 916.

131 "I accuse all those . . . unmask": Robespierre, Speech of 8 Thermidor Year II, in Vellay, ed., *Discours et Rapports*, 392 note.

131 Every citizen and politician came under suspicion . . . only Robespierre knew the truth: See Patrice Gueniffey, "Robespierre," in Furet et al., *A Critical Dictionary of the French Revolution*, 302.

133 "Perhaps Heaven is calling me . . . glorious destiny": Robespierre, Speech of 27 April 1792, in Vellay, ed., *Discours et Rapports*, 170.

133 "Great men do not die in their beds": Saint-Just, "Fragments d'institutions républicaines," in Saint-Just, *Oeuvres complètes*, ed. Duval, 966.

134 "The day when I will become . . . I will stab myself": Saint-Just, "Fragments d'institutions républicaines," ch. 2, "De la société," in Saint-Just, *Oeuvres complètes*, ed. Duval, 977.

134 "Certainly, I would be leaving . . . mute witness of evil": Saint-Just, Speech of 9 Thermidor Year II, in Saint-Just, *Oeuvres complètes*, ed. Duval, 908.

134 "If Brutus does not kill others . . . kill himself": Saint-Just, Letter to Daubigny, 25 July 1792, in Saint-Just, *Oeuvres complètes*, ed. Duval, 364.

134 Carol Blum on Jacobins' rage redirected against themselves: See Blum, *Rousseau and the Republic of Virtue*, 167 and 248.

134 "I, who do not in the least believe . . . we await your blows": Robespierre, quoted by Blum, *Rousseau and the Republic of Virtue*, 248.

134 "Let us rejoice . . . tyranny's daggers": Robespierre, quoted by Blum, *Rousseau and the Republic of Virtue*, 249.

134 "the grave and immortality": Robespierre, Speech of 8 Thermidor Year II, in Vellay, ed., *Discours et Rapports*, 397.

134 "For my part, I consent . . . not to govern": Robespierre, Speech of 26 July 1794, in Vellay, ed., *Discours et Rapports*, 424 and 427.

135 "The good and the bad . . . immortality": Robespierre, Speech of 26 July 1794, in Vellay, ed., *Discours et Rapports*, 425.

135 "honorable whispers"; "shameful applause": Robespierre, Speech of 27 April 1792, in Vellay, ed., *Discours et Rapports*, 163.

135 "Yes, there is another [sacrifice] . . . tear it to shreds": Robespierre, Speech of 27 April 1792, in Vellay, ed., *Discours et Rapports*, 170.

135 "I wanted my reputation . . . country": Robespierre, Speech of 27 April 1792, in Vellay, ed., *Discours et Rapports*, 170.

135 "O sublime people! . . . die for your happiness!": Robespierre, Speech of 7 May 1794, in Vellay, ed., *Discours et Rapports*, 351.

135 leave "to posterity a spotless name . . . imitate": Robespierre, Speech, summer 1791, in *Ecrits*, ed. Mazauric, 124–125.

136 "the Temple of Emptiness": Mona Ozouf, "Le Panthéon," in *Lieux de mémoire*, vol. 1, *La République*, ed. Pierre Nora (Paris: Gallimard, 1984), 141.

136 "It is ordained . . . cannot be free": Edmund Burke, "Letter to a Member of the National Assembly" (1791) in his *Further Reflections on the Revolution in France*, ed. Daniel Ritchie (Indianapolis: Liberty Fund, 1992), 69.

5. DECLARING—AND DENYING—RIGHTS

137 **"A bill of rights . . . no just government should refuse":** Jefferson to Madison, 20 December 1787, in Jefferson, *Writings*, ed. Peterson, 915–916.

137 **"What think you of a Declaration of Rights? . . .":** Adams to Jefferson, 10 November 1787, in Cappon, ed., *Adams-Jefferson Letters*, 1:210.

138 **federalists rebuffed demands of Gerry and Mason for a charter of rights:** Ketcham, *James Madison*, 226.

138–39 **a frustrated and disappointed Gerry announced that he would "withhold his name":** *The Complete Bill of Rights: The Drafts, Debates, Sources, and Origins*, ed. Neil Cogan (New York: Oxford University Press, 1997), 101 and 548–549.

139 **Mason left . . . "in an exceeding ill humour indeed":** Madison to Jefferson, 24 October and 1 November 1787, in *The Republic of Letters: The Correspondence Between Thomas Jefferson and James Madison, 1776–1826*, 3 vols., ed. James Morton Smith (New York: W. W. Norton, 1995), 1:503.

139 **On Magna Carta and bill of rights of 1689:** See Gordon Wood, "The Origins of the American Bill of Rights," *The Tocqueville Review*, 1993, 4, 1, 33–47.

139 **"Were I in America . . . annexed to it":** Jefferson to William S. Smith, 2 February 1788, in Boyd, ed., *Jefferson Papers*, 12:558.

139 **Exceptionally talented men . . . overbearing Northern interests:** Bernard Schwartz, *The Great Rights of Mankind: A History of the American Bill of Rights* (Oxford: Oxford University Press, 1977), 106.

140 **"Living in splendor . . . friend of our happiness":** Patrick Henry, Speech of 9 June 1788, in Elliot, ed., *Debates in the Several State Conventions*, 3:314.

140 **Washington maintained that a federal bill of rights . . . bills of the states:** George Washington to Lafayette, 28 April 1788, in Washington, *Writings*, ed. Rhodehamel, 678–679.

140 **"if federal law is to be supreme . . . no security":** Mason, quoted by Schwartz, *The Great Rights of Mankind*, 106.

140 **"our lives, our property, . . . our public faith":** Mr. Holmes, 30 January 1788, Mr. Tredwell, 1 July 1788, in Elliot, ed., *Debates in the Several State Conventions*, 2:109, 111, and 401.

140–41 **While the prosperous seaboard cities . . . the small inland towns:** James MacGregor Burns and Stewart Burns, *A People's Charter: The Pursuit of Rights in America* (New York: Alfred A. Knopf, 1991), 50; Ketcham, *James Madison*, 235–236.

141 **"always been in favor"; "material defect":** Madison to Jefferson, 17 October 1788, in Boyd, ed., *Jefferson Papers*, 14:16–21.

141 **"half a loaf . . . permanent, affecting and irreparable":** Jefferson to Madison, 15 March 1789, in Boyd, ed., *Jefferson Papers*, 14:660–661.

141 **Some historians attribute . . . his campaign promise:** Robert Allen Rutland, *The Ordeal of the Constitution* (Norman: University of Oklahoma Press, 1966), 297.

141–42 **"The constants and continuities . . . ratification":** Jack Rakove, "James Madison and the Bill of Rights: A Broader Context," *Presidential Studies Quarterly*, 22, 676.

142 **Madison championed a bill of rights . . . check over the legislature:** Madison, Speech of 8 June 1789, mentioned in Rakove, "James Madison and the Bill of Rights," 675.

142 **As for the federalists' objection . . . inferior status:** Rakove, "James Madison and the Bill of Rights," 676.

142 **"A few *milk-and-water* amendments"; "diet drink":** Fisher Ames to George R. Minot, 12 June 1789; Pierce Butler to James Iredell, 11 August 1789, in Cogan, ed., *The Complete Bill of Rights,* 82.

142 **Again and again, Madison tried to raise the question of a bill of rights:** Edward Dumbauld, *The Bill of Rights* (Norman: University of Oklahoma Press, 1957), 35–36.

142 **"Without revenue the wheels of government . . . postpone":** George Clymer to Richard Peters, 8 June 1789, in Cogan, ed., *The Complete Bill of Rights,* 80.

142 **Others asked for a year's moratorium:** James Jackson of Georgia; see Irving Brant, *The Bill of Rights: Its Origin and Meaning* (Indianapolis: Bobbs-Merrill, 1965), 42.

142 **Even antifederalists had lost their enthusiasm for a bill of rights:** Jack Rakove, *Original Meanings* (New York: Alfred A. Knopf, 1996), 330.

142 **"They will meliorate . . . indispensable liberty":** Tench Coxe to James Madison, 18 June 1789, in Cogan, ed., *The Complete Bill of Rights,* 82.

142–43 **In March 1789 he began sifting . . . not sufficiently protected:** Burns and Burns, *A People's Charter,* 56–57. See also Madison, Speech of 8 June 1789, in *The Mind of the Founder: Sources of the Political Thought of James Madison,* ed. Marvin Meyers (Hanover, N.H.: University Press of New England, 1981), 161.

143 **"We have . . . nothing to lose":** Madison, Speech of 8 June 1789, in *The Mind of the Founder,* ed. Meyers, 163.

143 **"All the world . . . bill of rights":** Jefferson to James Currie, 20 December 1788, in Boyd, ed., *Jefferson Papers,* 14:366.

143 **Jefferson seemed to be everywhere . . . trial by jury:** Jefferson to Madison, 18 November 1788, in Boyd, ed., *Jefferson Papers,* 14:188; Jefferson to James Currie, 20 December 1788, ibid., 14:366.

143 **chiding Americans . . . give up so soon on a bill of rights:** Gordon Wood, "The Origins of the American Bill of Rights," 41.

143 **trying to galvanize a stalled James Madison . . . draft of a bill of rights for France:** Jefferson to Madison, 12 January 1789, in Boyd, ed., *Jefferson Papers,* 14:436.

143 **"merely as a canvas . . . to work on":** Jefferson to Rabaut de Saint-Etienne, 3 June 1789, in Boyd, ed., *Jefferson Papers,* 15:166–167.

143–44 **Americans were awakened by the French passion for rights . . . October 1789:** David Brion Davis, *Revolutions: Reflections on American Equality and Foreign Liberations* (Cambridge, Mass.: Harvard University Press, 1990), 30.

144 **"community of ideas":** R. R. Palmer, *The Age of Democratic Revolution,* 1:487.

144 **"energy of the American declarations":** Robespierre, quoted by Marcel Gauchet, *La Révolution des Droits de l'homme* (Paris: Gallimard, 1989), 53.

144 **"must not servilely follow the United States":** Rabaut Saint-Etienne, quoted in Stéphane Rials, *La Déclaration des droits de l'homme et du citoyen* (Paris: Hachette, 1988), 365.

145 **"national catechism":** Georges Lefebvre, *The Coming of the French Revolution,* trans. R. R. Palmer (Princeton, N.J.: Princeton University Press, 1947), 155.

146 **it guards "liberty against . . . government":** Jefferson to Francis Hopkinson, 13 March 1789, in Boyd, ed., *Jefferson Papers,* 14:650.

146 **"no" means "no!"**: Brant, *The Bill of Rights*, 225.

146 **William Lee Miller on "mandatory" nature of Amendments**: Miller, *The Business of May Next*, 267.

147 **While ordinary legislation calls for . . . supreme law of the Constitution**: Denis Lacorne, "Le Débat des Droits de l'homme en France et aux Etats-Unis," *The Tocqueville Review*, 14, 1 (1993), 22–23.

147 **"a Constitution established by the people . . . alterable by the government"**: Madison, *Federalist* No. 53, 348.

147 **"The freedom of the press was never understood . . . God deliver us from such liberty"**: John Allen, quoted by Brant, *The Bill of Rights*, 253–254.

147–48 **there have been few governments . . . arouse hatred against them**: James MacGregor Burns, *The Vineyard of Liberty* (New York: Vintage, 1983), 127.

148 **On "Spitting Matt" Lyon and Thomas Cooper**: See Burns and Burns, *A People's Charter*, 64–65.

148 **On Luther Baldwin**: See Burns, *The Vineyard of Liberty*, 129.

149 **Bellah on conceiving rights less in terms of the individual and more in terms of the community**: Robert Bellah, *The Good Society* (New York: Alfred A. Knopf, 1991), 130 and 126.

149 **"hyperindividualism . . . collective responsibilities"**: Mary Ann Glendon, *Rights Talk: The Impoverishment of Political Discourse* (New York: The Free Press, 1991), x.

149 **Legal historian Akhil Reed Amar . . . citizens entitled to act together**: Akhil Reed Amar and Alan Hirsch, *For the People: What the Constitution Really Says About Your Rights* (New York: The Free Press, 1998), xi.

149 **the "essence" of the Bill of Rights was "majoritarian"**: Akhil Reed Amar, "The Bill of Rights as a Constitution," *Yale Law Journal*, 100 (1991), 1133.

149 **"In our Governments the real power . . . truth of great importance"**: Madison to Jefferson, 17 October 1788, in *The Republic of Letters*, ed. Smith, 1:564.

149 **the greatest threat to rights . . . acting through government**: Madison, Speech for the First Congress, 8 June 1789, in Cogan, ed., *The Complete Bill of Rights*, 54.

150–51 **"You must ferret the people out . . . if they are soft"**: Thomas Jefferson to Lafayette, 11 April 1787, in Jefferson, *Writings*, ed. Peterson, 893.

151 **The jury system as a "*school* in which . . . civil duties as well as rights"**: Jefferson to John Adams, 22 January 1821, in Cappon ed., *Adams-Jefferson Letters*, 2:570.

153 **"The emphasis is not on the rights of each against all, but rather the reverse"**: Tony Judt, "Rights in France: Reflections on the Etiolation of a Political Language," *The Tocqueville Review* 14, 1 (1993), 72.

154 **"no written prohibitions on earth"**: Madison to Jefferson, 17 October 1788, in *The Republic of Letters*, ed. Smith, 1:566.

154 **"I confess that I do conceive . . . majority against the minority"**: Madison, Speech for the First Congress, 8 June 1789, in Cogan, ed., *The Complete Bill of Rights*, 54.

154–55 **"a right against the Government . . ."; "annihilated"**: Ronald Dworkin, *Taking Rights Seriously* (London: Duckworth, 1977), 194.

155 **"legislative despotism"**: James Wilson, Speech of 16 June 1787, quoted in Stourzh, "The Declaration of Rights," in *La Révolution américaine et l'Europe* (Paris: CNRS, 1979), 357.

155 **"Restrictions, precautions, and conditions . . . free man of nature":** Mirabeau, quoted in Rials, *La Déclaration des droits de l'homme et du citoyen*, 403.

155 **language of the Tenth Article of the Virginia Declaration of Rights of 1776:** State constitutions, Due Process Clause, see Cogan, ed., *The Complete Bill of Rights*, 349ff.

155 **As William Lee Miller points out . . . "the law of the land":** Miller, *The Business of May Next*, 264.

156 **not to create rights but rather to guarantee them:** Stéphane Rials, "Des Droits de l'homme aux lois de l'homme," *Commentaire*, 34 (1986), 285.

156 **"there is no authority in France higher than the Law":** Constitution of 1791, title 3, ch. 2, section 1, article 3, quoted by Stourzh, "The Declaration of Rights," 355.

156 **Revolutionaries like Condorcet . . . thwart the resistance of counterrevolutionaries:** Mona Ozouf, "Revolution," in Furet et al., eds., *A Critical Dictionary of the French Revolution*, 812–813.

157 **the judiciary had not only preserved . . . arbitrary acts of the royal government:** Tocqueville, *L'Ancien Régime et la Révolution*, ed. J.-P. Mayer, 1:174.

157 **But if any judicial tribunal . . . censuring the General Will:** Stourzh, "The Declaration of Rights," 361.

157 **In 1790, the National Assembly prohibited judicial tribunals . . . execution of the laws:** Stourzh, "The Declaration of Rights," 361.

157 **the judiciary would have to report to it periodically:** See Constitution of 1791, title 3, ch. 5, articles 21, 22, and 8, in Jacques Godechot, ed., *Les Constitutions de la France depuis 1789* (Paris: Garnier-Flammarion, 1979), 61.

157 **As Montesquieu had prophetically observed . . . freedom becomes arbitrary:** Montesquieu, *De l'esprit des lois*, Bk. 11, ch. 6.

158 **"Under a constitutional regime . . . factions that attack it":** Robespierre, Speech of 25 December 1793, in Vellay, ed., *Discours et Rapports*, 312, 316.

158 **"I shall rejoice . . . happy order established in France":** Burke to Depont, November 1789, in Burke, *Further Reflections on the Revolution in France*, ed. Ritchie, 10–11.

159 **a "mass" existing in the place of individuals:** Alexis de Tocqueville, *Fragments et Notes*, 2:337.

160 **Robespierre regretted that the Declaration of 1793 . . . ensuring economic justice:** Robespierre, Speech of 24 April 1793, in Vellay, ed., *Discours et Rapports*, 246–254.

161 **Franklin Roosevelt's economic bill of rights:** See James MacGregor Burns, *Roosevelt: The Soldier of Freedom* (New York: Harcourt Brace Jovanovich, 1970), 34.

6. ENLIGHTENMENT LEGACIES

163 **Davis on United States as adversary of popular revolutions:** David Brion Davis, *Revolutions*, 3.

163 **Successful foreign revolutions were essential . . . "to protect liberty at home":** Jefferson to George Mason, 4 February 1791, in Boyd, ed., *Jefferson Papers*, 19:241.

163 **After his election in 1860 Lincoln observed . . . "all should have an equal chance":** Lincoln, quoted in Garry Wills, *Inventing America: Jefferson's Declaration of Independence* (New York: Vintage, 1979), xix–xx.

163–64 **It was France's sacred duty . . . "regain their freedom":** Article 8, Act of 19 November 1792, in *Les Constitutions de la France*, ed. Faustin-Adolphe Hélie (Paris: Librairie de Jurisprudence, Edouard Duchemin, 1880), 346.

164 **Ortega y Gasset on the intellectual at the center of the revolutionary stage:** José Ortega y Gasset, *The Modern Theme* (1931), trans. James Cleugh (New York: Harper Torchbook, 1961), 131.

164 **"George Washington . . . a terror of the slaveholders":** Frederick Douglass, "The Dred Scott Decision," 1857, in *The Life and Writings of Frederick Douglass*, ed. Philip S. Foner (New York: International Publishers, 1950), 2:422–423.

165 **"I was not only a child . . . a king upon his throne":** Frederick Douglass, *My Bondage and My Freedom*, in *Autobiographies*, ed. Henry Louis Gates, Jr. (New York: The Library of America, 1994), 154–155.

165 **A slave "should know nothing . . . learn to obey it":** Waldo E. Martin, Jr., *The Mind of Frederick Douglass* (Chapel Hill: The University of North Carolina Press, 1984), 7.

165 **"I am quite willing . . . uncultivated mother":** Frederick Douglass, *My Bondage and My Freedom*, in *Autobiographies*, ed. Gates, 156.

165 **Douglass's father was probably Aaron Anthony:** Martin, *The Mind of Frederick Douglass*, 3.

165 **"I say nothing of *father* . . . shrouded in mystery":** Douglass, *My Bondage and My Freedom*, 151.

165 **"Slavery . . . does away with families":** Douglass, *My Bondage and My Freedom*, quoted in Martin, *The Mind of Frederick Douglass*, 3–4.

165–66 **"I do now and always have . . . humanity is broad":** Douglass, Speech of 3 September 1894, quoted in Martin, *The Mind of Frederick Douglass*, 1.

166 **"at war with itself"; "radically at fault":** Douglass, 5 April 1850, *The North Star*, in Foner, ed., *Life and Writings of Frederick Douglass*, 2:117–119.

166 **The Constitution, he announced . . . not "impostors":** Douglass, "The Meaning of July Fourth for the Negro," in Foner, ed., *Life and Writings of Frederick Douglass*, 2:201.

166 **"brains, heart and soul". . . despised slavery:** Douglass, Discussion of 20–21 May 1857, in *The Frederick Douglass Papers*, ed. John W. Blassingame, Series One (New Haven: Yale University Press, 1985), 3:158.

166–67 **Douglass on Washington, Jefferson, Franklin, and Madison:** Douglass, "The Proclamation and a Negro Army," 6 February 1863, in Blassingame, ed., *The Frederick Douglass Papers*, 3:558.

167 **"the gross injustice and cruelty . . . *I* must mourn":** Douglass, "The Meaning of July Fourth for the Negro," in Foner, ed., *Life and Writings of Frederick Douglass*, 2:192 and 189.

167 **Turning away from Garrison's philosophy of nonviolence and nonresistance:** Martin, *The Mind of Frederick Douglass*, 24.

167 **one hour of bondage "is worse than ages . . .":** Douglass, "Is It Right and Wise to Kill a Kidnapper?" in Foner, ed., *Life and Writings of Frederick Douglass*, 2:288.

167–68 **"I should welcome the intelligence . . . liberty for the enslaved of America":** Douglass, "The Meaning of July Fourth for the Negro," in Foner, ed., *Life and Writings of Frederick Douglass*, 2:200.

168 "Oh! that we had a little more . . . Heroes of the American revolution": Douglass, "The True Remedy for the Fugitive Slave Bill," 9 June 1854, quoted in Martin, *The Mind of Frederick Douglass,* 51.

168 "We can scarcely conceive . . . the war for independence": Douglass, "The Proclamation and a Negro Army," February 1863, in Foner, ed., *Life and Writings of Frederick Douglass,* 3:322.

168 "an evil of Colossal magnitude": John Adams to William Tudor, 20 November 1819, quoted in Ellis, *Passionate Sage,* 140.

168 Adams countenanced women's authority in the private sphere of the home: Ellis, *Passionate Sage,* 185.

168 "the most strange, radical . . . ever witnessed": Douglass, quoted in Martin, *The Mind of Frederick Douglass,* 162.

168 "No man should be excluded . . . burden of the Government": Douglass, Speech of 14 May 1868, in Blassingame, ed., *Frederick Douglass Papers,* 4:173.

168 "Let women go to the polls . . . than we have now": Douglass, Speech of 20 November 1866, in Blassingame, ed., *Frederick Douglass Papers,* 4:148.

169 Elizabeth Cady Stanton's racism: See Martin, *The Mind of Frederick Douglass,* 158.

169 On the stone statue of Robespierre in Moscow: A. Z. Manfred, "Robespierre dans l'historiographie russe et soviétique," in *Acts du colloque Robespierre* (Paris: Société des études robespierristes, 1967), 237.

169 Lenin on political liberalization and on separating socialism from democracy: Richard Pipes, "The Origins of Bolshevism: The Intellectual Evolution of Young Lenin," in Richard Pipes, ed., *Revolutionary Russia* (Cambridge, Mass.: Harvard University Press, 1968), 39, 50, 49.

170 "One cannot be a Marxist . . . struggle against feudalism": Lenin, quoted in Anne P. Young, "Lenin and the French Revolution as Myth and Model," in *The Consortium on Revolutionary Europe, 1750–1850,* Proceedings (Athens, Ga.: The Consortium on Revolutionary Europe, 1985), 177.

170 "A real revolutionary Social Democrat". . . recklessly undermining the idea of the dictatorship of the proletariat: Nikolay Valentinov (pen name of N. V. Volsky), *Encounters with Lenin,* trans. Paul Rosta and Brian Pearce (London: Oxford University Press, 1968), 128–129.

170 Jacobin leaders . . . energetically defended the people: Manfred, "Robespierre dans l'historiographie russe et soviétique," 245.

170 "a struggle without kid gloves . . . resorting to the guillotine": Valentinov, *Encounters with Lenin,* 129, 128.

171 "monstrous and criminal"; "just and legitimate": Lenin, quoted in Young, "Lenin and the French Revolution as Myth and Model," 182.

171 "The dictatorship of the proletariat . . . without Jacobin coercion": Valentinov, *Encounters with Lenin,* 128.

171 "one of the highest pinnacles . . . emancipation": Lenin, quoted by Manfred in "Robespierre dans l'historiographie russe et soviétique," 245.

171 "We are reproached . . . shall not use": Lenin, quoted in Young, "Lenin and the French Revolution as Myth and Model," 180.

171–73 **Steinberg on Kadets, Trotsky, Lenin, and his own imprisonment:** See I. N. Steinberg, *In the Workshop of the Revolution* (New York: Rinehart & Co., 1953), 59, 60, 136–139, 145, 157, 161.

174 **Serge on Kronstadt, Lenin, and New Economic Policy:** See Victor Serge, *Memoirs of a Revolutionary, 1901–1941* (Oxford: Oxford University Press, 1963), 126–129, 131, and 135.

174 **"retreat for a new attack":** Lenin, quoted in Edward Hallet Carr, *The Russian Revolution: From Lenin to Stalin* (London: Macmillan, 1979), 37.

175 **In September 1945 . . . French residential quarter:** See Archimedes L. A. Patti, *Why Viet Nam? Prelude to America's Albatross* (Berkeley: University of California Press, 1980), and see also Stanley Karnow, *Vietnam, A History* (New York: The Viking Press, 1963), 135.

175 **"All men are created equal . . . happy and free":** Patti, *Why Viet Nam?*, 248–251.

176 **"The entire people of Viet Nam . . . independence and liberty":** Ho Chi Minh, *On Revolution, Selected Writings, 1920–1966,* ed. Bernard Fall (New York: Frederick Praeger, 1967), 145.

177 **"starry-eyed revolutionary . . . cause of a free Viet Nam":** Patti, *Why Viet Nam?*, 86.

177 **Ho explained to Patti . . . that was all the American could remember:** Patti, *Why Viet Nam?*, 223.

177 **Sun Yat Sen admired the American Revolution and the Civil War:** Sun Yat Sen, *The Three Principles of the People* (Taipei: China Publishing Co., 1963), 86.

178 **Indochinese independence a "near-obsession" for Roosevelt:** Burns, *Roosevelt: The Soldier of Freedom,* 591, and Patti, *Why Viet Nam?*, 52.

178 **Roosevelt's ideals unquestionably anticolonial but he lacked strategy for achieving goals:** Burns, *Roosevelt: The Soldier of Freedom,* 593.

178 **"France has milked Indo-China . . . something better than that":** Memo from Roosevelt to Hull, 24 January 1944, in Allan Cameron, ed., *Viet-Nam Crisis: A Documentary History, Vol. 1: 1940–1956* (Ithaca, N.Y.: Cornell University Press, 1971), 13.

178 **"the Indochinese were people . . . since she had the colony":** The Yalta Conference: Exchange of Views of Roosevelt and Stalin on Indochina, 8 February 1945, in Cameron, ed., *Viet-Nam Crisis,* 21.

178 **Ho hoped that his case . . . would reach . . . "the great president Roosevelt":** Ho Chi Minh, quoted by Patti, *Why Viet Nam?*, 54.

179 **American State Department's Far Eastern Bureau . . . respect French sovereignty in Indochina:** Jean Lacouture, *Ho Chi Minh* (London: Allen Lane, 1968), 217.

179 **"agent of international communism":** Patti, *Why Viet Nam?*, 382.

179 **"prevent expansion of communist aggression . . . expansion in Southeast Asia":** Patti, *Why Viet Nam?*, 402–403.

179 **Truman government backs French military effort in Vietnam:** Jean Lacouture, *Ho Chi Minh,* 218.

180 **Ho's open letter to Eisenhower:** Ho Chi Minh, *Textes,* ed. Alain Ruscio (Paris: L'Harmattan, 1990), 180.

180 **Kennedy dismissed the warning of Charles de Gaulle:** Stanley Karnow, *Vietnam* (New York: The Viking Press, 1983), 248.

180–81 T. E. Lawrence appeals for independence for Syria and Mesopotamia: Liddel Hart, *Colonel Lawrence* (New York: Dodd, Mead, 1934), 313.

181 Ho inspired by President Wilson's Fourteen Points: See SarDesai, *Vietnam: Trials and Tribulations of a Nation* (New Delhi: Promilla & Co., 1988), 66.

181 Ho's "eight points" for Vietnam: Ho Chi Minh, 1919, in *Textes,* ed. Ruscio, 22–23.

181 "haves of the world against the have-nots": Conor Cruise O'Brien, quoted by Joseph M. Skelly in *Irish Diplomacy at the United Nations, 1945–1965* (Dublin: Irish Academic Press, 1997), 97.

181 Ho in Paris to study "what lay behind . . . liberté, égalité, fraternité": James Pinckney Harrison, *The Endless War: Fifty Years of Struggle in Vietnam* (New York: The Free Press, 1982), 38.

182 French authorities forbade translation of Rousseau and Montesquieu into Vietnamese: See Ho Chi Minh, *Textes,* ed. Ruscio, 55.

182 Zhou Enlai, Deng Xiaoping, Phan Chu Trinh in Paris after World War I: Stein Tonnesson, *The Vietnamese Revolution of 1945* (London: Sage Publications, 1991), 95.

182 Ho wanders streets of Paris with his friends: Lacouture, *Ho Chi Minh,* 15.

182 Ho joined French Socialist party: Ho Chi Minh, in *On Revolution,* ed. Fall, 5.

182 "dirty Negroes and dirty Annamese . . . rot on the battlefields of Europe": Ho Chi Minh, "French Colonization on Trial," in *On Revolution,* ed. Fall, 68.

182 French colonial strategy robbed the colonized people . . . sense of oneness: Ho Chi Minh, *On Revolution,* ed. Fall, 113.

183 Brothers were turned against brothers: Ho Chi Minh, "French Colonization on Trial," in *On Revolution,* ed. Fall, 73.

183 France's revolutionary decree of November 1792: Article 8, 19 November 1792, in *Les Constitutions de la France,* ed. Hélie, 346.

183 "personification of universal fraternity": Hồ Chi Minh on Lenin, Moscow, July 1924, in *Textes,* ed. Ruscio, 66, 68.

183 "the radiant sun . . . Socialism and Communism": Ho Chi Minh, in *On Revolution,* ed. Fall, 7.

183 "this aggressive war . . . besmeared . . . Washington and Lincoln": Ho Chi Minh, in *On Revolution,* ed. Fall, 369.

183 "Frenchmen in Indochina! . . . liberty, equality and fraternity": Ho Chi Minh, in *On Revolution,* ed. Fall, 154–155.

183 "The French Revolution sacrificed many people without flinching . . .": Ho Chi Minh, quoted in Hue-Tam Ho Tai, *Radicalism and the Origins of the Vietnamese Revolution* (Cambridge, Mass.: Harvard University Press, 1992), 180.

184 "the authority of France in Algeria liberated . . . of morality": Michel Debré, quoted by Frantz Fanon, *Toward the African Revolution,* trans. Haakon Chevalier (New York: Grove Press, 1964), 158.

185 Fanon sympathized solely with the goals of Algerian nationalists: See Conor Cruise O'Brien, "The Neurosis of Colonialism," Review of *The Wretched of the Earth* by Frantz Fanon, *Nation,* 200 (21 June 1965), 674–676.

185 Fanon wished to see Algeria liberated . . . "a new man": Frantz Fanon, *The Wretched of the Earth,* trans. Constance Farrington (New York: Grove Press, 1963), 252–255.

185–86 **history of FLN and FIS in Algeria:** Robert Malley, *The Call from Algeria: Third Worldism, Revolution, and the Turn to Islam* (Berkeley: University of California Press, 1996), 229.

186–87 **Burgat on three stages of decolonization:** François Burgat, *L'Islamisme au Maghreb*, quoted by Martin Stone, *The Agony of Algeria* (New York: Columbia University Press, 1997), 147.

187 **"No models hold for us . . . on our own":** Sebastian Mallaby, *After Apartheid* (New York: Times Books, 1992), 8.

189 **both sides spoke of "democracy . . . rule of law":** Mervyn Frost, "Preparing for Democracy in an Authoritarian State," in *Launching Democracy in South Africa*, ed. R. W. Johnson (New Haven, Conn.: Yale University Press, 1996), 24.

189 **"History on the whole . . . parliamentarism":** Leon Trotsky, *Between Red and White: A Study of Some Fundamental Questions of Revolution* (Westport, Conn.: Hyperion Press, 1922), 76.

189 **The government instituted by the new South African Constitution . . . eleven official languages:** South African Constitution, 1/6.

190 **"As freedom fighters . . . moved to act":** Nelson Mandela, *Long Walk to Freedom* (New York: Little, Brown, 1994), 508.

190 **one promising new party . . . 5 percent of the vote:** Suzanne Daley, "South Africa Takes Notice of a Multiracial Party," *The New York Times*, Monday, 29 June 1998, A6.

191 **alternative power bases outside of politics:** Patti Waldmeir, *Anatomy of a Miracle: The End of Apartheid and the Birth of the New South Africa* (New York: W. W. Norton, 1997), 274–275.

192 **Tocqueville remarked that in America . . . revolutionary ones:** Tocqueville, *De la Démocratie en Amérique*, vol. 2, pt. 3, ch. 21, 2:316.

7. ON "HER MAJESTY'S LOYAL OPPOSITION"

194–95 **Shays's Rebellion and Whiskey Rebellion:** See Burns, *The Vineyard of Liberty*, 14–15 and 98.

196 **"To say where 'the government' . . . metaphysics":** Robert Dahl, "The American Oppositions: Affirmation and Denial," in Robert A. Dahl, ed., *Political Oppositions in Western Democracies* (New Haven, Conn.: Yale University Press, 1966), 34.

197 **during Kennedy's first two years in office . . . two times out of three in the House:** Dahl, "The American Oppositions," 60.

198 **Years earlier, when he was a senior . . . Wilson had warned against:** See Burns, *The Deadlock of Democracy*, 120.

198 **transactional, not transformational, national leadership:** See James MacGregor Burns, *Leadership* (New York: Harper & Row, 1978), 9–28.

198 **"no society can make a perpetual constitution":** Jefferson to Madison, 6 September 1789, in *Writings*, ed. Peterson, 959.

199 **"An opposition . . . what good there is in an opposition":** Napoleon, quoted in C. J. Herold, *The Mind of Napoleon* (New York, 1961), quoted by Ghita Ionescu, *Opposition: Past and Present of a Political Institution* (London: C. A. Watts & Co., 1968), 59.

199 **Since the Revolution, the legitimacy . . . Indochina and Algeria:** See Alfred Grosser, "France: Nothing But Opposition," in Dahl, ed., *Political Oppositions in Western Democracies,* 289ff.

199 **De Gaulle's Constitution for the Fifth Republic:** See François Furet, "La France unie," in *La République du centre,* ed. F. Furet, J. Julliard, P. Rosanvallon (Paris: Calmann-Lévy, 1988), 53.

200 **"The paradox . . . democratic deliberation":** Pierre Rosanvallon, "Malaise dans la représentation," in *La République du centre,* eds. Furet et al., 169.

200 **revolutionary left lost its polestar, right lost its best foil:** François Furet, "Chronique d'une décomposition," *Le Débat,* 83, January–February 1995, 84.

201 **"the frightening emptiness of . . . discourse":** Cornelius Castoriadis, "L'idée de la révolution," *Le Débat,* 57, November–December 1989, 221.

201 **"politics is becoming empty of meaning":** See Nicholas Tenzer, "Reconstruire la politique," *Le Débat,* 63, January–February 1991, 162–163.

201 **"rush to acquire . . . welfare state":** François Furet, "Chronique d'une décomposition," *Le Débat,* 83, January–February 1995, 84.

201 **"If citizens continue to close . . . renew themselves":** Tocqueville, *De la Démocratie en Amérique,* vol. 2, Bk. 2, pt. 3, ch. 21, 2:324.

202 **"a more civil, respectful and consensual body":** Richard Gephardt, quoted by E. J. Dionne, Jr., in "Radical Moderation," *The Washington Post Weekly Edition,* 11 May 1998, 22.

203 **"sown in the nature of man":** Madison, *Federalist* No. 10, 55.

203 **"Whether we speak . . . under the sun":** Daniel Defoe, quoted by Lawrence Stone, "The Results of the English Revolutions of the Seventeenth Century," in *Three British Revolutions: 1641, 1688, 1776,* ed. J. G. A. Pocock (Princeton, N.J.: Princeton University Press, 1980), 75.

203 **dominant features of modern English parliamentary democracy:** See Allen Potter, "Great Britain: Opposition with a Capital 'O,'" in Dahl, ed., *Political Oppositions in Western Democracies,* 6–8.

204 **limits on verbal abuse:** Stone, "The Results of the English Revolutions of the Seventeenth Century," 98.

205 **there must not be too much conflict—or too little:** Dahl, "The American Oppositions," 65.

205 **"a society where dissent . . . suppressed":** Dahl, "Epilogue," in Dahl, ed., *Political Oppositions in Western Democracies,* 392.

205 **Wilson wanted to see American institutions mirror English ones:** See Burns, *The Deadlock of Democracy,* 121.

205 **"for any people . . . it has grown":** Burke, "A Letter to a Member of the National Assembly" (1791), in Burke, *Further Reflections on the Revolution in France,* ed. Ritchie, 65.

Index